NEIL FINDLAY was born in 1969, the son o
teacher. Brought up in the working class vil
after leaving school at 16 he was an apprent
years with his father's small business, becam
struck up a great friendship with Tam Daly
he worked in social housing before becomi
Councillor for nine years, he was elected to the Scottish parliament in 2011, ... g
in various front bench posts and contesting the Scottish Labour leadership election
in 2014. Scottish campaign manager for Jeremy Corbyn's two leadership elections,
Neil is current chair of the Scottish Parliament's health and sport committee. He
enjoys fishing, golf, gardening and going for a pint.

Socialism & Hope

A journey through turbulent times

NEIL FINDLAY

with

JEFF HOLMES

Luath Press Limited

EDINBURGH

www.luath.co.uk

First published in 2017

ISBN: 978-1-912147-27-4

The author's right to be identified as author of this book
under the Copyright, Designs and Patents Act 1988 has been asserted.

The paper used in this book is recyclable. It is made from low chlorine pulps
produced in a low energy, low emission manner from renewable forests.

Printed and bound by
MBM Print SCS Ltd, East Kilbride

Typeset in 10.5 point Sabon by Main Point Books, Edinburgh

This book is dedicated to Fiona, Chloe and all my family, friends, colleagues, neighbours and comrades whose friendship, humour, advice and help I have enjoyed over the years; also, to my great friend and mentor Tam Dalyell, who died the day after I finished writing. I miss him greatly.

Thanks to you all; live life to the full – you're only here once!

Contents

Foreword by Jeremy Corbyn MP

I AM DELIGHTED to have been asked to write this foreword for my friend and comrade Neil Findlay.

Becoming leader of the Labour Party has given me the opportunity to meet people from across the Labour movement – and one of the personal highlights for me has been getting to know Neil. I value enormously the support and friendship he has given me.

Of course you know a true friend when they are prepared to be honest and forthright with you and tell you the things you sometimes don't want to hear. Neil is one such person, as most people who know him will confirm: he is not one for pulling his verbal punches! When Neil calls he is always clear, of course very friendly, but always robust. So no one should be in the least bit surprised that this diary is an honest, frank and challenging – as well as humorous of course – account of his time in the Scottish Parliament and at the forefront of Scottish politics.

Neil has observed and been part of a tumultuous time in Scottish and British politics. In Scotland, unfortunately, the changing political landscape has seen difficult times for the Labour Party. One of the brighter spots amongst an often rather miserable period was Neil's election in 2011. He was elected on a platform of an uncompromising determination to create a better, fairer and more equal Scotland and Britain. Nobody should be in any doubt that he has used his position to throw himself with 100 per cent commitment into the campaigns and issues for which he cares passionately.

A tireless campaigner, Neil fights on the side of justice and against injustice at all times. He has supported and stood alongside blacklisted construction workers, unjustly sacked and victimised miners, local government workers and women who have been injured and left disabled by polypropylene mesh medical devices which were meant to make their lives better, not worse.

To state the blindingly obvious, Neil is a very active Parliamentarian, introducing a member's bill to establish a lobbying register in Scotland, which was subsequently passed by the Scottish Government (though to his great regret significantly diluted).

During the 2011–2016 Scottish Parliament, Neil was also a key Shadow

Cabinet Member, holding the SNP Scottish Government to account for their failings in health and social care. Never one to think that holding them to account was simply about criticising the Government of the day, Neil always looked for positive and progressive alternatives, shown when he commissioned two radical reports into social care and the persistent scandal of stubborn health inequalities.

And whilst engaged with all of that, Neil also found time to be a key protagonist in the debate about Scotland's constitutional future. He spoke at countless meetings, arguing with energy and conviction for Scotland to remain part of the UK but within a federal and decentralised set up. Alongside his colleagues from across the broad left, he was part of the 'Red Paper Collective' and worked with leading Labour and Trade Union movement figures who argued for Scotland to stay tied to the UK for reasons of solidarity and socialism.

He also found time to stand for the post of Scottish Party Leader and put up a brilliant fight, which, although ultimately unsuccessful, was very important in ensuring that a strong, socialist vision of Scotland was heard during that particular campaign.

Reflecting upon this rich experience, Neil's book provides entertaining insights into remarkable and transformative political machinations over six years. What he has to say in relation to normal parliamentary dynamics is in itself interesting; against the backdrop of the Scottish Independence referendum, Brexit, his own Scottish Labour leadership campaign and the Labour leadership elections, Neil's observations become a must-read for all those wanting to better understand this fascinating period of Scottish and British political history.

Our movement should value Neil for his energy, commitment and dedication as a trade unionist and socialist. However, there is much more to Neil. He is a thinker and someone who has the heart and the imagination to lead people out of drudgery and isolation to a better society.

I count Neil as a good and real friend and one who teaches us to think and act.

Jeremy Corbyn MP
August 2017

Preface

SOCIALISM IS ABOUT optimism and hope. And by God, over the last few years, as a member of the Scottish Labour party, that optimism has been tested. These years have taken us from a position of power to a point where people were questioning our continued relevance.

This existential crisis has been enough to take even the greatest optimist to the edge of despair.

However, politics is nothing if not unpredictable.

As this book goes to print, we enter into another Scottish Labour leadership election. It comes at a time when Labour is winning trust across the nations of the UK with a policy manifesto that truly addresses the needs of our communities. A manifesto that embodies a vision of full employment, fairness, equality and, crucially, solidarity, it reflects the socialism that I have always believed in.

Throughout the 20th century, it is the labour movement that has brought about radical social change – from council housing and the National Health Service, to devolution and the National Minimum Wage. I believe that, in a spirit of newfound optimism, Labour will build on these historic achievements and rise to the challenges of the future, with policies to 'Transform Our Society For the Many, Not the Few'.

Neil Findlay MSP
August 2017

From Bangour to Holyrood

WE ARE LIVING through one of the most turbulent periods in UK political history. The last few years have seen a Scottish independence referendum, a couple of General Elections and a vote on whether or not we should remain in the European Union. Throw in two uncompromising Labour leadership battles at UK level and a couple in Scotland, and it would be true to say that nothing less than a political whirlwind has swept through the corridors of the Scottish Parliament since it 'reconvened' in 1999.

I've been an MSP since 2011, but things could have been so different had the navigation skills of a certain Lithuanian maritime skipper been more accurate. To explain, my great-grandfather Kazimere Dekyritis – my ma's grandfather – had decided to leave his Baltic homeland in search of a better life. The family paid for passage to the United States and after being on the open seas for quite some time, were told the land they could see on the horizon was America when, in reality, they were a few thousand miles short – in Leith. From there, they moved on to Stoneyburn, in West Lothian, and the prospect of a future Congressman Findlay was forever lost.

Kazimere's son Bernard broke his back in a mining accident before my ma was born, and found himself working nightshift in the lamp cabin handing out and taking in miners' lamps, but by day he was a fixture at the street corner outside the Stoneyburn Co-op, collecting bookies lines long before gambling was legal. My ma and her siblings would jump on the bus to Blackburn to pick up lines and money from contacts there. It was a family concern.

My ma excelled at school and went to Edinburgh University to study, before attending Catholic Teacher Training College at Craiglockhart, and she taught in primary schools for 40 years. She was also an EIS shop steward.

My parents were chalk and cheese. My da was a hairy arsed and hairy faced, larger than life character (I can't recall seeing him in the flesh without his trademark beard) who loved the banter and camaraderie of the building site and the pub. He played the big drum in the Livingston and Pumpherston Pipe Band and was a world champion in 1984. When he passed away, his legacy to me was three kilts and the highland dress to go with them, and I was a proud recipient.

As a kid from a church-going Protestant family, it couldn't have been easy for him, in those days, hooking up with my Catholic ma. But it was the mark of him as a person and my two grannies and granda that they gave my parents their full blessing and support to marry and not once was religion an issue. It's my da's hatred of sectarianism that has instilled in me the same intolerance of religious bigotry and racism, and I thank him for that.

While my ma and da weren't political, neither were they apolitical. Whether it was taking our old clothes in for needy kids in my ma's school or raising money for a local charity, running the school badminton club or sitting on the St Kent's School PTA, their goodness, decency and humanity impacted on many people. They lived their lives with a commitment to their community, class, faith and family, and although they may not have thought it, they were the living embodiment of communitarianism and collectivism.

I have two siblings. Anna is the brainy Findlay. Always an A grade student, she went to Edinburgh and Strathclyde Universities before fulfilling her dream of becoming a stewardess with British Airways, where she worked with Tommy Sheridan's wife, Gail. She travels the world and has visited all the places I've only ever read about.

My older brother John was the rebel. He always had attitude and girls telling him they fancied him and always had a new haircut/colour and new clothes. He was a skilled engineer, and a shop steward at one time, but his life changed dramatically in the late '90s when he was diagnosed with MS at the age of 30. He has battled this illness heroically and only recently had to give up work at the age of 50. His stubbornness, feisty character and attitude have seen him through some tough times.

I was born in Bangour Village Hospital (once called Edinburgh District Asylum), near Broxburn, in March 1969. It closed as a functioning hospital in 2004, but has since seen use as a film location for the 2005 movie *The Jacket*, which starred Keira Knightley and Adrien Brody. The hospital grounds were also used as the site for a counter-terrorism exercise run by the Scottish Government to test decontamination procedures in the event of a nuclear, chemical or biological incident.

Until I was five, we stayed in Blackburn, which lies halfway between Edinburgh and Glasgow, and has a population of around 5,000. It grew exponentially in the early 1960s as firms like British Leyland moved into nearby Bathgate. At its peak they employed around 8,000 but the closure of the factory in 1986 saw the population of Blackburn fall accordingly.

Even after moving to Fauldhouse in 1974 I continued to attend Our Lady of Lourdes Primary in Blackburn, because my ma taught there and it made things easier all round. My Aunty Mary lived a few minutes from the school and I would pal about with the McCafferty family. There were five brothers and one sister, so there was always someone to play with. They sold papers to workers at the huge British Leyland plant nearby at 5 o'clock each night and we would walk or cycle the mile to the factory gate and set up a wee metal stall and punt copies of the *Evening Times*. Someone else would be selling the *Evening News*. The *Evening Times*, traditionally a Glasgow paper, sold more copies as many workers were 'Glasgow overspill'. We sold dozens each night for 5p and on the way home we would pass the queues of traffic from Blackburn Cross, backed up through the town to the factory gate. It was a busy, bustling town in those days.

We played badminton at the school club my da ran (I was County singles champion), football, hide and seek down the burn, kick the can; we went runs on bikes and swam in the 'dookie' – a wide and deeper part of the River Almond.

St Kentigern's Secondary School wasn't my favourite place and I showed little interest in my subjects. I was more interested in having a laugh and pissing about. I loved cooking. I enjoyed Mrs Jenkins' food and nutrition class, but everything else was a chore. I was useless at maths and couldn't grasp it at all. I got a dreadful report card in third year – all Ds and Es for attainment and effort and two As for cooking. My ma went mad, but I sat my exams and remarkably passed O-Grades in English, Chemistry, Food and Nutrition, Art and Arithmetic. We were all baffled.

Our John's love of Mod and Punk music rubbed off on me and the hours that should've been spent poring over school books were taken up listening to The Jam, a band that wrote the soundtrack to my childhood, and even when I became heavily involved in politics they remained the perfect fit as Paul Weller's beliefs just about mirrored my own.

Coming from a mining village, we were on the front line during the miners' strike. My da would give striking miners a few shifts labouring, and donate to collections for pals on the picket line. My ma would take stuff into school for the kids of miners on strike and her union, the EIS, offered support too.

My best pal Jimmy's da was responsible for pit safety, so he was given permission by the unions to work throughout the strike to prevent the pit flooding or being beyond use when it was over. In the end, Polkemmet was deliberately flooded by the Coal Board, with millions of tonnes of coal and hundreds of jobs lost in the process. It was an act of industrial vandalism. I watched every twist and turn of the strike on television and was engrossed by Scargill, Heathfield and McGahey. These men became my heroes: clever, working class, great orators and uncompromising leaders. This was my political awakening: I just couldn't understand why Thatcher wanted to put my pals' das, uncles and brothers out of work. What did she know about our lives, our community and communities like it? I really did grow to hate her because she was everything my ma and da weren't, and everything I would come to oppose.

Of course the strike was lost and unemployment reached 26 per cent in my village, which was such a waste of talent. Young people went years without a real job – just a £20 a week Youth Opportunities Scheme. When the pit closed, miners got their redundancy and without financial advice, many handed it over to greedy bookmakers or smiling publicans. Others were milked dry by ruthless fair-weather friends.

It was around this time I started going out, and I had my first alcoholic drink – a half pint of cider – in a bar in Edinburgh after the Christmas badminton tournament at Meadowbank Stadium. This was closely followed by my first big adventure to the centre of the West Lothian dancing scene – the Bathgate Palais. I would steal our John's blue leather jacket before meeting up with my mates. We were on a strict budget of a fiver but it was enough to ensure a good night as long as we were careful. We loved the music at the Palais: Duran Duran, Spandau Ballet, The Smiths and U2, and the night always finished with the evocative Green Onions by Booker T and the MGs.

It was at the Palais that I met Fiona Miller – the girl I would marry. She went to Blackburn Academy and lived in Stoneyburn. On our first meeting, we shared a taxi home and she bought me a pizza – all to myself! We started going out and the first time I went to Fiona's, my nerves got the better of me and I spilled scrambled egg all down the side of her sofa. I then tried to scoop it out without Fiona, her parents and two wee sisters seeing me. They said nothing at the time, but years later confessed they had all spotted me trying in vain to scoop the scrambled egg back onto the plate without making a mess or leaving any evidence.

But Scrambled-Egg-Gate didn't prevent me enrolling on a catering course at West Lothian College in Bathgate. I was a decent cook and becoming a chef sounded interesting. It was long before the days of the celebrity chef, when there was far more to preparing meals than screaming and shouting at everyone. But the college was great. You got your chef's whites, a set of knives and a waiter's uniform. We learned the basics of the kitchen, the theory of catering and worked in the college restaurant both cooking meals and operating silver service.

I enjoyed the kitchen but needed to earn some money. Fiona was studying hairdressing at college and worked in a shop on a Saturday, and I was determined to pay my way. So after the first year of a two-year course, I left when I was offered a job at the brand new four-star Hotel de France in Edinburgh, owned by Rangers chairman David Murray. I was placed in the bistro and worked various shifts, but each presented its own problem. For a 6am start, I had to stay with my brother in Whitburn and get the 4.30am bus to be in on time, as there wasn't any public transport from Fauldhouse at this ungodly hour. After six months, it was clearly unsustainable and despite so much support from my family, I quit. But my da had a plan. He offered me an apprenticeship as a bricklayer. It was a bit different from preparing stroganoff but I talked it over with Fiona and decided to accept. My brief career as a chef was over but I retain a lifelong interest in cooking.

I started as a YTS bricklayer on £27.50 per week and even though I knew it wasn't a 'job for life', it was undoubtedly one of the best things that has ever happened to me. The work was hard, bending and lifting bricks and concrete blocks all day, working in high summer heat and freezing winter frost. We did mostly private work; single houses, extensions, garages, garden walls, patios and the like. I met the best, brightest, funniest and most entrepreneurial people I have ever come across – many without a single academic qualification, but geniuses in the ways of the world, making money and in being all round good folk. I discovered comradeship, sharing, fairness and appreciating the rewards of hard work. I learned to treat people like I wanted to be treated myself. I learned my trade and how to work as part of a team. I could lay brick and blocks quickly and make money for the team. Mind you, winters were hell. We would often have to shovel snow out of deep muddy foundations before we could even think about building something. We had to lift frost-covered scaffolding poles with bare hands or set fires on the sand pile to defrost it. I hated winter so much.

After eight years on the tools, I decided to go to night school to study Higher English; probably to prove to myself that I wasn't as daft as I thought, but I went for six months, got bored and decided to chuck it. My ma urged me to sit my exam, as it was paid for. It was still a few months away, and I was reluctant but agreed. I did zero revision and to my utter astonishment I got a C pass! What could I have achieved had I really put the time and effort in?

The following year I studied modern studies in the afternoon and history in the evening – and my da gave me one afternoon off a week. I achieved an A for modern studies and a B for history, and my ma, my sister and her partner Jim suggested I apply for university. Me, university? Aye, maybe to work in the canteen! But they were right. It was time to get off my arse and do something about it. I sent off applications and was accepted by Edinburgh, Glasgow and Strathclyde. I was now shitting myself, as three universities had called my bluff. My ma and Anna had gone to Edinburgh and advised me against following in their footsteps, telling me I'd hate it. Jim was at Strathclyde and gave it a glowing report, so I chose there.

At the time Fiona and I lived in a four-in-a-block council house in Lanrigg Road, in Fauldhouse: a real traditional council house, among the best ever built. It was a one-bedroom 'upstairs' flat with a coal fire and the rent was £21 a week. Fiona was working in the Mitsubishi electronic factory, having been sickened by the derisory wages in hairdressing. We had a reasonable income, enough to pay the rent, run a banger of a car, go on holiday once a year and out at the weekend, so the time was probably right to go to university – and I'm glad I did. Strathclyde was unpretentious and had a broad mix of people. I still worked with my da during the summer holidays so I had the best of both worlds.

I was a teenager when I got into politics and joining the Labour Party seemed a logical move. It was 1988 and I had voted in my first election the year before – an experience I'll never forget. The night before voting day, I came within a raised gearbox of getting myself killed. I was 18 and driving along in my wee Mini – my £300 pride and joy – when I pulled out at a blind junction in front of a hulking great Nissan turbo. We collided and had I not been shunted across into the empty passenger seat, because the gearbox in the Mini wasn't as high as other cars, I probably wouldn't be here today. I was very lucky. I was charged and fined for driving without due care and attention, but I had no complaints. It was my fault. The car was a write-off and I got an awful fright, although not quite enough to make me vote Tory the next day!

Mind you, Annie Somerville would've made sure that didn't happen. She was my pal John's mum, and my earliest political influence. Annie was chair of the Fauldhouse Labour Party and was always talking politics. She influenced me the best way, by speaking to me rather than preaching.

I attended my first Labour branch meeting in the Fauldhouse Miners Welfare Club, the social and political heart of our community, where a thrusting young council leader called Jack McConnell was the invited guest. He talked of devolution and the need for a Scottish Parliament. Earlier that day I had listened to Dennis Canavan talk at an anti-poll tax meeting about organising working-class communities to resist the tax. My sympathies lay and still do lie more with the Dennis Canavans of the late '80s – although I disagreed with him on his views about independence – than the Jack McConnells, but after that evening I was hooked.

I got drawn more and more into politics and helped out at council elections for Robert Lee and Alex Bell, and we won both battles easily. Fauldhouse was a solid Labour town back then. I was soon a delegate to my constituency party and met some great people, although one man more than most proved such an inspiration: my MP, the irrepressible Tam Dalyell. Through time, Tam would become my close friend and mentor, even though our backgrounds couldn't have been more different. He was an Old Etonian living in a family ancestral home, The Binns, near Linlithgow, and went to Cambridge University where he chaired the Conservative Club before marrying Kathleen Wheatley, daughter of Labour MP and social housing pioneer John Wheatley. Kathleen had gone to St Mary's Secondary in Bathgate with my ma.

Kathleen's father held a lofty position in the first ever Labour government in the mid-1920s under Prime Minister, Ramsay MacDonald. He was Minister of Health in 1924 and was succeeded in the position by future Prime Minister Neville Chamberlain. The Conservatives had garnered the most votes in that election, but lost their parliamentary majority and a shared government was set up with MacDonald's Labour Party, which was just 24 years old, and the Liberals, under the stewardship of Asquith. Because Labour had to rely on the support of the Liberals, it was unable to pass any socialist legislation in the House of Commons, the only significant measure being the Wheatley Housing Act, the brainchild of John Wheatley, which began a building programme of 500,000 homes for rent to working-class families. Wheatley's Housing Act sparked a council housing revolution throughout the country, and changed people's lives for the better.

Tam rarely missed a constituency party meeting and valued the opinions of members. He was also brilliant to listen to and learn from, and insisted that being educated at Eton and Cambridge had taught him to be unembarrassable. He would get into issues others wouldn't touch with a barge pole. He led a one-man crusade in the '70s against devolution, then had Thatcher on the brink of resignation over the Falklands. Once he got his teeth into an issue he didn't let go. He was relentless, which made him so effective. He also had integrity by the bucket load.

During my second year at university Tam asked if I wanted to go to the Scottish Grand Committee of the House of Commons, in Kilmarnock. I was a bit puzzled, but accepted the invitation. After a bizarre day of standing around in my denim jacket and trainers and being introduced to various MPs, including Donald Dewar, we started out on our journey home. A few miles from Fauldhouse, Tam asked if we could draw into a lay-by. I suddenly thought, 'I know he went to Eton but bloody hell...'

But what followed was astonishing. He was considering standing down as an MP and wanted me to succeed him. I was 26 – the same age he had been when elected – and he told me I had made my mark and that he would help me. I was gobsmacked, but there wasn't a snowball's chance in hell of it happening. I wasn't confident or knowledgeable enough and certainly didn't believe it was the type of thing I could do.

Tam was a political giant; I was at university and Fiona and I had just had Chloe and were living in a one-bedroom council house. Fiona was working in the factory and we were just trying to get by, so it wasn't an option. I don't see it as an error of judgement on Tam's part. He clearly didn't view age as a barrier, as he had been in there as a young man and gone on to be a parliamentary legend. The answer was a firm 'no' and Fiona was the only person I told.

Whenever Tam stood up in parliament to argue or debate with anyone, on any subject, he was convinced he was right and would argue his case with tenacity, always fully briefed. He had the courage and confidence to face anyone. Me? I had gone to St Kentigern's Academy, and great school though it is, it didn't instil in me the self-belief of the Eton elite. Confidence is massive in life, although too much or too little can be a problem. It took me a while to become that near-confident person, and I'm convinced Tam was trying to bring it out in me, because he wanted someone local to replace him. He was always against candidates being parachuted in from other areas.

When I eventually became an MSP, the time was right. I was better prepared than I had been earlier. I had a university education, which obviously isn't essential, as there are some great people out there who haven't been to college or university, but that and a couple of different jobs had certainly helped me. I'd met many people, and also accrued a more developed socialist view of the world.

I was an active member of the Labour Party locally but never got involved in the university Labour club, as it was full of wannabes. Those who floated around student politics and the Labour club/NUS gang were people I had nothing in common with. They were clearly carving out some sort of political career, whereas I saw politics as a means of improving the lot of my pals, my family and my community. My socialism was developing not through text books or studying philosophers and economists but through observing the lives of people around me. I didn't particularly realise it at the time but it was class politics I believed in. I didn't study Marxism and say, 'that's the boy for me!' Through time, I discovered that Marx's philosophy chimed with me and my view of the world. It was class that determined almost everything in life: your school, where you lived, your career, how long you lived. Those with power and wealth went to private school, and through connections, had access to the best universities and jobs. They were healthy and lived longer than the poor and working class. Of course people could climb the social ladder but money didn't necessarily change a person's class because it was also a mind-set. A set of values and beliefs; a set of values that were ingrained in me and which I respected greatly. Fauldhouse for me epitomised those values – community, solidarity, people caring for each other – a tough place, yes, but with a huge caring, loving side to it. The people know who they are and are fiercely proud of being Scottish working class.

Mind you, the Labour Party and Marx were soon forced to take a back seat. I had graduated from university with a BA in geography and was proud of my achievements. It was 1996 and under normal circumstances I would've stayed on to do my honours, but our daughter Chloe came along.

To rewind a little, Fiona and I were overjoyed when we discovered she was pregnant and started planning for the new arrival. I was a little apprehensive at the thought of becoming a father, but also excited. When we told our parents, they were very happy and supportive. Mind you, criticism would come from a different, and unexpected quarter. After work one night, Fiona popped in to tell my Granny Lena the happy news. An hour later, she was standing in our living room in tears. There was no consoling her and it was a few minutes before her mumbled words started to make any sense. My granny had given Fiona the sternest of rows (think Alex Ferguson's infamous hairdryer treatment – and multiply by ten!). Apparently she was furious with us for daring to have a child out of wedlock. Fiona was close to my granny and was stunned at being spoken to in such a manner. I was furious and called my granny to say I would be down to see her the following day, and I also told my da. He went straight over to have it out with her, and when I arrived the following day, she couldn't apologise enough and explained that it was her old traditional views that had provoked the stormy reaction. I accepted her apology and normal service was resumed. Fiona and I married two years later, and if my granny wasn't happy at the length of time we took to tie the knot, she never did say!

When the time came for Fiona to go into hospital to give birth, I was there throughout. It was a lengthy labour, but an experience I couldn't miss. Thankfully everything went smoothly and baby Chloe came into the world at 2.45pm on the 16 January 1996.

Chloe's arrival hastened the need to get a job. Fiona was still at the Mitsubishi factory in Livingston but we needed extra money in. We discussed how best I could use the qualifications from university but agreed I should go back on the tools with my da in the short term. It would bring in a regular wage while I looked around for something else. When I eventually started sending off my CV, I awaited the replies – but heard nothing. I then met a friend, Brian Gunn, a former manager with Coca Cola, and explained my situation. He made a few minor adjustments to my CV and, lo and behold, I started to get interviews and job offers. The simple changes he made had a positive effect and I was offered a position with a local housing association. Result. I thoroughly enjoyed that job, even though it was completely different to anything I'd done before. I was working in Craigshill, Livingston, where my job was to help folk who simply needed a hand up, whether that be with benefits or to plan their budget, and make sure they were paying their rent. I also helped them navigate their way through a complex system. All the while I developed expertise in welfare rights, and I got a great sense of job satisfaction.

At the beginning it was tough and upsetting, going in and out of houses where some people didn't even have carpets on the floor. Some of the young people I met were surviving on £30 a week dole money, so you would try and help them make their money stretch till the next giro cheque. There were people who had been abused; folk with mental health issues, and also quite a few neighbour disputes to deal with. Some were complex, like an individual constantly claiming his neighbours were noisy when in fact he had mental health problems and was hearing noises.

We were also told of the drug dealer caught by police concealing heroin in a baby's nappy.

Once we were called out to a house where a man had died and been lying for three weeks. I will never forget the smell when I walked through the front door. And then we had someone with a cannabis farm in his house, which we discovered because the trickle of water being used to feed the plants had overflowed, and flooded the house below.

But one of the most bizarre cases I heard of from a housing officer involved a guy living upstairs from his partner, and they had taken a power saw to the floor, cut a massive hole out and put a staircase in! No engineers involved, no planning permission. 'Grand Designs' indeed!

But there would also be the most heart-warming stories of people going the extra mile to help out their neighbours; people with little, working hard to raise huge amounts of cash for charity, and giving their money, possessions or time, firmly believing others to be much worse off than them.

Some of the stories housing officers could tell are just unbelievable. I worked with the housing association for around five years and while the work was good, the pay was much lower than other local housing associations or councils. I regularly pressed management for a wage increase and better conditions, and we joined the Transport and General Workers Union, but struggled as many of my colleagues refused to join. Management weren't best pleased and after a while I moved on. I got a start with a sheltered housing association, but while it offered the best pay and conditions I'd ever had it was completely dull because everybody paid their rent on time and the neighbours all got on well, which meant there was little challenge. Not long after that, I began my teacher training. It had been on my mind for some time, and it was good to finally get started. The base for my training was Glasgow University. I say 'base' because the course runs for nine months, and half of that takes the form of a school placement. The training was tough, but enjoyable, and I managed straight As in everything I did – until the final piece of work. I'd had a run-in with one tutor about a placement issue, and she had been really intransigent about it, so I made a complaint. She, in turn, gave me a fail. Not even a B, C or a D, a complete fail. It was really infuriating because an 'A' would've seen me graduate with an Honours Degree with Distinction, but that fail meant I had to rewrite the whole thing. Still, I got my qualification in 2003 and in the same month I was elected onto West Lothian Council, and that threw up a new set of problems. I had completed my final placement at Taylor High School in New Stevenston, and they wanted me back. I wanted to return to do my probation year so I wrote to North Lanarkshire Council to inform them I was now a councillor, and that I also had my probation to do, and they insisted it wasn't a problem. I would get time off for public duties and wasn't to worry.

The General Teaching Council had other ideas, though. They wouldn't allow me to do both as it was a one-year full-time probationary teaching proposition. I asked if I could do two years part-time, and they said no. I asked what would happen if I had been female and pregnant, or was in the TA and was forced to go abroad to participate in the Gulf War, or many other scenarios that would prevent me being there full-time. It mattered not, and I eventually got my MSP and the union involved, but still they refused to budge. In the end I had to resign my probationary post at Taylor High the week before I was due to begin. I had to register as a supply teacher and do my probation the old way – clocking up days on supply; so what should have taken around nine months, took three or four years. At one point I was ready to quit, but encouragement from my family kept me going. In hindsight it worked out well, as the supply system allowed me to do two days teaching and three at the council.

The two provided a good contrast and offered variety in my working life. I was teaching modern studies, which allowed me to bring my politics into the classroom and make it lively. It was the perfect combination.

At the time I didn't realise it would take me a few years to clock up my probationary hours, so I approached it with great enthusiasm and worked at a number of different schools. Councillors can't work in their own local authority area, so my training took place in Falkirk and North Lanarkshire. I was at Falkirk High School on and off for about three or four years. It was a good school with good kids, although it had quite a different culture from West Lothian; the pupils had a different accent and used different local slang words, which I love. It's amazing how things can be so different just 10 or 15 miles apart.

I worked as a supply teacher, which can be quite tough, because in many ways they are the most abused in the education system. However, the opposite was the case at a school in Grangemouth. The head teacher was tremendously supportive and insisted on meeting us every morning. He would tell us we weren't there to take rubbish; but to do an important job. What a revelation, because in some schools you would get grunted at and handed a timetable.

I am hopeless at maths, and think I may even have dyscalculia, a brain disorder that makes it difficult to understand arithmetical calculations, so if ever I received a timetable that said I was taking sixth year advanced higher maths, I would walk into the class and say, 'I'm taking the class but I'm not quite sure where you're up to at the moment.' I would scan the classroom and pick out one of the brightest students and they would be in charge. They quite liked the idea of being teacher for a while, and it was my trick to overcome my complete inadequacy in that subject. They also respected honesty. Children are good at seeing through fake people, and I'm sure I would've been rumbled immediately. It's important to have a bag of tricks when you're a supply teacher because if you don't catch the kids in the first few minutes of a lesson, it can be an hour of hell.

I also did a year at a primary school which turned out to be one of the best experiences of my life. I took a group of about 10 kids who needed extra assistance and different strategies to learn. I worked hard at developing a programme of outdoor education, and insisted that no matter the month of the year, we would be outside if possible. I was determined it was going to work and the kids bought into it from the beginning. We constructed a school garden, a greenhouse and bird boxes. We worked with older folk at a care home for dementia sufferers – and we won a photography competition organised by the local rotary club.

Meanwhile, the kids didn't realise they were actually doing maths and English, but they would be measuring trees, logging the height of plants, and keeping a daily diary, so they were constantly learning and all coming to school regularly. Their behaviour and focus improved.

That lasted a year until budget cuts ended the post and the harsh reality was it ended the extra stimulus that some of the young people had benefited from. When I spoke to a former colleague later on, she said that education wise, the kids had gone backwards, which was sad to hear. It had been a satisfying year for me and, I hope, for the kids too but this was the reality of austerity politics impacting on the most needy.

My ma was a teacher and my da a brickie, and I've sampled both. To me, they are equally as important, although it was a bit warmer in the classroom! But I was soon on the move again. In 2011, the opportunity to become a Member of the Scottish Parliament presented itself, and I grasped it with both hands. Mind you, with just 12 months until the next council elections, I decided to stay on as a councillor and do both jobs rather than resign and prompt a by-election.

Most people – a number of councillors became MSPs at the same time – also remained in situ for that year. It worked out fine as my colleagues at the council took on part of my official workload. It did mean increased hours, but it was a case of managing your diary as efficiently as possible, which was helped by having a great team around me. I also decided to forego my council salary. Money has never been a key motivation for me, so that cash went back into the council pot.

At that time, we weren't in the grip of grinding austerity so there was cash around and we could do things to improve communities. In Fauldhouse, I drove a project to build a partnership centre which means we now have a community centre, swimming pool, gym, library, housing office, two GP surgeries, a dentist and a pharmacy all in one brand new building. It cost £7.5 million but it's a tremendous facility and benefits everyone in the village.

I was also instrumental in setting up the Fauldhouse Community Development Trust. We were awarded a £500,000 lottery grant, which meant we could bring together a whole range of projects in a new community hub. It's run by locals and represents community working at its best.

Becoming a councillor was one of my better decisions. When Councillor Robert Lee was retiring I was asked to put my name forward. I'd stood before, in 1999, in Armadale and Blackridge but only as we didn't have a candidate, and also to gain experience. This time, I was elected as councillor for Fauldhouse with 64 per cent of the vote and a near 700 majority, which presented an opportunity to try and make a difference for the people of the town. When it came to the end of my term, I had no hesitation in standing again, and thankfully I topped the poll by 500 votes.

Having a good councillor who is active in the community and knows how to get things done is worth his/her weight in gold. I was pleased when the BBC recently produced a short series called 'The Council', because it showed the type of work that council workers typically do and how, on a daily basis, they help ensure our society remains a civilised one. Because it is public services paid for collectively through our taxes that educate our kids, look after the elderly and keep our streets safe. If we allow these services to crumble through underfunding, we all pay the price.

When I half-heartedly put my name forward to be considered as a candidate for the Scottish Parliament, never for a second did I expect to be elected. Initially I didn't believe the Labour party would allow someone who has always been firmly on the left to clear the vetting process, but to my great surprise I did. I then expected to finish 17th of the 16 people who moved forward to a ranking ballot of Lothian members. To my astonishment, and probably theirs too, I came third. That's right, third. How on earth did that happen? But ultimately my fate lay in the quirks of the Scottish electoral voting system, which is now a hybrid of first-past-the-post and an Additional Member System. Previously, it was quite straightforward and whoever polled most votes won the constituency seat. That still happens, but a proportion of the seats are decided by a top-up system called the list. A party might win 50 per cent of the overall vote across the parliamentary region (in my case, Lothian), but on first-past-the-post votes they take just 25 per cent, so if you get 50 per cent of the vote across the region they top it up from the list to take you up to your 50 per cent. So as Labour seats were lost in constituencies across the Lothian region my chances on the list increased. In the end I was elected as a list MSP with Labour colleagues Sarah Boyack and Kezia Dugdale – two people I had never met prior to turning up at the decleration of our result.

When I turned up for my first day at Holyrood I knew very few of my own party colleagues, never mind my opponents. There were none I regarded as close friends, just people I'd met once or twice, or had previously seen on TV. So I went into the Scottish Parliament with no real connections, which I think was a good thing.

My first job was to find a parliamentary researcher; someone I could work easily alongside and preferably someone who shared many of my beliefs and ideals. I had been introduced to Tommy Kane through a mutual friend, Alan Brown, but we got to know each other much better during a week-long charity cycle trip across Cuba five years later. Tommy is from a family of political activists and lives in Addiewell. He worked as a market trader, pipe fitter and in a tyre factory before returning to further education in his late 20s, where he thrived. After gaining an HNC he went on to Stirling University and earned a PhD in sociology. An outstanding achievement. Tommy was as close to the perfect candidate as I could find. There was no interview, just a straightforward chat and an understanding of how we would work. We hit it off right away and he has worked with me since June, 2011. We are both driven by a desire for justice and fairness for our class.

In 2016 Tommy joined Labour leader Jeremy Corbyn's team of advisors, which was a well-deserved recognition of his talent and abilities. His role was to advise the Corbyn team on Scotland, but this didn't mean an end to our working relationship as he is still with me part time.

There is plenty of ding-dong political debate in the Holyrood chamber and I enjoy it best when it's lively and 'robust' and laced with a bit of humour. If you give it out you must be able to take it back and I try not to take it personally. The 2011 Scottish Government elections saw the SNP voted in with their first ever clear majority – the first time a ruling party had secured a majority, which wasn't meant to happen. The electoral system was designed to produce coalition governments and not a one-party majority. It was a remarkable achievement and almost inevitably there would be an independence referendum.

The Scottish Labour Party – dominant for the previous 30 years – had been trounced by the SNP. Labour MPs in the House of Commons reacted by pointing accusatory fingers at MSPs. Our Westminster cousins had long been portrayed by the media as the country's political elite, and sadly many of them believed that: the clever folk, the people who did the politics. They believed it was the Z-Listers who walked the corridors of Holyrood. Perhaps some of my colleagues felt a bit intimidated after that, but my attitude was, 'I have nothing to lose here – I am absolutely going to go for it.' I'm convinced that helped me early on as I was willing to robustly take on the opposition, argue my case and do so with a bit of passion, and a slice of humour at times. My mantra was, 'Why should I be scared of you lot?'

The primary function of an MSP is to represent those who voted you into office. Most people come to you with local issues. When I was a councillor I held regular surgeries – and still do – but over time technology has changed the way we operate. Why turn up at a draughty community centre on a wet Monday night when you can send an email straight from your phone? We have an office in West Calder where lots of people still drop in to speak to us, and it's staffed all the time, but technology is without doubt changing the way we work. We receive on average around 200 emails per day.

In the summer of 2012, I was privileged to be asked to go to Venezuela to be an observer at their national elections and saw it as a fantastic opportunity to learn how this complex South American country did their politics. Venezuela sits in one of the most heavily politicised regions in the world and the Socialist, Hugo Chavez had been in power for over a decade before his death from cancer which precipitated the election. We were there for a week and looked at every aspect of the election. Early polls suggested the Socialist candidate was 12 per cent ahead, but in the end Nicolas Maduro won by less than one per cent. Before we left, the situation had become extremely tense. Ten people had been shot dead and street violence was rife throughout the capital city, however there was no doubt the result was fair. As observers, we examined every aspect of the elections and signed off our report unanimously with just a few minor recommendations.

I returned to the day job at Holyrood where Parliament sits on Tuesday, Wednesday and Thursday afternoons. People probably see the chamber half empty and assume the rest of us are in the bar or having coffee, but what goes on in the chamber makes up only a fraction of what actually happens in Holyrood. Your time is taken up by dozens of meetings, covering a variety of topics. In 2016 I was elected as chairman of the parliament's Health Committee. As a former Shadow Health Spokesman for Labour, that's something I'm comfortable with and enjoy.

Each MSP is responsible for sorting out their own diary, and you put into it as much as you want. I like to have a wide range of interests and campaigns on the go. The thing that motivates me most is campaigning on grassroots issues, like with the mesh-injured women who are trying to get a faulty medical product banned, or to get justice for blacklisted construction workers, and that is the Tam Dalyell influence; the dogged campaigner who gets an issue and runs with it until he gets a result.

Some politicians adopt a tactic which sees them pick up on an issue that helps make their name, but an issue they will never resolve, so they can keep campaigning until the cows come home. I have no interest in that. The reason I campaign is to try and achieve a positive outcome, because ultimately people are hoping something will change for the better.

My office deals with thousands of cases every year and I'm fortunate to have a really good staff in Tommy, Marion Kirk (now retired), Andrew McGuire, Lesley Brennan and Frank Toner, as all go above and beyond to help people. As it turned out, I needed all their help, and more, when Scotland clicked into referendum mode in September, 2014. The country was set to go to the polls to vote on their constitutional future for the first time since 1979. It would prove to be quite a year.

2

Referendum Diary: January 2014

'Ladies and gentlemen, I Mary Pitcaithly, Chief Counting Officer at the Scottish Independence referendum held 18th September 2014 am pleased to confirm that all ballot papers have now been verified and counted and I am content the results are accurate. Accordingly, I hereby certify and declare... The total number of votes counted in the referendum for the whole of Scotland is 3,623,344. The turnout was 84.6 per cent. The total number of votes cast in favour of each answer to the referendum questions for the whole of Scotland is as follows... Yes – the number of votes is 1,617,989. No – the number of votes is 2,001,926. There were 3429 rejected papers.'

Mary Pitcaithly – Chief Counting Officer, Scottish Independence referendum
September 18, 2014

1 JANUARY: This will be a momentous year no matter the referendum result. One way or another, Scotland is going to be a different place by the end of the campaign, so I will keep a diary of the year just for my own interest. Chances are no one will ever see it but I want to record it from my own perspective.

As with every New Year I spent Hogmanay at my ma's. Fiona is working nights at the hospital and Chloe is at a New Year party, so I'm at my ma's with my brother John and his partner Sharron, my sister Anna, her husband Jim, my cousin Mick, who hails from Liverpool, and his wife Pam, and their kids Ali (mad hippy idealist, and fabulous musician who runs an annual music festival in Wales), Faye (biology teacher at the international school in Copenhagen), her husband Patrick (half Irish, half Danish), their one-year-old Flynn, who is absolutely gorgeous, and Fraser, who has just graduated in agriculture and works as a dairy farmer.

A fabulous night of music from Ali, Mick and Jim with everyone singing along. Plenty of beer, whisky, gin and wine, and some great crack. Hobbled off to bed at 5am – great start to 2014.

Referendum thought: early polls show big lead for No, but many folk are undecided and could sway the outcome. Labour *must* have a bold radical devo offer; the Devolution Commission must deliver, and deliver BIG. I have said from the moment I was elected that Scottish Labour MPs don't get it and are just an 'X' on a referendum ballot paper away from their P45. Indeed, when I said this at a meeting of MPs and MSPs in May 2014, Jim Murphy said I should keep such views to myself and that they were not required – such arrogance!

Working on a speech for our return to parliament next Tuesday and will use it to promote the position of the Red Paper Collective, of which I am a member. We are calling for radical federalism across the UK, retaining a redistributive system of taxation and the Barnett formula but with double devolution to regions and communities; if only Labour would say the same, I'm sure the referendum would be won quite easily.

2 JANUARY: The Liverpool gang went off to Edinburgh for the day – and they loved it. Edinburgh is a beautiful city, and we often take it for granted, but it's a great place.

Had a curry at my ma's with everyone before listening to Radio 4 documentary on miscarriages of justice from the miners' strike. I took part in the programme as part of my campaign for a review of the cases of miners arrested in Scotland during the momentous strike of 1984/85. That campaign will run and run – and I am determined to make progress with it this year.

3 JANUARY: Started working out campaign plan for this year. Political priority is the referendum, and I hope to expose the crisis in social care and health inequalities, as well as continuing my work on blacklisting and miners' justice. Personal priorities are the constituency selection and planning for the list selection which may become important post-referendum.

Today, the UK government released Cabinet papers from 30 years ago, the year of the miners' strike. The papers vindicate Arthur Scargill's claims that 75 pits were earmarked for closure, and also that the government was prepared to call in the army as the National Coal Board crumbled – and that on almost every count Thatcher lied, lied and lied again.

4 JANUARY: Radio 4 miners story has provoked another 150 people to sign up to my campaign for a review of convictions – now up to more than 2,500.

Went to the cinema with Fiona to watch *Long Walk to Freedom*, the Nelson Mandela story. Thoroughly enjoyed it and the actress who played Winnie Mandela, Naomie Harris, was fantastic.

5 JANUARY: *The Herald* splash with the story that John Mulvey – former leader of Lothian Regional Council, and someone I tried to help win the nomination to become our MSP in 1999 – has come out in favour of independence. He is another who made his name in the Labour Party before turning against us when his career was winding down. I have more respect for the likes of Jim Sillars and Alex Neil, who left the Labour Party years ago, before or in the middle of their careers on a point of principle.

6 JANUARY: Attended the funeral of family friends Brian and Kit McLaughlin in the local chapel. It is most unusual for a mother and son to be buried on the same day. Two really good people.

It was then over to Cowdenbeath to help at the by-election caused by the sudden and very sad death of Helen Eadie, a lovely, caring woman with a great Labour pedigree. Alex Rowley, Gordon Brown's right hand man, is our candidate. He is a shrewd operator and was excellent at the campaign launch. I suggested to Johann Lamont that we should stage a meeting in one of the miners' clubs and get Nicky Wilson from the National Union of Mineworkers along, as well as others, and tell them that when back in power we will hold a review into the convictions of miners in Scotland. This will go down a storm in Fife coalfield villages such as Lochgelly, Lochore and Ballingry, which are covered by the by-election. Johann isn't against it but has left the final decision to James Kelly as he is running the by-election with Gordon Banks MP – so that will be that kicked into touch. I guarantee we won't hear another word of this.

I also took 10 minutes to speak to Ian Price, the party's Scottish secretary, and urged him to re-think the pairing of the Almond Valley constituency with Falkirk East – (miles apart, no shared history, culture or understanding) but he looked at me in that vacant disinterested way he does and said he couldn't do anything about it. The SEC will decide on Saturday.

7 JANUARY: Tommy has taken a week's holiday in an effort to finish his eight-year-long PhD!

I take part in an SNP debate on Scotland's future, which focuses on child care and free school meals (not introduced by the SNP, but by Barnett consequentials from the coalition's decision to introduce them). The debate was dreadful, and it seems the new buzz phrase is 'transformative childcare'.

Every SNP automaton spews out this line as no doubt a focus group told them it was a fantastic phrase and of course *only* independence in their eyes can deliver it. They have the powers to deliver it but hey-ho that doesn't matter, as all they have to do is repeat the phrase!

The front bench position was poor. Instead of saying that of the two positive things – free school meals and childcare – we would put money into childcare as this is the best way to help families increase income through work, Johann and Kez got into claims that there is no evidence of the benefits of free school meals etc. This is simply not the case. There is a large body of evidence that suggests free school meals help children develop, concentrate and learn free from stigma. Predictably, this results in the SNP giving us a good kicking. I expected this would happen.

8 JANUARY: The papers have given Labour a hard time over the free school meals vote, which is hardly a shock. Why could people far more experienced than me not see this coming? Apparently Kez (Dugdale) said on TV last night that we may get rid of the small business bonus to fund childcare, and this was repeated by Patricia Ferguson today. I can just imagine the reaction had I said that. It is actually a decent suggestion, as the bonus is a £500 million gift to small businesses for zero return. They don't need to create a single job or pay the living wage to qualify. At the very least there should be conditions attached. We need to call out the SNP on this as there is no evidence of the policy delivering any of their objectives, but without a doubt it will deliver votes for them.

Went to Lochgelly Business Centre for the by-election launch. Former Dunfermline FC manager and Fife Provost Jim Leishman introduced Johann Lamont and Gordon Brown. Alex Rowley then spoke and was passionate, articulate, unscripted and Fife through and through. An excellent candidate!

It has been quite a day, and it ain't finished yet. I attended an evening group meeting on SNP plans to end corroboration. Women's groups believe its abolition will bring more prosecutions for sexual assault and rape cases, but this would be a huge and fundamental change to Scots law, which I fear would open the door to further miscarriages of justice. Not an easy issue, but at this stage I cannot support it, and will urge the Shadow Cabinet to oppose.
My mate Alan Brown and his partner Rebecca had their fourth child today.

They called him Keir, after Keir Hardie, founder of the Labour Party. A good name choice.

9 JANUARY: *The Herald* headlines today with the story of Dr Jane Hamilton, who headed up the perinatal ward at St John's, Livingston. This was supposed to be a national centre of excellence dealing with vulnerable women and their newborn babies, but she was suspended after raising a series of concerns about the safety of the unit and the procedures it follows, or doesn't follow to be more precise. I spoke to her at length and find it appalling that she is being gagged from speaking the truth. The NHS's handling of whistleblowing is very poor. Instead of dealing with these serious matters, and using them as an opportunity to improve services, there appears to be a culture where they attack, discredit or gag the person raising genuine concerns about patient safety. Not a good situation.

I asked Alex Salmond about this at First Minister's Questions and his retort was sharp. He was clearly unhappy about having to reply, but this is now on the record and I intend pursuing it as I find Jane a credible and committed person who has done nothing wrong. Time will tell if my judgement is right. After FMQs, NHS Lothian came out strongly against her saying everything has been investigated and they have no concerns.

Met with Anas Sarwar, Labour's deputy leader in Scotland, and he has given me two weeks to write a health paper for our devolution offer. Anas is well-mannered, ambitious and extremely well connected. His father was an MP and multi-millionaire businessman and became a Governor in Pakistan in 2016. He and I have differing political views on some things but there is a mutual respect and we get on well personally.

I then attended a meeting called by 38 degrees on lobbying (In 2012 I introduced the Lobbying Transparency (Scotland) Bill, which sought to introduce a register of lobbyists). Mike Crockhart, the Lib Dem MP, defended the awful UK government bill which is really just a naked attack on trade unions and their funding of Labour. Martin Sime, of the Scottish Council for Voluntary Organisations (SCVO), came out strongly against the UK bill, saying it was outrageous etc, but went all defensive when I tackled him on SCVO leading the charge against my bill in Scotland. The reality is he is Salmond's mate from university and does whatever the Scottish Government ask.

Tonight it was revealed that the French president Francois Hollande has been having an affair with a 41-year-old actress. I thought this was one of the qualifications for being the French President!

10 JANUARY: To Cowdenbeath for canvassing. I feel at home here; very much the same type of community and people as where I live. Cowdenbeath is an ex-mining town with lots of council housing, a football team and great people. I think I will enjoy this by-election.

11 JANUARY: Delivering election newspapers in Inverkeithing and it's a beautiful winter's day.

The Scottish Executive met today and agreed not to twin Almond Valley with Falkirk West. This is good news for me and helps if I go for the constituency nomination.

I was really saddened to hear of the death of local man Brian Welsh, who was only in his mid-50s. Cancer is soon to be the killer of one in three Scots and eventually one in two. Depressing stuff.

13 JANUARY: It's my surgery today, and the agenda includes a disturbing assault case, housing issues and need for drainage at local football pitches. I write to the relevant people and agencies on behalf of my constituents. Surgery and constituents' cases are the most important things I do and I take great care and pride in replying to everyone who contacts me. After all, they've taken the time to do so and deserve to be dealt with respectfully.
Housing is one of the greatest issues of our times. The under investment in council housing and selling off of homes has been a disaster. It is always a topic at my surgeries.

Chloe's first day on placement as a student occupational therapist. She is at the Orchard Clinic within the Royal Edinburgh Hospital. This is a place for high tariff violent mental health offenders and patients. Her mum and I were naturally anxious about this but she showed no sign of apprehension. She had an excellent first day talking to staff and patients and was unfazed by it all. Chloe has the right attitude for this type of work. Proud as punch.

14 JANUARY: Shadow Cabinet meeting with Scottish Trades Union Congress (STUC). They should be our greatest allies but stupid decisions over the years, and the advent of New Labour, have strained relations, and the SNP have cunningly built up a rapport with them. It was, however, a good meeting with Dave Moxham saying he thought the STUC wouldn't take a position on the referendum. This is as good as we are likely to get as unions are under strong pressure from their members, many of whom support a Yes vote.

15 JANUARY: Shadow health team meeting. Richard Simpson still off after cancer surgery but he calls in via Skype, which is quite effective. Truth is, we are fire-fighting just now without him, as his knowledge and advice is invaluable.

Was due to attend a meeting with Brian Connelly, father of junior doctor Lauren Connelly, who tragically died driving home after a long stretch of 12-hour-plus shifts. I had asked for a meeting with Salmond on this, and he agreed, but I can't attend, due to a debate I am leading on; so Tommy, and Margaret McCulloch one of his MSPs, agreed to attend. Tommy reported back that Linda Fabiani, MSP for East Kilbride, was there – Salmond must have invited her. I will call Brian tomorrow to talk further on what is a very serious matter.

Labour debate today calling for a wholescale review of the NHS. We need this as every element of the NHS is teetering on the brink. The call has been echoed by the Royal College of Nursing, British Medical Association, Royal College of Physios etc. Health Secretary Alex Neil's tactic is to dismiss all concerns and personally abuse me! This means we are being effective. If you can't answer the substantive point have a go at the man. Good speeches by Jackson Carlaw for the Tories, and Hugh Henry and Michael McMahon, with Alex Neil all bluff and bluster. Government rejects all calls for a review.

16 JANUARY: Chloe's 18th today, which is hard to believe. She is a confident, funny, young woman who is quite a character. She enjoys a night out, likes a bit of fun and can work hard. She doesn't get everything given to her on a plate and knows she has to contribute.

I went to watch the Standards and Procedures Committee evidence session concerning their inquiry into lobbying. Spinwatch, the Alliance for Lobbying Transparency and Unlocking Democracy, gave evidence. They were clear and confident with sound evidence, and spoke of the need for a register. In contrast, the reps from the lobbying industry looked smug and self-protecting. Alistair Ross was the best of them, while the others came across as vacuous.

At First Minister's Questions, Ruth Davidson accused Salmond of 'misleading people'. The Presiding Officer urged her to withdraw her statement, saying it was unparliamentary. Davidson was quick on her feet and instead said he was 'detached from the truth'! It was an interesting exchange as misled or misleading has been used over 70 times this session. I thought someone would raise this at the end as a point of order but as no one did I went ahead and asked Patricia Marwick for advice and consistency in its use. She isn't the greatest Presiding Officer, and can be rather partisan, even though she does give me quite a lot of opportunities at FMQs etc. I personally get on okay with her.

17 JANUARY: To Cowdenbeath to deliver hundreds of leaflets in a block of flats. Response on doorstep is decent and we are hoping for a 5,000 majority. If the weather is good on the day it will definitely help.

Chloe's 18th birthday party tonight in the house. Fiona put in a huge effort with lots of photos up on the walls, great food, home baking etc. Around 50 people, young and old, appeared and it was fantastic – music, banter, dancing till the early hours. I do love a party in the house and the young folk's company was great.

18 JANUARY: Lie in till 12 noon, and then it's the big clear-up after the party. Actually, the house isn't too bad. Several trips to the bottle bank though!

Excited for tonight. Going to Bathgate to see The Underground Jam tribute band. It will be like a school reunion. The Jam are my all-time favourite band so I expect the place to be bouncing.
    The gig was fantastic. The music was spot on and I knew lots of folk there: Tossy McDonald, Elaine and Damian Byrne, Sean, Mikey, Tony Fairley, Gee McCafferty, Toyer, Martin Rennie, our John, Alan Findlay, Brunton. Best gig in ages.

20 JANUARY: Surgery at the office in West Calder. Today's issues included fishing rights on the River Tay, anti-social behaviour and access to GPs and podiatry.

Off to Cowdenbeath for by-election campaigning and I was out with Councillor Billy Pollock (elected on the same day as Cara Hilton, our victor in Dunfermline) and Harry Cartmill from Bathgate. It was a good session. Ed Balls is in town to do some campaigning. I was leaving just as he arrived. I have to say he looks a real ruthless bastard, but maybe you need that to get to the top in politics.
    Alex Rowley has the support of Councillor Willie Clarke, a Fife legend and the last Communist councillor in the UK. It's amazing to think

Cowdenbeath used to have a Communist-run town council. The SNP are trying to discredit Willie locally – and he is a Yes supporter too!

21 JANUARY: Shadow Cabinet meeting with Ian McNicol, Labour's UK General Secretary. Complete unanimity from members telling McNicol to wake up to what is going on. I spoke out saying I was appalled that Labour were sleepwalking towards independence and MPs would be on the dole at this rate. I don't think he gets it but he was left under no illusion about how we felt. I feel that as a Scot, McNicol should have known better but it appears he is just reflecting the UK party's complete lack of understanding of the situation in Scotland.

Spoke in debate on suicide today. A friend of mine, Des Murphy, holds an annual concert in our village to raise money for the charity Touched by Suicide. The community show massive support and raise thousands of pounds each year. Des's boy committed suicide about six years ago, and his family do so much to help the charity.

22 JANUARY: Spoke to a friendly lawyer today about a letter I received from ex-MP Jim Devine, who is to appear in court in Edinburgh in a defamation case with a former employee, Marion Kinley. The letter says Devine will call me to give evidence. I worked for Devine for about four hours before realising the madness I could be getting involved in, and walked out – sending him a stinging email on the way out. My lawyer pal says he will handle it; that the Irish law firm has no jurisdiction in dealing with this and that the whole thing looks a bit iffy. I feel a bit better now. Devine is a capable man from a very good family, but has lost the plot. I feel sorry for him but more so his family.

To the Bonham Hotel where I was the main speaker on health at a dinner hosted by the Centre for Public Policy. Twenty health people there, including board chiefs, academics, drug company reps, etc. I spoke about health inequality, social care, falling budgets, staffing issues etc. and repeated my call for a wholescale review of the NHS in Scotland. Interesting that the Chair of one of Scotland's largest health boards supported this but would not commit to saying it publicly. Good event and I think I got my points across well.

23 JANUARY: Met with my brother, John and sister, Anna. John had just crashed his car on the motorway but thankfully didn't sustain any injuries. They were in for my members' debate on discrimination by airlines against

disabled passengers, and wanted to speak about issues like the lack of small wheelchairs to move passengers etc. John said that each time he goes on holiday it's an unmitigated disaster with regards to wheelchair and disabled provision, and that many disabled people have had similar experiences. Roberto Casteglioni of the Reduced Mobility Rights passenger group says this happens all over and that the EU must tighten up on it.

I led the debate, and Alex Johnston and Jackie Baillie were excellent and supportive, while Colin Keir, who chairs the cross party group on aviation, was the apologist for the airline industry. He had clearly been lobbied. Afterwards, easyJet rep said they would change their policy and carry on-board aisle wheelchairs. It was a small victory, but made the effort worthwhile. Let's hope others follow. The Minister agreed to write to the airlines and the EU about this matter. This has been a good day and hopefully I have made a difference to the lives of some disabled passengers.

Over to Cowdenbeath for five hours of door knocking. It was bloody freezing but hopefully worth it!

24 JANUARY: Stayed up late for Cowdenbeath result. Eleven per cent swing to Labour with 5,488 majority – a brilliant win for Alex Rowley. However, there is still a big worry that working class voters feeling shafted by Tory and Blair Governments are saying 'to hell with it – independence can't be worse than this so let's vote Yes'. I completely understand this, so we need a response that is more coherent than saying Better Bloody Together. It's clear to me the SNP will go all out to target Labour voters who hold the key to the referendum result.

25 JANUARY: After some union work it was off to the pub to 'wet the wean's heid' with Alan Brown, his family, and our mates. I'm a bit worried that my mates Scotty and Toyer, both solid socialists, are voting Yes. These guys are a good barometer for me.

27 JANUARY: Devolution health paper due in today. I gave it to Richard Simpson for a final look and his fresh pair of eyes was a godsend. We were getting bogged down in detail but he nailed it and I'm very pleased with our contribution.

Received a briefing from Kez Dugdale on her childcare campaign called 'every step'. It is straight from the 'movement for change' manual and 'Progress' crib sheet. Kez is ambitious and capable. She appeared recently on BBC Question Time and was very good but it is being over promoted too early by certain people in the party.

Went to surgery at South Queensferry and came home to check emails – one from a regular who is always abusive and threatening, although this one went a bit further. Might have to alert the police to this guy's behaviour. It turns out he is a council employee, so I may also have to raise this, albeit reluctantly, with the chief executive of the council.

28 JANUARY: To Shadow Cabinet – report from Cowdenbeath is that Labour's returns show 59 per cent of Labour voters against independence and 17 per cent in favour. I think this is complete bollocks, said so and was supported by others. If folk believe this they are mad!

29 JANUARY: Saw on Twitter this morning that Labour at Westminster will call for an apology for miners arrested at Orgreave, as well as the release of all papers – plus an inquiry. This is fantastic news on one hand but hugely frustrating on the other. I had urged the Scottish party during the Cowdenbeath by-election to announce that we would hold a Scottish inquiry on coming to power. As predicted, the Scottish party dilly-dallied and James Kelly and Gordon Banks failed to lead on this. It would be an understatement to say I am furious. I contacted Johann's office and urged them to lead with it at FMQs. Again they took a conservative approach and simply put out a press release, eventually, calling for a review. I will push on with my campaign as many people have signed up to support my efforts.

Today Mark Carney, Governor of the Bank of England said that the sterling zone proposed by the SNP would mean a loss of sovereignty. At last. The Red Paper Collective have been arguing this for two years. Amongst the Yes camp it is difficult to find people who agree with the SNP on this. The Greens don't, SSP don't and Dennis Canavan doesn't, but none of that matters. The SNP hierarchy dictates the line and the others must go along with it.

30 JANUARY: Papers are full of Carney's criticism – the SNP policy is being savaged but Salmond and Sturgeon bluster on. Their brass neck and ability to say black is white is remarkable.

As chair of the Public and Commercial Services (PCS) union parliamentary group I work across parties with colleagues who support the work of the union. Today I met Scottish Secretary Lynne Henderson to discuss the likely outcome of their consultation with branches, and the position of the union in relation to the referendum. To date no trade union has come out for a Yes vote but Lynne suspects PCS will. Sturgeon has promised them the world: no redundancies, living wage and new jobs! It's complete rubbish but she just does this anyway – anything to get folks' votes. PCS has a small but influential number of Socialist Party of Britain and SSP members in their leadership team and some of their branch activists are pro-independence so not the biggest surprise to me. It won't change the way I deal with Lynne and her team, or any of their members, but it would be significant if they came out for Yes.

3

Referendum Diary: February 2014

1 FEBRUARY: Enjoyed a rare long lie before taking Chloe to her work (weekend cleaner at the local hospital) then onto the Midlothian CLP Burns Supper where I spoke, told some jokes and enjoyed the banter. We then heard from Jim Leishman, the main speaker. He is a natural raconteur and story teller, and lived up to his excellent reputation. Fiona O'Donnell gave the reply from the lassies (which was filthy, but very funny).

Alex Rowley's daughter, Danielle, was one of the organisers so I got a chance to have a good chat to Alex, who came along with Fife MSP Jayne Baxter. Alex will be a good addition to the group, but he isn't impressed so far and won't sit quiet for long. He told me during the campaign they had booked a venue to announce the miners' justice stuff, which the campaign team then pulled – idiots!

Left a wee bit early to attend my sister-in-law Lynne's 40th birthday meal in Linlithgow. Fiona was on nightshift so I went myself.

2 FEBRUARY: To Ardrossan to speak to Cunninghame South CLP about some of the campaigns and issues I'm involved in; miners' justice, blacklisting, social care and the Red Paper Collective. Alex Gallacher (a councillor in Ayrshire and prolific writer of letters to newspapers) and Alan Wilson (former MSP and government minister) were there and were very hostile to any further devolution and, it seemed, devolution itself! They reckon we should just argue for a No vote and forget any other offer of powers. These guys are seriously deluded if they think that's the answer. They are so far out of touch it frightens me. We agreed to disagree.

3 FEBRUARY: Michael Sharpe started in the office today for a few months over the summer. He is the son of MP Cathy Jamieson and a really bright, switched-on young guy from a very political family. He will be a great asset.

Thousands of emails coming in about same-sex marriage vote this week. The overwhelming majority in favour. As a Catholic I thought I would get a lot of heat from the church as I fully support the proposal, but opposition has been limited. I think they are putting up a token resistance because they know so many people in their congregations support it.

4 FEBRUARY: This morning's Shadow Cabinet meeting was a cards-on-the-table session with concerns raised about policy, lack of strategy, our devolution offer – or lack of it – the trade union link etc. I spoke of the failure to grab the initiative on the miners' justice campaign, using this as an example of us having the chance to lead on a UK-wide issue and blowing our chance – which was completely ignored by Johann, James Kelly etc.

This afternoon's historic debate on same-sex marriage saw parliament vote overwhelmingly in favour of the bill and I was proud to support it. There were excellent speeches from across the political spectrum, including Ruth Davidson, Patrick Harvie, Jim Eadie and James Dornan. It was a passionate and often moving debate with many personal reflections and insights being aired. It was parliament very much at its best. Some of the social media abuse aimed towards people who took part on either side of the debate was regrettable, but in general it is good for our democracy. For the LGBT community this was a huge issue, with jubilant scenes across the country and much celebration. The first gay marriages are scheduled for the autumn. In a year or two we will reflect and wonder what all the fuss was about.

5 FEBRUARY: Met with Christina Taylor and her sister. Christina worked as an activities co-ordinator at Pentland Hills care home, owned by Bupa. She told me the story of how her mum went into the home and she thought that as she worked there, she would be able to keep an eye on her and ensure she was well looked after. However, the care was horrendous. Her mum was assaulted by a staff member and had to go to hospital. The management lied, covered up the story and fabricated evidence. The place exploits migrant labour on low pay with little resources. Ultimately the person who assaulted Christina's mum got off, while the managers who were supposedly dismissed were simply moved to another home. While this is shocking, it's not surprising and is sadly too common in social care. It is nothing short of a national disgrace. Poverty pay, zero hours contracts, poor standards, inadequate inspection regime and contracts based on lowest tender are at the root of it all. This issue will only get worse.

Budget debate today, but I still don't get it. There seems to be some principle or convention that we are supposed to agree the budget across parties. Why? Anyway, we secured funding to mitigate the bedroom tax despite (John) Swinney saying he didn't want to do this and 'let Westminster off the hook!' The reality is I went to Jackie Baillie and suggested we bring in a members' bill on the Bedroom Tax, and she ran with the idea and worked with Mike Dailly at the Govan Law Centre on a bill. Only when the SNP knew the bill was proceeding were they forced to act, claiming it was their actions that mitigated it. Regardless, we have done well by some of the poorest people in Scotland and I'm very pleased to have suggested the route to do that. Jackie Baillie played a blinder in pushing this through at breakneck speed, which forced the Government's hand.

6–13 FEBRUARY: I won money from the bookies on a football bet just before Christmas. I put a coupon on most weeks but realise it's usually just a donation. Not this time, although you could say I won it by default. For a start, I changed my bookie for some reason and the bet I put on was construed as something else (I like to think that, but it was actually me who messed up!). Anyway, instead of getting a treble and a four-fold up, I got a seven-team accumulator up, although Derby County made me sweat. I will always have a soft spot for the Rams now. I won the grand total of £3,000 for a £14 bet (I have never won anything close to that before and probably never will again) and instead of frittering it away on this and that, I decided to take Fiona to Egypt for a week's holiday – total relaxation: and thank you Derby County!

14 FEBRUARY: Huge row as George Osborne, Ed Balls and Danny Alexander insist there will be no sterling zone. Why do they keep doing this? It's bonkers and feeds the SNPs victim mentality – they will now say look at Labour teaming up with the big bad Tories and useless Liberals to stop Scotland using our own currency! The strategists thinking this through are hopeless.

15 FEBRUARY: The currency row shows no sign of abating.

16 FEBRUARY: On *The Andrew Marr Show*, Manuel Barroso, President of the European Commission, said that (in the event of independence), Scotland would have to apply to join the EU just like any other state and access would not be automatic. Swinney said this was 'preposterous'. He is once again using the black is white tactic!
On currency zone proposals, the arguments rumble on – but the

bottom line is, the SNP will need a plan B. Their proposal is just piss poor – Jim Sillars called it 'stupidity on stilts'? Why would you let the central bank of another country (England in this case) determine your interest rates etc. and why would you allow the Chancellor of another country to determine economic policy – it is just madness! We should have kept this argument for later in the campaign as it's so damaging. If Osborne is seen to be coming north to tell Scots what they can and can't do it will backfire badly as he is hated up here. The SNP are trotting out the bluff, bluster and bullying claim.

Paul Sinclair, Johann Lamont's chief of staff, has been tweeting that there is a cancer around the independence debate – this isn't clever either as it will be used mercilessly against us.

17 FEBRUARY: Currency debate is fierce, and Salmond is trying to invoke Obama's 'yes we can' in relation to using sterling. Meanwhile, Balls, Alexander and Osborne say No! Salmond's line is that the Bank of England is part-owned by Scotland and we have every right to use that asset and if we don't then Scotland will default on its debt and refuse to accept our share. Salmond's tactic is to pitch it as Scotland v. England – this is simple nationalism at play and not the civic kind!

Met with 20 Labour council leaders in Glasgow today to discuss crisis in social care – only one woman there out of 20 people! Everyone agreed social care is in crisis and that funding is key. All want to see the introduction of a living wage, end of zero hours contracts and improved standards, but they have to be able to fund it and cannot do this with the SNPs all-out attack.

18 FEBRUARY: Met Ranald Mair of Scottish Care. He agreed with the 'social care in crisis' line, and with much of my analysis. He said that in Edinburgh, 15 per cent of social care beds are vacant due to concerns over poor care. In Glasgow the figure is 20 per cent, and 15 per cent in the Highlands.

Shadow Cabinet presentation by Anas Sarwar on the document 'Together we can' to be presented at conference. It looks decent. Met afterwards with Anas, Susan Dalgety and Danny Phillips, who have been commissioned to write the report. The health section looks good – our big commitments are all there, including the call for a 'Beveridge style' review of the NHS, social care etc. I've a good feeling about this. If we can promote it professionally it could be a turning point in showing what enhanced devolution could mean, and that is a modern, progressive Scotland with fully-funded, quality public services financed by the UK's wide redistribution and devolved Scottish taxes.

19 FEBRUARY: Health team welcomed Dr Richard Simpson back after being off for around six months following cancer surgery. He looks weaker but in good spirits and it's great to have him back. He is such an asset and a good man who cares deeply about the NHS.

Went to SECC to speak at UNISON social care event. They have published a terrific report called 'Time to Care', highlighting the scandalous terms and conditions experienced by care staff. One in 10 are on zero hours contracts. Back at 6pm to vote, and then to the STUC Trade Union Week reception. It was great to meet so many friends there.

20 FEBRUARY: Met BMA junior doctors' rep to discuss excessive hours and punishing rotas being worked by young medics. Mentioned the Lauren Connelly case which struck a chord with them, and agreed to work with them on this.

Met my niece Eleana for lunch and a tour around parliament – she is really bright and is studying accounts at Strathclyde. Thoroughly good company.

Hosted 'Unions into Schools' event for Trade Union Week and discussed the referendum with the young people. On a show of hands very few seemed to be supporting independence.

Spoke in the debate on public procurement, highlighting the opportunity to address blacklisting and tax avoidance through public procurement by stopping companies getting contracts if they don't address blacklisting and self-cleanse, and if they don't pay their taxes. Nicola Sturgeon was lead minister on the bill. She doesn't attempt to hide her dislike of me because I don't roll over to them, but I won't lose any sleep over it. What is clear is that the government will do nothing on some of the major procurement issues. It will be a huge missed opportunity.

21 FEBRUARY: Leafleting with the team in Fauldhouse today and noticed the headline in *The Herald*. It screams 'PCS Union to Vote Yes to Independence'. Oh well, if this is true the weekend PCS conference will be lively. I am debating the referendum with Sturgeon.

22 FEBRUARY: To Glasgow for the PCS one-day conference to decide the union's position on the referendum. Outside, the ultra-left groups are selling newspapers. I bought a *Morning Star* and chatted with friends. Inside was a bit different though. I made a point of speaking to Sturgeon (or trying to as we sat together on the platform) but she was having none of it – ice cold and dismissive of my attempts at small talk, so I gave up.

Lynne Henderson spoke first about the PCS and its democratic processes, and how they had consulted widely with workplace meetings etc. She appealed for the union not to take any position on the referendum and allow members to make their own minds up. Given yesterday's *Herald* headline this would be a great result if Lynne's position was passed. I don't know what Lynne's personal position is on the question, but naturally she doesn't want the union to be divided, which is understandable.

Sturgeon then spoke and offered a list of bribes, some of which she cannot deliver, in the event of independence. No compulsory redundancies, facility time, check off, living wage etc. How can she guarantee no compulsory redundancies with the austerity that would follow the end of Barnett and setting up of a new state?

I had no bribes to offer but did have a class analysis of the SNP position and what it would mean for workers, the trades unions and ordinary people across the UK – corporation tax cuts, tax competition, new currency, divided trade unions and a reduced role for DFID and HMRC etc. After some intelligent and lively contributions, the conference voted – 18,500 to take no position, 5,500 for a Yes position and zero to support a No vote. Sturgeon left straight after she spoke, whereas I stayed to the end and went for a few beers in the Griffin Bar with delegates and enjoyed the chat. This was the best zero vote ever, and I would love to have seen Sturgeon's face as the result was announced, but she was gone by then. This was the one big union they thought they had in the bag. I have no doubt a great many PCS members will vote Yes, but the union will not officially campaign for a Yes position – result. Looks like the *Herald*'s Magnus Gardham is up for this year's Tartan Bollocks award for one of the biggest bullshit stories of the year!

24 FEBRUARY: Fiona off to Pitlochry for a few days with her mum and sisters.

25 FEBRUARY: Richard Baker has been undertaking a review of public spending commitments, such as free bus passes and prescriptions, following Johann Lamont's 'something for nothing' speech which questioned these polices. That was an ill-judged, badly-written speech which, had it been pitched better, could have opened up a real debate, but quoting Thatcher

killed it before she had sat down. Anyway, we received Baker's paper 20 minutes before the Shadow Cabinet meeting. I complained bitterly that we hadn't time to read or digest it before the meeting. I made my position clear that I would not support cutting any of these universal benefits but instead recommend we argue for devolved tax powers and use them to tax the wealthy and middle classes who gain from them. I also said the red leaflets we put out during the Cowdenbeath and Dunfermline by-elections, which stated we would keep these policies, should have put the issue to bed. I feel isolated as people probably share my views but won't say so.

Met Paul McCarthy and Neil Smith from the GMB to discuss my idea for a class justice conference. We would bring together the blacklisting, miners' justice, Shrewsbury pickets, Cammell Laird workers, phone hacking and Hillsborough campaigners, and we would learn from each other about individual campaign successes and failures. They're keen on taking this forward.

Tonight, Sturgeon and Johann Lamont went head-to-head on a TV debate – and it was appalling. Two intelligent, principled women reduced to stairheid rammy. If the cameras weren't there it could have ended up with fistfuls of hair and blood and snotters. Truly awful stuff – I switched it off.

26 FEBRUARY: Met with James Kelly, the chief whip. I had to get to the bottom of what happened with the miners' justice stuff at Cowdenbeath. He said everything had been arranged. Miliband had agreed it and Gordon Brown was going to speak. The venue was booked etc and one of Johann's advisors kyboshed it. What the hell for? Miliband then announced it in the House of Commons and we lost any initiative or recognition in the Scottish coalfield communities. Crazy!

Went to Royal College of Nursing (RCN) conference in Glasgow and spoke about the pressures of the NHS. We did a Q&A that went well and the feeling was I got a decent hearing from them.

27 FEBRUARY: It was revealed today that Joan McAlpine, Salmond's parliamentary aide, has been exposed having an affair with an ex-SNP researcher and is now implicated in an expenses probe. McAlpine spouts bile in her weekly column in the *Daily Record* and has been critical of MPs cheating with their expenses. What goes around comes around!

News today about Standard Life – who employ 6,000 in Scotland – saying they will leave if Scotland goes independent. Mind you, they said they would do the same with devolution and didn't.

Today's vote on corroboration saw the opposition united against it and the government win by just three votes. Kenny McAskill really is so right wing on justice issues and he tried to deflect by saying that everyone who voted against was a Tory. What childish nonsense.

To Lothian UNISON Health branch to debate referendum with Dennis Canavan. 100 members there and a largely good-natured meeting. Many voting Yes and have bought the line that we only need a Yes vote to deliver socialism in Scotland whereas the reality is we will deliver a free market, neo-liberal, low-taxed society. I enjoyed the meeting even though it was undoubtedly a Yes audience, but it was comradely. One thing to note is that Michael McGahey, Mick's son, who is a UNISON officer, is voting Yes. I wonder what his da's view would have been as many communists are split on the issue.

I remember meeting Mick in 1992 at the Labour Party conference when as a young delegate I attended a meeting of the newly formed 'Scotland United', a group campaigning for a Scottish Parliament following John Major's election victory. The panel at the event consisted of George Galloway, Irene Adams, John McAllion and Dennis Canavan and the entire audience consisted of me and Mick! Despondent at the lack of interest, I left the meeting only to hear Mick call out to me, 'There might only have been two us at the meeting son, but we are right'! And so he was.

Afterwards went to speak at Edinburgh East CLP and got home at 10.30pm.

28 FEBRUARY: Went to old Tom Rodgers' funeral. He was a quiet, well respected man and known throughout the village. Good turnout at the chapel, and the choir, of which Tom was a long-standing member, were in fine voice. The Catholic Church at its best.

Then to the Royal Infirmary in Edinburgh to host the annual charity quiz for staff members. Good crack – enjoyed it.

Phone call from Adrian Weir at Unite in London asking if we can put pressure on the Foreign Office as they have refused a visa to Rene Gonzalez, one of the so called 'Miami Five' Cubans recently released from a US jail after serving 13 years on falsified spying charges. I called Hugh Henry, Elaine Smith and Sandra White to ask them to do the same.

4

Referendum Diary: March 2014

2 MARCH: Have been privileged to speak at several *Morning Star* conferences, including this one. John Foster and the CP folk are great and always draw a crowd of very serious, knowledgeable people from across the broad left, so you always get a fair hearing. There are about 100 people present to debate the referendum. Dennis Canavan and Zara Kitson of the Green Party are up against Richard Leonard of the GMB and me. Richard is sound in his politics. He is the GMBs political officer and a really clever and articulate man; someone who knows their Labour movement history inside out. Canavan was his usual bitter anti-Labour self. Mind you, he has a lot to be bitter about given the way they treated him. Zara was okay. Richard and I gave a good account of ourselves and put forward the Red Paper line that the debate shouldn't be about borders and flags but what constitutional settlement will be in the best interests of the UK working class. Some of the so-called Radical Independence folk were there, like Cat Boyd, who fancies herself as some sort of left superstar. She actually asked what the plan is to bring about socialism in the event of a No vote! Bloody hell, what is the plan to bring about socialism with a divided working class and trade union movement in the low-taxed, free market, neo-liberal Scotland that Salmond and Swinney are planning?

3 MARCH: Met Jim Forrest and Alison McCallum to discuss concerns over cancer rates in West Lothian. I urged them to look into this. After the meeting I felt awful – coughing and spluttering. Man flu, perhaps?

4 MARCH: Off to London with Tommy Kane and Lawrence Cowan to meet Andy Burnham about health issues and take part in a series of other meetings. I coughed, sweated and spluttered the whole way down. Feeling awful. Graeme Morrice is hosting us and is always very hospitable when we are in London. Bumped into Jim Sheridan who is depressed at Unite's

failure to come out for a No vote. They won't because of pressure from members but MPs don't get this.

Spoke to Davie Hamilton and briefed him on the miners' justice campaign. He was scathing about (Jim) Murphy and Douglas Alexander's recent pronouncements about the referendum. I then caught sight of Murphy at a table with the Scottish press pack, briefing them about something – no doubt derogatory towards Johann, MSPs and everyone else except him.

Met with Andy Burnham and his advisor Kevin Lee. Andy has produced the Oldham report into social care. He wants to integrate physical, social and mental health needs under the same principle as the NHS, paid for by taxation and a tax on estates. This would mean everyone paid and everyone could access care without having to empty their bank accounts, which often eats into a legacy for children. I really like it.

I raised our upcoming conference and the call for Beveridge '21, which he liked, and encouraged us to go for it. A very positive meeting and my feeling is if Labour win the election he would go for this right away and try to take the heat out of it early.

I feel like I'm dying so it's back to Graeme's flat and in bed for tea time.

5 MARCH: After an awful night, I'm up early to get to King's Cross for the train home. Slept all the way and went straight to bed.

6 MARCH: I don't really do birthdays but it's mine today and I'm still feeling rotten, but into parliament as I had a question to ask the First Minister on the failure of the Scottish Government to meet A&E waiting times. Not my best FMQs but the problems of the NHS grow by the day and cover almost every area of our health service. This is not a political comment from me; just what staff are experiencing every day in their jobs, and patients in the service.

Catch up with Alex Rowley. He appears exasperated by the lack of any strategy within the parliamentary group. These reflect the feelings I have had since joining parliament and they have become deeply engrained since entering the Shadow Cabinet. Alex is experienced and thoughtful. I think we can work together on a number of things if we get the chance, but the party is a mess and I don't think the people advising Johann know how to get us out of it.

Straight home for birthday tea with family and relatives. Nice way to unwind.

Got word tonight that there are major problems/disagreements with the Devolution Commission paper. It appears Ed Balls is digging his heels in over the devolution of taxation. I texted Johann and party chairman Jackson Cullinane, urging them to stand firm and tell Balls to piss off. If we get this wrong and look timid we are done for.

7 MARCH: Phone call from Unite to say Mark Lyons (union convener at INEOS Grangemouth, sacked by Jim Ratcliffe following the Falkirk Labour/INEOS debacle) has his interim tribunal hearing today. He has a strong case as he was treated dreadfully by INEOS. They asked if I would give a press comment if required. Of course I will. Mark and his colleague, Stevie Deans, have also been treated appallingly by the Labour Party. Neither have done anything wrong, yet they've lost their jobs, had their reputation trashed and the police investigating them. All claims of wrongdoing are unfounded, yet I haven't heard the Labour Party or anyone else apologise.

News came through later that Mark has won his interim hearing and will be on full pay until the hearing in around a year. The tribunal judgement reckon he will win his case when heard. This is fantastic news and at least some justice has been delivered.

9 MARCH: To Livingston for the CLP meeting to commemorate the 30th anniversary of the miners' strike. Ex-miner Brendan Moohan read poetry, while John Cunningham performed some great folk songs. We had posters and memorabilia from the strike and people recalling their activities at the time. Great event.

10 MARCH: Busy constituency day. Met Carers of West Lothian to discuss the Carers Bill going through parliament. They are a fabulous organisation providing vital support for the thousands of local people who perform caring roles for family and friends daily.

Spent the afternoon leafleting the Craigshill area of Livingston with our team, before heading to Inveralmond High School in the evening to meet a ladies group and discuss the referendum. The women, aged 35 to 80, were all interested in the issues and asked serious questions about social care, pensions, local services etc. Some said they would pay more taxes to get better services. Observing the body language and reactions I would guess around 30 were No voters and perhaps only five Yes voters. I was surprised at how opposed they were. They even gave me £20 to cover my petrol but only took it back after a great deal of arguing. Really enjoyable discussion overall.

11 MARCH: As I was getting ready to attend the Shadow Cabinet meeting, news filtered through that RMT leader Bob Crow had died suddenly. I was stunned by this. Bob was one of the best and most high profile union leaders in the country. He led from the front, never flinched in the face of media hostility and had the full support of his members, as well as many in the wider Labour movement. He skilfully used his position and members' strengths to halt the transport sector to win higher wages and protect jobs and conditions on the railway and the wider transport sector. He described himself as a Communist and a militant, and didn't flinch when the RMT left the Labour Party. He saw it as an opportunity to act without any pressure from the party. I met him a few times as a member of the RMT parliamentary group. He simplistically and wrongly, in my view, conflated Scottish independence with Irish nationalism and supported independence. Despite some differences I liked Bob; I respected him greatly and am deeply saddened at his passing.

To Crosshouse Hospital for UNISON Ayrshire and Arran AGM and debate on constitution with Jim Sillars. I was late because of a huge traffic jam after a bad accident. I got there as Sillars was just starting. His rhetoric is good but his analysis is woeful! It can be summarised as: 'Scotland is a left wing country (is it?) and all we have to do is to vote for independence and socialism will follow. Oh, and I've written a book and it contains the manifesto for that socialist Scotland'. What planet is he living on? He also said I was 'a member of the political elite'! Me, an ex-bricklayer, who lives in a council scheme in Fauldhouse and is married to a nursing assistant is a member of the political elite, whereas he is married to a politician, lives in Morningside and has a holiday home in Portugal. You can draw your own conclusions as to who is a member of the political elite. I enjoyed it though and I like Jim, as he is able to discuss things afterwards and remain friendly. The fact that his wife Margo and I get along very well helps.

12 MARCH: Met with the RCN today. They have huge worries about social care and the NHS and said I had made a good impression on their members at the RCN conference a few weeks back. They are keen to work with us on the big health issues.

Papers again full of Joan McAlpine and her expenses.

14 MARCH: Awful news as my political hero Tony Benn has died at the age of 88. I first met him at the Clause IV rally at the Scottish Conference in 1994 where he made the case to retain our commitment to common ownership

with such clarity. He was simply the greatest political communicator of the last half century. He captured my imagination when I was a teenager as he could make complex issues easily understood and argue with passion, integrity and dignity. He didn't go in for personal attacks, preferring to argue about policy. He would have been a great, radical Prime Minister. The press vilified him and ran poisonous campaigns against him because they feared he could win. The Labour right hated him and set up the SDP. Tony inspired millions of people across the world and campaigned relentlessly, taking part in tens of thousands of public meetings, right up until his death. His great causes were peace, democracy, justice and socialism. A fine socialist preacher. This has been an awful week for the left. First Bob, and now Tony – solidarity comrades.

15 MARCH: To Edinburgh where I had been invited to an austerity rally planned by an organisation which was presumably a front for the Socialist Workers Party. We marched through Edinburgh to the square at Lothian Road. I was at the front with Jackie Baillie, who has been doing great work on the Bedroom Tax Bill, and forcing the government to act. Despite this a few people wearing Yes Scotland badges and scarves came to the front and started yelling through a loud hailer that Jackie was scum, Labour scumbags etc. This went on for an hour. Several times I asked a guy to stop abusing a woman in that way and if he wanted he could shout abuse at me. I gave him my name so he started shouting 'Findlay scumbag, Findlay scum'! He soon got bored and went back to abusing Jackie. Another guy kept chanting 'no banks, no money, the drug dealers are taking over the city'! As a catchy slogan it won't make the charts! At the rally, Jackie was booed and heckled by some of the baying mob. I spoke about Tony Benn and Bob Crow and the values they represented, values of solidarity, community and justice. I didn't get much heckling but some of these folk are clearly mad. They wouldn't understand unity and solidarity if it slapped them in the face. It is sheer political sectarianism and will only get worse as the referendum draws nearer.

16 MARCH: Fiona and Chloe are at work while everyone else is at my ma's for Sunday dinner. They came in after finishing at the hospital. I really enjoy these days when everyone is together.

17 MARCH: Leafleting in Addiewell. The houses have all been insulated and re-rendered and the place looks fantastic. What a transformation when the physical appearance of houses is improved so dramatically. I love Addiewell; it's a great place. Jobs, the living wage and security of

employment are the policy areas that would help so many people here. These have to be a priority for Labour.

Devolution Commission report out today and it's disappointing. They have come up with a convoluted 40 per cent of tax being devolved, devo of housing benefit and attendance allowance, health and safety admin, employment tribunals and other things, but it looks weak, unenthusiastic and limited. I fear we will get hammered for this. Labour MPs will like it as they will see it as protecting their power, but they will take a hiding and won't need to worry about power as many will be out on their ear.

Tensions in Crimea and Ukraine mounting – very worrying!

18 MARCH: Met with Bristol-Myers Squibb (pharmaceutical company). They are lobbying to get a new drug approved for Hepatitis C. They make a very good case and believe it could eradicate this awful virus. I do however get really angry and frustrated by these companies. They always come lobbying for approval for drugs that cost tens of thousands for treatment for one person and NEVER one that costs a few pence or a few pounds. They really do play God and extract huge amounts of cash out of the NHS. There must be a better way of developing new medicines, perhaps via public ownership, so we can develop drugs and maximise their impact on patients without being ripped off.

Today was the launch of Labour's Devolution Commission paper. Main points were 15p of income tax devolved, housing benefit, attendance allowance, tribunals, equalities legislation, double devolution to councils, etc. For me, it comes across as a set of proposals designed to keep the party together, rather than a coherent, radical and credible plan to deliver a fair and just Scotland within the UK.

Later on, it was off to a public meeting organised by the Blantyre *Morning Star* group, where we debated the constitution with Robin McAlpine of the Reid Foundation. It was an astonishing meeting. McAlpine is one of those guys who wants to be seen as a bit whacky, but also a deep-thinking intellectual (not a view I share). He used to be a Labour Party press officer and is now in the process of destroying the Jimmy Reid Foundation. His argument is that everything about the UK is rubbish and he backs this up with reams of statistics that no one can rebut because we don't have the real figures to hand, but in essence the UK is the most unequal, unfair, has the lowest productivity, poorest exports, lowest this, worst that, and if only we have independence we will be one of the fairest, richest counties in the stratosphere! It all sounds convincing to some because he makes these claims with confidence, so people think he must be right when in fact he talks utter bollocks. He repeated the Tory claim that Gordon Brown and Labour caused the banking crisis. I challenged him on this and asked, 'Did Gordon Brown cause the crises in Spain, Portugal, Italy and Ireland too?' He replied by declaring, 'you can't compare the UK with these countries as they aren't developed states like Britain!' Bloody hell, this guy is completely nuggets, but incredibly people nod along. The most frustrating thing about the debate is that good people on the left have totally abandoned their capacity to critically analyse what the Yes side tell us, and have a view that because it is from them it must be true. Remarkable and depressing.

19 MARCH: How about this for big news? The *Daily Record* runs a two-page spread saying Nicola Sturgeon wants to be First -Minister. Well, who'd have thought it? Of course she is desperate to be First Minister, and everything she has done is geared towards that aim, but in Scotland, in referendum year, this is indeed a revelation!

To Infrastructure and Capital Investment Committee to move amendments to prevent public sector contracts being given to companies who have failed to self-cleanse (own up, pay up and apologise) for blacklisting construction workers for trade union activity. Many of the biggest companies in the UK have been culpable, including Balfour Beatty, Laing, McAlpine, Skanska, Keir etc. I also moved an amendment to prevent companies who avoid their taxes being given public contracts. Nicola Sturgeon, the lead Minister, rejected both amendments. She did express support for the sentiment but wouldn't support the amendments, so it is all warm words but no action. Other Labour amendments on zero hours contracts, equalities and community benefit clauses were also refused. Indeed, every Labour amendment was rejected. Progressive my arse!

20 MARCH: A crowd of ex-miners, their families and supporters came to parliament for Iain Gray's debate on the 30th anniversary of the miners' strike. Gray (who I'm not close to) spoke very well, the best I've heard him. Meanwhile, the SNP's Adam Ingram shamefully decried some Labour politicians and failed to mention the thousands of Labour members, and many councillors and MPs, who work tirelessly on behalf of the miners. He singled out George Foulkes for criticism which was just wrong. He also turned on the tears and tremoring voice when speaking about the gallantry and bravery of the mining communities. I was furious. I don't want his

tears, I want action from him!

I called again for a review of the convictions and spoke of why we need an inquiry, as new evidence had come to light following the Hillsborough inquiry. The Scottish Government can and should act in the same way as they have with other inquiries (Shirley McKee case, Surjit Singh Chhokar etc). The Minister Roseanne Cunningham repeated the line that individuals need to complain to the Scottish Criminal Cases Review Commission or relevant police force. She just doesn't get it – or chooses not to. Good debate and I felt positive afterwards. The miners who attended, including David Hamilton MP, were pleased with the way it went.

To Perth for Scottish Labour Party pre-conference rally with speakers including Karen Whitefield (PPC Falkirk West), Harry Donaldson GMB, Ian Mearns MP (Gateshead), Owen Smith MP (Shadow Welsh secretary), Johann Lamont and Gordon Brown. Owen and Ian were very good, and talked about solidarity and common links with the North East and Wales. Gordon Brown was also on form, saying how Labour can ensure fairness, equality and justice for all. It was a good event, although I can't believe it wasn't filmed and put out to a wider audience. We should be sorting out basic stuff like this.

21 MARCH: Devolution Commission document 'Together we can' debate in the conference hall. The right wing press are portraying it as a lurch to the left (if only!). The *Daily Record* very positive about it and the *Herald* scoffing. In saying that, the *Herald* is really just an in-house SNP journal these days. The debate was decent with an excellent contribution from the GMB's Richard Leonard. He is always excellent and I hope he gets elected to parliament next time as he would be a great addition. He stood in Carrick, Cumnock and Doon Valley and was beaten by Adam Ingram – sickening as he would have significantly bolstered our group.

Ed Miliband's afternoon speech was pretty flat and short and in all honesty rather poor. He does it all from memory these days and when it works it is impressive but today it didn't.

Did fringe meeting on the scandal of social care, and heard from UNISON members about their experiences of caring for the elderly and vulnerable on low pay, insecure contracts and declining standards. This really is a huge scandal and no one in government seems all that interested.

To the CFS/Unite fringe meeting on common ownership. Very good attendance and people feeling a bit better about the left's position. We are beginning to get our act together.

22 MARCH: Up early and along to the conference hall to speak to lots of folk and have a coffee.

People in general are very friendly and I feel there is a lot of support in the party for the campaigns I am running. The left is definitely going in the right direction, but we must continue to organise properly. The ultra-new Labourites like Jim Murphy are the ones who aren't friendly. I don't give them much to attack me with as I talk to most people and remain on speaking terms, but they don't like that and their little helpers would like me to be openly hostile, which I won't be. I will stick to policy.

To the conference hall for the health debate. I had invited Christina Taylor to come along with her sister and speak about the scandal of social care; her experiences and that of her mum in the Bupa care home. She was magnificent and clearly and eloquently told her mum's story, and had the conference on their feet when she pledged to continue the fight for decent social care as a tribute to her mother. I was proud of her and glad I asked her to speak.

In my own speech I set out the case for a Beveridge 21 (making the NHS fit for the 21st century) full-scale review of the NHS, action of health inequality and the crisis in social care. David Conway of the Socialist Health Association outlined the plan for his health inequality review. I was pleased with how the health session of the conference went – the NHS is Labour's greatest creation and we should always be at the forefront of defending it against attack, whilst also meeting the challenges of a new age of health care.

Later, I spoke to a few people about arranging a tribute to Tony Benn in Glasgow. They seem keen.

Afterwards, Fiona came up and we went for a curry and a few beers. A good couple of days.

23 MARCH: To the conference hall for debate on blacklisting, which was very good, and then onto the stage for Deputy Leader Anas Sarwar's speech and the singing of the red flag.

Tony Boyle, a Unite delegate and West Lothian councillor, had to be rushed to hospital from the conference so I took his car home for him. Turns out he has gall stones and will be kept in hospital – we all got a real fright though.

24 MARCH: To the office and Marion, my case worker, has everything in

order. I really don't know what I'd do without her.

Tommy's daughter is seriously ill with ulcerative colitis. She has had ongoing problems that are really bad now, and there are concerns about her bile duct, pancreas etc. Worrying times for the family.

To Mid Calder for leafleting session, and then an evening surgery in Armadale.

25 MARCH: To Shadow Cabinet. People positive after conference, good feedback but polls still narrowing for referendum. We need to get the 'Together we can' document and message out. I hope there is some sort of cunning plan to do so. I asked for a strategy session for all members of the Shadow Cabinet and Westminster front bench team so we can work out what we are doing until September and beyond. Let's wait and see if it happens, but I wouldn't put a brass penny on it.

Father Paul Lee, newly ordained priest whose dad was the Fauldhouse councillor before me, came in to do 'Time for reflection' in the chamber. He spoke very well and enjoyed being shown round the building. We took him and his dad for a bite to eat and had a nice chat.

To Bathgate Regal Theatre for George Galloway's 'Just say Naw' event. Galloway and Brian Wilson are touring the country making the case against independence. Galloway in his fedora hat and tartan scarf looks ridiculous, but eloquently and powerfully took apart the case for independence. One memorable section of his speech focused on oil in his lifetime being priced at between $9 and $156 a barrel. How can you plan and deliver public services based on a commodity with such price volatility? Brian Wilson also spoke. They make an odd couple but are very effective. Around 150 people in attendance.

26 MARCH: Finance debate today. John Swinney and the Tory, Gavin Brown, trade stats and debating points. Brown is clever and a good debater; more than a match for Swinney. I used my speech to attack neo-liberalism and Swinney's desire to see Scotland even more enthralled to it, with low taxes and deregulation. I followed Willie Rennie (Lib Dem) and Chic Brodie (SNP, but ex-Lib Dem who fought seven elections for them before joining the SNP). I started by saying it was unusual to follow two Liberal Democrats! Brodie was fuming, shouting and gesticulating but he is a pompous git, and even his own side dislike him.

Today, Labour MPs at Westminster voted for a cap on the amount of cash spent on benefits. Only 13 Labour MPs voted against, including Michael Connarty and Katy Clark – good on them. This will be flung back at us time and again over the next few months.

27 MARCH: Tony Benn's funeral today. I framed the front page of the *Morning Star* which said 'Another Legend Has Gone'. A group of us are meeting in a fortnight to plan a Scottish tribute. Benn's passing is a momentous event for the left. He has educated and inspired activists across the world for decades. I must have poured over his diaries a dozen times. Essential reading for any socialist. I regularly go back to them when in need of inspiration.

28 MARCH: Met student Andrew McGuire to discuss past Labour election campaigns for his dissertation. Had to go over the agony of 2007 and the NHS issues in West Lothian, where the SNP crudely but effectively exploited local NHS issues for party political advantage and won the seat from us in Livingston. We also covered 2011, especially the infamous 'Iain Gray Subway' incident. During the election campaign, Iain Gray was met at Central Station by serial protestor and all round strange bloke Sean Clerkin. He followed Gray and his assistant through the station, shouting in their faces, and to get out of his way they took refuge in a Subway takeaway shop. It was all caught on camera and looked terrible, being presented as him running away from voters. It was without doubt a very significant moment.

30 MARCH: Day off so went through to Glasgow for a wander. Going for a few drinks and lunch with Fiona – bliss.

5

Referendum Diary: April 2014

1 APRIL: Shadow Cabinet/STUC joint meeting today. We discussed the Public Procurement Bill and Labour's Devolution Commission. I suggested to Johann Lamont that she bring together all the stuff from the Devolution Commission; the procurement policies, blacklisting work, miners' justice, FAI, corporate homicide proposals etc into a charter on workers' rights, and that she announce it in her STUC congress speech. We should push hard on this with an ongoing campaign. I hope they listen.

2 APRIL: Met with Mike Donnelly, who has been brought in to help out with strategy. Thank the Lord we now have a strategist. There is a mountain to climb but at least it's a start. He is obviously a very smart and experienced guy and is someone I hope to build a good rapport with.

Lib Dem debate on mental health today. I raised the issues of social care and the failure to fund local government as two huge issues affecting mental health services.

To Bathgate Chapel hall to speak to Scottish CND marchers who are on their way from the Scottish Parliament to Faslane. I mentioned Tony Benn and his commitment to peace and a nuclear free world. I called for well-funded services and a halt to spending on killing machines. A film crew were present and interviewed me but tried to make it all about the referendum and asked aggressive and divisive questions. Surely CND should be about building unity and not creating division.

3 APRIL: FMQS was awful. It was clearly something Paul Sinclair thought would be a good ruse – Johann going on and on about Salmond's junketing in relation to the Ryder Cup. It lasted 22 minutes! Questions and answers were torture. Some folk cannae afford to feed their weans

and this is what we choose to lead on.

In the afternoon I attended a meeting of health spokespersons from all parties, which was called by Health Secretary Alex Neil. Senior civil servants showed a lot of slides about Scotland's NHS problems, of which there are many. Alex Neil clearly doesn't have his troubles to seek and wants us brought into the tent to nullify the political fall-out by building a consensus around primary care, social care and centralisation (What happened to 'Keep Healthcare Local?'). He is a wily fox and will do anything, and I mean anything, to get his way. I raised social care, GP shortages, the need for a review across the NHS etc. The meeting was okay but there was a lot of shadow boxing going on, although we agreed to meet again soon.

In the evening it was off to the McSense Business Centre in Dalkeith for a referendum hustings. On the No side it was myself, Councillor Adam Montgomery, a former Midlothian Provost, and Councillor Alex Bennett, ex-NUM chairman. Opposite was Green Councillor Ian Baxter, Colin Beattie MSP, and former Tory and now Independent Councillor Peter De Vink, who was dressed in Rupert the Bear tartan trews. I enjoyed this meeting immensely. Alex and Adam are good 'old Labour' socialists and were a great contrast to Beattie, a Porsche-driving former merchant banker, and De Vink, a right wing venture capitalist. De Vink argued for flat taxes, lower corporation taxes and free market economics, which is as far from the 'progressive beacon' as it gets. Adam said his flag was not the Union flag or the saltire, but that his flag was red! Alex raised the issue of miners' pensions and industrial injuries benefits – important issues in the mining areas. Beattie was hopeless and Baxter was well meaning but pretty poor. If we could've hand-picked our opponents we couldn't have come up with better than this lot. I really do like going through to Midlothian, the people are great and very much like West Lothian folk. One really noticeable element of all referendum debates is that the numbers turning out to take part are growing. Tonight there were around 70 at the event.

4 APRIL: To Glasgow's Marriott Hotel for a UNISON conference on the referendum, where I debated with Carolyn Leckie, a former Scottish Socialist Party MSP. She has a reputation for being vicious but I didn't find her at all like that and we enjoyed a good and civilised debate. Audience probably more Yes than No, but certainly more No voters than the Edinburgh UNISON branch.

Returned home to discover Margo McDonald had died after a long illness. Margo had Parkinson's and did everything she could to continue working despite obvious difficulties. She used an electric scooter around parliament, which was the butt of many jokes. I liked her a lot and I think she liked me. In my first year of parliament we worked together to expose the actions of pay-day loan companies. I also took her through to Blackburn to meet the credit union. We spoke and gossiped often, and when she offered advice I took it, but she was also interested in my opinions. She was a political icon who had a great way with people. I disagreed with her on independence (she was a fundamentalist) but we agreed on a lot more. A huge loss to parliament.

5 APRIL: A lot of good coverage of Margo in the newspapers and on TV, reflecting the genuine affection people had for her. One of her greatest qualities was that she could disagree with people vigorously, but remain friends.

8 APRIL: First proper day off in ages and I'm painting the bloody spare room. I hate painting!

9 APRIL: Still bloody painting. Went to Pizza Express for a bite to eat with Fiona – to escape the brush and emulsion!

10 APRIL: A crown fell out of one of my teeth today. There was little of the tooth left so the dentist had to pull the root. After much tugging it came out. Sore when the painkillers eventually wore off.

Went to meeting with Excite, the leisure trust that runs the local community gym. They want to cut opening hours and close early at weekends. It's all about money and nothing to do with health and wellbeing. Local gym members Kathleen Swift and Elaine Fisher, Councillor David Dodds and I put the case for keeping opening hours and building up the membership rather than cutting back. Kathleen and Elaine were brilliant and had obviously done their homework. They argued the case so well that the officials are to rethink their plans. We may just win the day on this.

Opinion polls for the Holyrood elections are bad: SNP on 41 per cent, Labour on 32, Conservatives 12 and Lib Dems nine. So, despite seven years in power, and major problems in the NHS, local government, education and the police, the SNP show no sign of decline. Quite remarkable. They are very clever at deflecting blame for their decisions onto someone else, with Westminster (formerly an area of London, now a term of abuse), councils (Labour, of course), the Labour Party and anyone else you care to mention as long as it's not them. Surely at some point the electorate must see through them.

11 APRIL: David Kelly is chairing a meeting of the Quality Care Commission, an initiative I set up to develop policy on social care. I know David from my West Lothian Council days, where he was deputy chief executive. He is a real visionary in this area and West Lothian was a trailblazer in his day, sorting out bed blocking etc, which saved millions of pounds, but more importantly, something which helped older people live independently at home for longer. I am pleased at this initiative as social care is one of the biggest problems in Scotland just now.

12 APRIL: To Aberfeldy for a night with my oldest friends, Jimmy and Kathleen, at the caravan. A nice dinner, a few beers then the next morning trout fishing on the Tay. My idea of heaven.

13 APRIL: Off to Livingston for a constituency party meeting. They agreed unanimously not to support an all-women shortlist for the Scottish Parliament selection, which is good news for me.

14 APRIL: Morning leafleting in Seafield before meeting Peter Hastie from McMillan Cancer Care to discuss new support services at St John's. It looks like our campaign to get the services reinstated, after they had been withdrawn, has been fruitful. No details yet but something is being developed.

15 APRIL: To the STUC congress in Dundee. Sat in on the morning debates before listening to Alex Salmond's speech, which was surprisingly quite flat. A significant number of trade unionists have bought into the Yes campaign, believing that a progressive agenda will follow independence despite the fact the SNP are promoting a low-taxed, neo-liberal agenda. Salmond's speech was received with lukewarm applause. I truly was surprised at the lack of enthusiasm. Milled around for a while and met lots of people. Bumped into Patrick McGuire from Thompsons Solicitors. He has been very supportive and helpful to me. He has just completed his final dose of chemotherapy, following his cancer diagnosis but remains positive and upbeat. I'm really worried about him but his attitude is exemplary. We went for a few beers with some union friends and had great fun sitting in a big group telling stories and enjoying the crack.

Attended *Morning Star* fringe meeting with Unite's Agnes Tolmie, John Hendy, a QC from London, and Richard Bagley, the paper's editor. As with all meetings just now it focused on the constitution. The *Morning Star* used to be called the *Daily Worker* and is the paper of the Communist Party. It has been going since 1930 and is the world's only English language socialist daily. It is great for getting an alternative view of the world and covers the Labour movement brilliantly. I get a copy delivered to my parliamentary office every day.

16 APRIL: I went into congress to hear Johann Lamont's speech. She spoke well, best I've heard her in a while. I had advised her to be positive, upbeat and to promote the Charter of Workers' Rights we had pulled together. She did it well and got a good reaction. When we promote a positive Labour agenda we do so much better.

I spoke at a packed 'United with Labour' meeting with Agnes Tolmie, Kevin Lindsay (ASLEF) and Pauline Rourke (CWU). A number of Yes people attended, ranging from former Labour MEP Hugh Kerr, who is a pompous git, full of his own self-importance, to a woman from the SWP who seemed to believe that everything from global warming to the Israel/Palestine conflict will be resolved if we vote Yes. I spoke of how the choice for workers should be between the radical federalism of the Red Paper, or the neo-liberal economics of the White paper. Agnes was brilliant and explained why as a feminist, socialist and trade unionist she supports the principles of solidarity and trade union unity over division and flag waving. Kevin Lindsay was funny, real and as always straight to the point.

What is interesting at these meetings is that when a left argument is made on the basis of our core values then people get it, and are much more willing to listen to the case for No. Yes campaigners understand this, which is why Labour voters are their key target and they are now using the language of social justice in their campaign. It's just a pity the Labour Party don't fully get it.

20 APRIL: Easter Sunday and an ICM opinion poll shows a narrow four per cent lead for No. I've had a bad feeling for months and this has confirmed it. The No campaign is awful. We should have had a strong Labour campaign, radical and distinct from the woeful Better Together effort, who appear not to have a clue what they are doing. The Yes camp are getting huge media coverage and will tell any lie to get support. The debate is so polarised that people appear willing to accept whatever they are told as long as it suits their side of the debate and that all critical faculties have been set aside.

22 APRIL: Parliament returned after recess, and it was straight to a Shadow Cabinet meeting with Labour Party General Secretary Ian Price and Anas Sarwar (deputy leader). Price has the charisma of a lump of concrete. There was real unease about the referendum, with the party appearing clueless over what to do. I can see no strategy and we appear unable to run with the same issues for any length of time. Some members have been calling for us to identify five or six key issues such as the living wage (the SNP voted it down in the Procurement Bill), pensions, childcare, housing and the NHS. These things mean much more to people than debates around currency unions and technical issues about the economy. I heard Gordon Brown suggested the same and fell out with some senior party people about it. I despair – they are throwing this away. We also discussed Gordon Brown's re-entry into the debate this week, when he will talk about pensions and the need to pull resources across the UK to provide universal UK pensions.

To the chamber for tributes to Margo McDonald. Good speeches all round, which captured Margo's likeable, mischievous, and principled character. She was no angel and would hate to have been cast as one but I liked her a lot because she would speak about things other than just politics.

Attended Green MSP Alison Johnston's debate on fan ownership in football. Alison has been effective at campaigning on niche issues. I spoke about how I have fallen out of love with football and how the involvement of the money men was spoiling the experience by changing the atmosphere and, as a result, the game was losing its honesty. As usual with the government, when they are caught out with something, they want to kick it into the long grass while pretending they support it. They fumble around by announcing a working group, a task force, a consultation or whatever allows them to avoid doing anything. Today, Shona Robison did the same on fan ownership.

23 APRIL: In the chamber for a debate on fuel poverty, with Margaret Burgess. She must be one of the worst Ministers in the history of devolution. Housing and related issues like fuel poverty are so important yet they put someone so clearly out of their depth in charge.

At Justice Questions, McAskill announced a pause on corroboration. After months of arrogance and bravado, and claiming opponents were on the side of criminals and other such tripe, he is trying and failing to sound conciliatory.

To a Labour group meeting to discuss referendum tactics. A lot of unease

about. People being reasonable but there is a real undercurrent of anger –
WE NEED A MESSAGE, AND WE NEED IT NOW!

24 APRIL: To Inverness for a referendum debate at the health campus of
Stirling University, which is sited in the highland capital. Met Mike Robb,
our PPC for Inverness, on the train. He is doing the debate with me. He's a
decent bloke and it would be great if he (or indeed anyone) would take the
scalp of 'the ginger rodent' Danny Alexander.

At the campus we met with students and had a cup of tea and a good
chat about their training, their recent placement experience as part of
their nursing course and life in general. It was great to hear their genuine
enthusiasm for the job and optimism about their future, but they also
spoke of the very real pressures on the NHS. Much of this chimed with
what Fiona tells me day in day out about life on the frontline of our NHS.

We were in Inverness to take part in a debate in front of students and
academics. Alex Neil, who is speaking for the Yes camp, turned up 15
minutes late, whooshing into the car park in his Range Rover with an
entourage who were missing only rose petals to throw in front of him. On
his side was Maree Todd, a local pharmacist.

The debate itself was interesting with the students asking about
pressures on the NHS, the crisis in social care, mental health etc. Alex Neil
is usually a good robust debater but he tried to get past tough questions by
using statistics about patient satisfaction, waiting times etc. but the students
– just back from placement – weren't impressed. They'd just witnessed
the pressures first hand and were having none of it. The pharmacist was
better, much more relevant. Mike did well and I tried to keep things real
by relaying some of the things I've heard from friends, relatives and staff I
know. This seemed to strike a chord with them. Afterwards, Alex Neil got
his photo taken and whooshed out as quickly as he had appeared, whereas
we stayed and chatted. All in all I think we made a good impression.

Afterwards I had been asked by party headquarters to go into Inverness
city centre to do some campaigning with Yvette Cooper, who originates
from the town. She was personable enough and we campaigned for an
hour or so with local activists. I thought it was to be a Labour event but it
turned out to be a Better Together stall. I felt really uncomfortable but did
my duty and got away at the first opportunity. The reality is most people
wouldn't have had a clue who she was, nor indeed I, but it was good to get
out of the central belt for a day and see a lovely part of the country. On
the train home (what a spectacular journey) I reflected on the value of this
referendum debate personally. Yes it's a grind at times, and appears to have

gone on forever, but what it has given me is priceless experience in dealing with the public and debating with some of our big-name politicians, such as Sturgeon, McAskill and Neil. I'm enjoying it immensely and hope I haven't been outdone in any of the head-to-heads.

25 APRIL: Margo's funeral today. I didn't go as I felt a bit uneasy about it in amongst the current referendum atmosphere, but regretted my decision afterwards. Jim Sillars read out her appeal for people to respect each other, and to come together after the result whoever wins. Fine and genuine sentiments and I'm sure Margo would have tried to do that, but I doubt it will happen as the atmosphere is getting more and more stark, polarised and bad natured by the day.

Visited Hampden with Andy Burnham. We went to see the 'Fans Into Football' scheme, which is helping football fans get fit by training at their local team's stadium. We were allowed to walk round the track that is being laid for the Commonwealth Games – it looks superb.

26 APRIL: Canvassing in Craigshill with a group of local folk. I was under the impression it was just Labour members, but it turned out to be a Better Together crew of half Labour and half Tories. As soon as I realised this, we (the Labour members) disappeared on our own never to go near them again. One of the Tories turned up in a kilt! Canvassing in Craigshill in a kilt – clueless!

27 APRIL: NHS in the news more and more – turns out more beds have been cut in Scotland than anywhere else in Europe!

28 APRIL: Met with David Martin MEP to campaign in Mid Calder for the European Elections. He is very frustrated at the lack of a Labour campaign for these elections. The reality is people don't really give a toss about them – a situation made worse by the end of the European constituencies and introduction of the list system. Most people haven't a clue what MEPs do!

To Balbardie Park in Bathgate for the annual International Workers' Memorial Day service. Run by the trades' council, it was brought to Scotland by my great friend Jim Swan, former convener of the British Leyland plant at Bathgate. We heard speeches from David Martin, Angela Constance MSP, and STUC President June McMinnery. Along with many others, I laid a wreath in memory of workers killed and injured at work. It is always a very poignant event, but it was noticeable that a number of SNP people attended this year, having rarely ever been seen at this event before!

The newspapers are giving Salmond pelters for praising Vladimir Putin, who he thinks has made Russia strong.

29 APRIL: To Shadow Cabinet to present the paper on the work of the health team and the introduction of our health inequality and social care reviews. These are the major challenges in health and we need radical policies to address them as we have growing inequality and a rapidly ageing population that will put huge demands on our NHS if we cannot support people at home for longer. We cannot sit back and watch people in communities like mine dying 21 years before those in more affluent communities and do nothing about it. This is Scotland's shame. As is the low pay, zero hours culture of social care, where our elderly and vulnerable are 'cared for' with a 15-minute visit – or as Johann Lamont has said, 'just long enough to hear the ping of a microwave'. I was surprised and depressed at some of the reactions to this. After all, if these aren't core Labour issues, then what are? I was gobsmacked at the lack of enthusiasm by some colleagues who seem so conservative in their approach and are more concerned about the fear of structural change to NHS boards or appeasing the articulate, sharp-elbowed middle classes than addressing the serious problems that are making people die early or live their lives lonely and with poor care.

Craig Davidson, Johann Lamont's adviser, came to see me afterwards to say he was disappointed with the response and encouraged me to continue this work and be bold. I don't know if that is Johann's view but I suspect it is as she speaks about the scandal of social care a lot.

In the chamber, Tricia Marwick selected the Lib Dems' topical question on bed losses in the NHS over mine. She is punishing me for being vocal and awkward with her. Alex Neil tried defending the loss of beds, which combined with the social care crisis, is a disaster. If social care was working well there would be no need to maintain the current number of beds, but it isn't, so beds are needed. This has a huge financial strain as to keep someone in hospital costs £3,000 per week, whereas to look after that person at home costs £350. We need to end social care tendering based on price, which drives down standards, implement a living wage for all carers and end the scandal of 15-minute visits.

Visited the Ryder Cup exhibition in the parliament entrance area. Can't wait for the tournament to come to Scotland in the autumn.

It's the annual Multiple Sclerosis reception at the parliament. I invited my brother John and his partner Sharron so they could meet representatives of the MS Society. The Minister, Michael Matheson urged the drugs companies to make new drugs available and promised to improve care (we hear that every year). John Swinney and his wife Elizabeth Quigley were there. She is struggling to walk and uses a walking frame, my brother is permanently in a wheelchair. Elizabeth spoke very well about the 'secret' of MS, where no one tells you anything; no one tells you about new drugs or new developments and you have to ask and fight for everything. It shouldn't be like that. This struck a chord with everyone. I congratulated her afterwards and introduced her to John and Sharron. She was really impressive.

Today the report into the Edinburgh baby ashes scandal was published. It is truly awful and very traumatic for parents who have lost children. There are calls for a public inquiry. I have urged our side to go on this at FMQs tomorrow and leave the Putin stuff aside as it's trivial by comparison.

6

Referendum Diary: May 2014

I MAY: The baby ashes report is the big issue – Kezia Dugdale is working on this in Edinburgh and has done a really good job building relationships with the parent groups. There was a statement today with Johann leading for us. (Michael) Matheson rejected calls for a public inquiry but said Lord Bonomy will investigate. It now emerges the same may have happened in Aberdeen, Falkirk, Glasgow and other areas.

To West Lothian College for the annual Livingston Lecture. This year the trades' council (of which I am an active member) approached the college asking them to host a lecture on cooperatives. Professor Robert Raeside, Hugh Donnelly (Cooperative Scotland) and Dr David Endal spoke passionately about the development of cooperatives and how they could be used to increase productivity, promote investment and a sustainable economy. It was an excellent event. Mind you, not a single SNP elected representative turned up – they don't really get this kind of thing.

4 MAY: Shock, horror – the least surprising newspaper revelation of the year – the *Sunday Herald* has come out in favour of independence! The fact that its circulation has dipped below 24,000 may have had some bearing on their decision.

To Fauldhouse Miners Welfare Club for the annual concert by local musicians in aid of SOBS (Survivors of Bereavement and Suicide). Organiser is Des Murphy, whose son Christopher inexplicably took his own life a few years back. The support from the people of my village for this event is amazing. Around 20 local singers and musicians performed to a packed hall of 300, raising around £5,000 in the process. They always have a speaker from SOBS to remind people why they are there, and provide information about suicide and related education. Despite the tragic subject, people still enjoy themselves and the place is rocking by the end. So typical of the care, friendship and generosity of local people. The best folk you could wish to be around.

5 MAY: To East Calder for European Election campaigning with Councillor Dave King. He is recovering from cancer, has heart trouble, is diabetic and has God knows how many other ailments, but is ALWAYS first to volunteer when campaigning is on the agenda. He is a remarkable man and just goes on and on. If only we could bottle and sell his spirit and enthusiasm.

6 MAY: To Shadow Cabinet where Graeme Pearson introduced a justice paper. He is an impressive guy and we might have different politics but he is experienced and genuine. He was a deputy chief constable and has seen a lot of action, dealing with tough criminals like Arthur Thompson senior.

After months of frustration and calls for a Labour Referendum campaign, as opposed to Better Bloody Together, we were advised that it will be launched after the European elections. Well, pop the champagne corks at last!

To a play called *From Wharf Rats to Lords of the Docks – the Henry Bridges Project*. It was a superb one-man play about the rise of the leader of the US dockers union. It was a tremendous show but disappointing that Hugh Henry, James Kelly and I were the only MPS to turn up despite all being invited.

7 MAY: Audit Scotland figures out today and show major delays in A&E with over 100,000 waiting more than four hours to be seen. We have decided to lead with the NHS at First Minister's Questions.

At a PCS parliamentary group meeting we discussed the dispute at the National Museum, which has been developing for a while as the management have withdrawn weekend allowances for new staff, thereby creating a two-tier system with low paid staff getting £3,000 less than their colleagues. Culture Secretary, Fiona Hyslop has refused to get involved. I will start to drum up support by asking PQs and putting down motions.

It was then into the chamber in time to hear that the Bedroom Tax will in effect be scrapped. The Scottish Government's proposal, based on the bill Labour's Jackie Baillie introduced, will be implemented. Great news, but it would never have happened without our input.

Went to the Crohn's and Colitis reception with Tommy's wife Diane, and daughter Caitlin, and my friend and constituent Steven Sharp. Steven has gone through hell with Crohn's, while Caitlin suffers from ulcerative colitis. These are very debilitating conditions and have a big impact on people, especially adolescents. It was very moving to hear how people's lives have been affected but also how they managed to get through it. Inspirational stuff.

8 MAY: To chamber for statement on continuing care, where patients are now going to be charged for this service. Alex Neil denied this, despite previously saying it would happen. It appears a very confused position, which Parkinson's UK and others think is illegal.

Afterwards I met with John Pentland MSP and Craig Davidson to look at Freedom of Information requests that John had submitted on mental health services in Monklands. Alex Neil has been caught red handed contradicting his own stated policy to save a ward in his own constituency against the wishes of patients groups, who want to see mental health services moved from hospital-based to community outreach.

9 MAY: After a busy week it was good to go with Fiona, Chloe and her boyfriend Lee to the Ashmaan in Linlithgow for a fine curry and a few beers.

10 MAY: Up at 4.30am to get to London for a conference on Venezuela. I was an International observer in their Presidential election so was invited to speak about my experience. The one-day conference discussed many issues with contributions from Billy Hayes of the CWU, Seumas Milne of the *Guardian*, Chris Williamson MP, and academics and activists from the UK and Latin America. Afterwards I spoke to Alicia Castro, the Argentinean ambassador to the UK. She knew I was a friend of Tam Dalyell and asked if I could arrange for her to meet Tam to discuss 'The Malvinas'. I will of course try to arrange this and am sure Tam will be happy to meet her.

Discussed the miners' strike and Scottish Justice campaign with Seumas Milne, who wrote the fantastic book *The Enemy Within*, about Thatcher's secret war against the miners. Seamus was very helpful and interested in some of my findings and research. I will send them to him.

12 MAY: Edinburgh University for Royal College of Nursing referendum debate with former GP, and SNP MSP, Dr Ian McKee. I felt a bit off form

and ill-prepared for some reason, but couldn't quite put my finger on it. Quite a number of SNP folk in the audience but also a feeling that there are a lot of people who are No voters, but who don't want to speak up. I think this may be an emerging theme with people perhaps feeling a bit intimidated and not wanting to say anything.

Headed home after it and went out for a run with Fiona. I hate keeping fit but really need to try and motivate myself to do something other than going for a pint and playing the odd game of golf!

13 MAY: To the STUC for UNISON retired members' debate with Tommy Brennan, former convener at Ravenscraig. Tommy spoke well and said Labour had left him, and that he now supported independence. His arguments were nationalist arguments tinged with a leftist agenda. This is odd because Tommy was no left winger. He would have been supportive of Blair's 'new realism' but now projects himself as socialist radical. Members of NUM hate Brennan because if he had supported them in 84/85, and refused to take coal into Ravenscraig, the strike may not have been lost. He did however make his arguments well in a relatively good-natured debate. The audience was split on the issue – reflecting the national mood.

Rushed back to the chamber for the Procurement Bill only to find out the 'progressive, left wing' SNP will again vote against our amendments to provide a living wage for workers engaged on public sector contracts. They will vote against action to stop blacklisting contractors getting public sector contracts if they have failed to self-cleanse, and they will vote against tax avoiders gaining contracts. They really are charlatans.

14 MAY: Met Clare Lally, Labour's Carers champion. She has twins, one of whom is disabled. I want to work with her on a carers' strategy. She is a really good person to front this. I also want to appoint Jim Leishman as our pensioners' champion (although I hate that term). I will approach Alex Rowley about this as he and Jim are close.

15 MAY: The *Herald* has run the story on Alex Neil's intervention in the Monklands mental health services fiasco – in his own constituency. Government policy is about 'shifting the balance of care' out of hospitals and into the community, and despite full support for this from the health board and mental health patients groups, who want to see more community outreach provision, he interfered for political reasons against the advice of clinicians and service users to overturn a decision to close

a ward. At FMQs, Johann Lamont asked Salmond four times to sack him, but of course he refused. No one ever gets sacked or resigns in this Government. They have no shame and are unembarrassable, even when they are caught red handed.

16 MAY: Been looking forward to this day for a while. Off to York for my pal Norrie Dixon's 50th birthday. Fiona, Jimmy and Kathleen Swift, and Phyllis and Norrie, are on the train first thing. Weather in York is scorching – quick change in the hotel and off to the racing. All ladies in their finery and the guys dressed up too. Fabulous day with only one 4/1 winner but Jimmy and Norrie did well with a 25/1 shot. Dinner and a few beers in the evening. Lovely day out, and getting away from it all was exactly what was required.

17 MAY: Up for a nice walk around York in the sunshine – what a beautiful place. This is my first visit and it's really impressive. We had a fish tea then jumped on the train home. A great few days. Nothing better than being amongst pals and relaxing.

18 MAY: St John's the Baptist Chapel for the first communion mass. Scotty and Lesley's wee boy Sean is involved. Lots of kids beautifully turned out for a special mass. Then to the Miners Welfare for lunch (steak pie – it's always steak pie in the club and it's fantastic). The whole Scott and Toner clan are there. Lesley comes from a huge family so they almost fill the hall themselves.

Papers continue to cover the Alex Neil 'Monklands' story, and are now saying he demanded to keep wards open that were full of asbestos. The pressure on him is mounting.

19 MAY: Campaigning in Bathgate with Councillor Harry Cartmill, then to Edinburgh University for the Healthcare Alliance referendum debate on health and social care with Alex Neil. He is a man under pressure but did his best not to show it. I actually quite like him. He is a ruthless operator and can be full of bluster and bravado, but you can have a political ding-dong with him and afterwards he will chat and keep on good personal terms – unlike others. His performance in the debate was remarkable. He spoke of his desire to see community-based services developed and for people to be treated at home or as near to home as possible, and all this despite being caught preventing this policy from happening in his own constituency! The brass neck of the man was something to behold. As

we were debating these matters, less than half-a-mile away, the party was submitting a vote of no confidence in him as Cabinet Secretary for Health. Rumour coming from some in the SNP is that he is to retire at the election. Now I need to prepare for the debate on Wednesday, which will be the first vote of no confidence in a Minister in over a decade or more and I will lead for Labour.

Newsnight Scotland with Jim Eadie MSP on the motion of no confidence, but I over-prepared and ended up doing a really shit interview. Annoyed with myself but you live and learn.

20 MAY: Into parliament and all the talk is of the forthcoming motion of no confidence in Alex Neil. The TV and papers are full of it and it's the buzz around the corridors of Holyrood. Spent all day working on my speech. Craig Davidson from Johann's team made some suggestions on language but after discussion with Tommy I ignored them and went with my gut feeling. Throughout the day I briefed the opposition spokespeople on our findings and why we were taking this route. I hope they are all on board. If we can unite the opposition we may just be able to get him to go. However the SNP are completely shameless, so I would be astonished if he did.

21 MAY: Up early for a radio interview on *Good Morning Scotland*, which thankfully went much better than the *Newsnight* rubbish. Spent all day preparing and running through my speech. The press are all over the story so I did several interviews for *Radio Forth, Kingdom* FM and BBC *News*. I sat beside Johann at FMQs, where she again raised the Alex Neil issue and called for his resignation. Salmond, as always, was in bullish mood.

The motion was taken right after FMQs (which is on a Wednesday this week because of tomorrow's European elections) in front of a packed chamber with Michael Matheson leading for the Government. My nerves disappeared when I stood up to speak and I was determined to prosecute the case in a deliberate and methodical manner, staying calm and not rising to the inevitable provocation from the SNP side. As the debate proceeded it became clear the SNP were going to ride this out and Matheson did so in an arrogant, uncompromising way with no humility. There would be no acknowledgement of wrong doing and certainly no apology.

Jackson Carlaw, for the Tories, who is a friend of Alex Neil's, said they would support the no-confidence motion, as did Jim Hume for the Liberals, but the biggest coup was securing Patrick Harvie and the Greens' vote. All opposition parties were now on board. John Pentland MSP for Motherwell and Wishaw, the MSP whose Freedom of Information request secured the information, spoke in a straightforward, caring and compassionate way about the service mental health patients in his area needed and that Alex Neil had denied them this for political purposes.

Richard Simpson MSP, an ex-psychiatrist, closed for us – credible, knowledgeable and hitting the right tone. Salmond closed for the SNP, and in an awful contribution said Alex Neil did everything right and stood up for his constituents – completely ignoring the fact that it was, according to patients and the NHS board, a decision that was the worst option available. He claimed this was a cyclical debate to coincide with the European Elections despite the fact it was SNP managers who scheduled the debate for this time and day! And it was his government who refused the Freedom of Information request for 18 months. In the end we won the debate hands down – no question, but we lost the vote 57–67, as the independents voted with the SNP.

I was happy with how I performed and how the debate went. We managed to get all opposition parties on board and forced the government to back a minister who had been caught reversing his own policy, and all for political ends. If that had been a Labour Minister they would have resigned, but the SNP are so brazen and arrogant that no one resigns, ever!

22 MAY: European Election day (joy.) I really am and always have been a fierce critic of the EU. Ever since the Maastricht debate I have objected to its lack of democracy and accountability. I am very internationalist and love travelling and experiencing new cultures, people, and enjoy seeing cities like London become cosmopolitan and exciting, but I cannot stand the way the neo-liberal economic orthodoxy is forced upon states, and where competition and the free movement of capital and people is seen as essential and a must when in fact all it does is enrich the super wealthy and drive down wages and services as the poor undercut the poor, who undercut the poorer.

Being an MEP must be one of the dullest jobs going. No constituency party to be held accountable to, no surgeries, huge allowances and salary and general anonymity. It sounds awful and utterly boring! I will probably vote to leave if there is a referendum in 2015 or 2016.

Up early with the team to put up posters at polling stations then to East Calder. We dropped leaflets all day in key areas for us. My prediction is UKIP will win at least one seat in Scotland.

Stayed up to watch some of the English council results – Labour picking up a few councils and seats but not as many as expected. The Lib Dems are being hammered and UKIP are picking up seats.

23 MAY: Media stories this morning are that the Lib Dems have taken a beating in the English council elections and Clegg is under pressure to go. Tories losing ground to UKIP and Labour not nearly doing well enough. Everything is focused on Farage – they have taken 18 per cent and have 125 councillors – taking both Tory and Labour votes. They took 10 seats from Labour in troubled Rotherham after the child abuse revelations. Good to see Liverpool almost totally red, with 81 out of 90 councillors Labour. Oh, and best of all, the BNP totally wiped out in Dagenham and Barking.

Good result for Labour in the Cowdenbeath council by-election, where we beat the SNP convincingly – and winning a council seat in Oban of all places.

To the Bombay Spice restaurant in West Calder for the Labour Party fundraiser. Great food, music with Alan Brown on fine form and brilliant poetry from Jim Monaghan. The place was packed out.

24 MAY: Salmond on TV moaning about the BBC and its constant coverage of Farage. He has a point as the little toad is never off the telly.

25 MAY: To St Margaret's High School, in Livingston, for the election count. Good results for Labour in the Breich Valley ward, although not so good in central Livingston.

The West Lothian results are: SNP 14,279, Labour 13,932, UKIP 5,228, Conservative 5,102, Greens 2,710, Lib Dems 1,425, Britain First 573, BNP 452, NO2EU 242.

Big news in Scotland is that David Coburn, a UKIP bampot, has taken the final seat north of the border. The SNP had targeted this and failed. They had talked up Tasmina Ahmed Sheikh as the new face of Scotland, but Scotland has voted for an old right winger. So much for us being so different! The SNP took 29 per cent of the vote, and Labour 26. In England, astonishingly or maybe not, UKIP won. Their MEP group will provide rich pickings for journalists as many are clearly bonkers. Nick Griffin and his BNP thugs are gone but Farage is now the receptacle for their votes. Very worrying.

I do, however, reject the assumption that all UKIP voters are racist, as they aren't. What they have done is allow voters somewhere to place their vote on issues that frustrate them most. Voting UKIP is a reaction to housing problems, low pay, job insecurity and fear. Labour should be the party tapping into and providing answers to these issues, especially amongst the working class voters of the midlands and the north. This is the challenge for Miliband.

I have spent a while reflecting on this result, as it might impact on our referendum. There were 850,000 votes cast for parties who are opposed to independence and 500,000 for pro-independence parties – this is the challenge the Yes campaign faces in the next four months.

26 MAY: Due to speak at a conference entitled 'A Healthier, Fairer Scotland' but received an email to say it has been cancelled as speakers had pulled out due to sponsorship by Nestle, who have a very poor reputation amongst health campaigners. Well done to those who have taken action.

27 MAY: Met a representative from a major Scottish charity today. I am amazed at how people have become conditioned to accepting austerity and cuts to budgets. They seem to have accepted the government's line that 'well, there really is nothing we can do until we get powers, so you will have to live with what we give you and don't complain about cuts or we will cut it more'. The voluntary sector has been totally silenced as critics of the government and have instead become, in effect, passive in the face of repeated cuts to their budgets, as well as council budgets. It's as if there is no action the SNP government can take to help the situation. Of course they can, but they have no intention of doing so. It's an amazing state of affairs. They have complete control over the voluntary sector.

Research for the UK and Scottish Governments has been released today and both sides are competing against each other over whether you will be £1,800 a year worse off with independence according to Cameron, or £1,000 better off according to Salmond.

28 MAY: Met relatives of elderly people who had been resident at the Bupa-run Pentland Hills care home. The stories are heartbreaking and horrendous. This place should be closed and some staff and senior management prosecuted. What happened to some of our oldest and frailest people is a scandal.

29 MAY: Met with the Royal College of GPs to discuss the crisis in general practice. 26 surgeries across Lothian have closed lists because of shortages and the situation will get worse as people turn their back on the profession.

A big crisis is brewing.

Up to St Augustine's Church for a Unite-hosted debate on the referendum with Kenny MacAskill. Mary Alexander of Unite was the chairperson. A grand total of eight people turned up (the excitement of hearing MacAskill and me was obviously too much for them). I find Kenny an odd character. He is one of the few MSPs I have never spoken to. He is aloof and has a lot of tricks and traits and seems very uncomfortable around people. He doesn't do small talk. We had an event discussion around the issues to an audience who had all made up their minds – all eight of them! So it was probably an entirely fruitless exercise for all.

30 MAY: To Glasgow Radisson Hotel for the national Care at Home conference, where I took part in a panel discussion with Jim Hume (Lib Dems), Susan Aitken (Glasgow SNP councillor) and a policy officer for a care organisation in England. What struck me was the absence of frontline care staff – it was all managers talking about managerial solutions. I raised political points about funding councils, ending competitive tendering that is driving down standards, raising wages, ending exploitation, providing job security and dignity for staff and clients and an end to the scandal of 15-minute visits. I'm very committed to all of this and it really gets me riled when I speak about it.

31 MAY: Played in the annual Silloth golf competition with my school pal Joe Murray. My golf was crap, but we had a great day, like a pair of 15-year-olds laughing at a load of nonsense!

7

Referendum Diary: June 2014

2 JUNE: Tommy's boy Dominic and his pal Jordan are in for a week's work experience. Took them to Broxburn to meet constituents who are having a problem with their water supply so we met with the housing association to try and resolve the matter. Back to the office for my weekly surgery and a list of case work.

Got a phone call in the afternoon to say George Galloway has agreed to do a referendum meeting with me in Fauldhouse in August. George can be brilliant or obnoxious and there are a number of things I disagree with him about, but he is an articulate socialist who can pull a crowd and will engage in the debate in an entertaining and clever way. It should be fun.

3 JUNE: Met Elaine Holmes and Oliver McIlroy; two women who are leading the campaign to end the use of transvaginal mesh implants. They were with campaigning journalist Marion Scott of the *Sunday Mail*. We have been working with them for over a year now, supporting them and doing lots of parliamentary work together. These women have been heroic in what they have done, bringing together women from across Scotland who have been horribly injured and affected by this product which is used to treat urinary incontinence or pelvic prolapse following childbirth. This is a growing global scandal, with 100,000 cases filed in just three US states alone. It is also Australia's biggest ever class action. Every week tens of millions of dollars are being paid out in compensation and yet despite being warned about this the Scottish NHS continues to implant this stuff.

We went along to the petitions committee where around 80 mesh sufferers were in the gallery. Women ranging from their early 20s to their 70s. Some have lost organs, others in wheelchairs, some women rely on crutches and sticks, while many have lost marriages and careers – tragic and upsetting.

Olive and Elaine presented their petition, which calls for mesh to be withdrawn from the NHS in Scotland so others can avoid similar injuries. As they were speaking, many of the women sobbed and hugged each other for comfort. Very powerful and had a big impact on the committee. It will get a lot of media coverage for the campaign. Afterwards Tommy and I and Graeme Morrice MP, who had come along to support the women, spent a lot of time with the campaigners – it was a moving but very rewarding day as we have taken their campaign a major step forward. Tommy's advice to bring forward the petition was a good call.

Through to the Old Fruitmarket, Glasgow, for the launch of the 'Labour Says No' campaign. It has taken an age to get here but it's now up and running. Thank the Lord! Opened by Gordon Mathieson, city council leader, who put on his gallus Mr Glasgow performance. We then heard from Johann Lamont, who spoke confidently and with clarity, putting across her case for a No vote – a really good speech.

Next up was Gordon Brown with his standard speech, which is self-deprecating, passionate and political, making the case for the 'pulling and sharing of resources'. At the end, Mathieson came back on to introduce a young singer who was to close the show. But instead of introducing her as Katie Murphy, he introduced her as *Karie* Murphy – the Labour candidate who was accused (and eventually cleared) of wrongdoing in the Falkirk Labour selection controversy. Comedy gold!

4 JUNE: Met with Stewart Stevenson, convener of the Standards and Procedures Committee, to discuss the lobbying inquiry. In 2012, I introduced a members' bill to bring in a register of lobbyists and open up lobbying to more scrutiny and transparency. After months of consultation, the Scottish Government grudgingly took over the bill with a promise to legislate. Since then nothing has happened and they are desperate to kick it into the long grass. They asked the committee to hold an inquiry, which is really just another delaying tactic. Stevenson has at least shown some interest in it.

5 JUNE: Met with Jim Leishman, Alex Rowley and Jackie Baillie to discuss appointing Jim as our pensioners' champion – he is keen and will be great at it.

7 JUNE: Presented medals at Livingston Gymnastics Club and then on to the Parkhead Gala day. It was then off to Bridgend to Sean Byrne's 50th birthday party at night. Busy day but great to see so many old pals again.

9 JUNE: 100 days until the referendum. There was a big Better Together event in Glasgow today hosted by Clare Lally and Alistair Darling. A lot of coverage but I don't go to anything that is Better Together.

Gordon Brown has come out today saying that David Cameron should debate with Salmond. What on earth is he thinking? Salmond would love that and wipe the floor with him! A lot of people really annoyed with this.

Spoke at length to Tommy Kane about what his daughter has gone through recently. It has been nothing short of hell. They are concerned about her travelling to Canada on holiday, but equally determined she should go. They are terrified she has a flare up while there. I feel for the family.

10 JUNE: Spoke to Alex Rowley and he is concerned about Jim Murphy's increasing involvement in the referendum, believing that he is lining up a leadership bid after September 11, which would be a disaster if true.

Came home and went for a run. Bloody hell; exercise doesn't get any easier.

11 JUNE: Off to Glasgow University to speak about alternative careers for people with an education degree – nice event, and I felt as though I gave the students a wee bit of food for thought about one alternative career.

I then headed a bit nearer home, to Bathgate Regal Theatre, for the West Lothian UNISON debate on the referendum. On my side were Councillors Angela Moohan and John McGinty, and we were up against Fiona Hyslop MSP, Bob Thomson (Labour for independence) and the bold Robin McAlpine. A lot of Yes folk in. McAlpine is a real chancer, full of simplistic garbage: the UK is the worst this, the lowest that, has the poorest this etc – and this is the positive campaign we are told! His analysis says all we need to do is increase wages and productivity and we will create a fairer, more prosperous country. Oh, and by the way, you can only do this with independence! Why do some intelligent people lap this up?

12 JUNE: Met a great set of pupils at the Scottish Parliament. They were from Bellsquarry Primary School, in Livingston. This is a part of the job I really enjoy. They are clever, alert and up to speed on the workings of parliament – great fun talking to them.

Went in to the chamber for FMQs straight afterwards and asked Salmond about mesh. I said, 'This week, a large group of women, including several from my region, attended the Public Petitions Committee calling for the suspension of polypropylene mesh implants, which are fitted to treat pelvic prolapse. Given the appalling injuries those women experienced, will the First Minister instruct the Cabinet Secretary for Health and Wellbeing to issue new guidance that would have the effect of suspending the use of the product until an inquiry is held into its safety?'

Salmond replied: 'As Neil Findlay should know, the matter is under serious consideration. We intend to move on it in conjunction with the other health departments across these islands. The Cabinet Secretary for Health and Wellbeing would be more than prepared to meet directly with the women concerned and explain the consideration that is being given to this fundamental and serious issue.'

Surprise, surprise, another non answer!

The Clare Lally issue is hogging the headlines. Campbell Gunn, Salmond's spin doctor, emailed the *Telegraph* (of all papers) telling them she was a Labour activist (not an ordinary mum as was claimed). He also told them she was the daughter of Pat Lally, the ex-Labour Provost of Glasgow, which is completely untrue. The cybernats have unleashed a wave of abuse at Clare. Salmond has defended Campbell Gunn. The press pack think Gunn will have to go, but he won't as they never resign, no matter how bad the accusation. All opposition leaders attacked at question time. Salmond looks bad defending this kind of abuse of a young mum.

14 JUNE: Fauldhouse Gala day – great atmosphere with lots of people enjoying the sunshine. Great day, then to Bathgate for my mate Norrie's birthday party. Good to see all the gang.

15 JUNE: Phone call from Kathleen Dalyell to advise that Tam is in hospital. He's fine but is being kept in for a few days. He has been speaking to the nurses who are complaining about the parking situation – it is appalling. Tam is always keen to listen to people's views or issues so he assured them he would speak to me about it. I will write to the health board again. The problem is the Scottish Government removed parking charges but failed to replace them with an efficient traffic management system. Now we have people using the car park as a park and ride service for the bus to Edinburgh, or a free car park for Livingston shopping centre, leaving patients and staff nowhere to park. It really is chaotic at times. I have had several chemotherapy patients speak to me about it as they have to turn up each day and spend up to an hour driving around trying to get a space. Not good enough.

Went to St John's to visit Tam. He was in fine form and we had a long chat about politics, the referendum, the NHS and just about everything else. He was scathing about the referendum campaign. He may be in his mid-80s but is as sharp as ever. His wife Kathleen and daughter Moira were there so we had a great catch up. They are such lovely people.

16 JUNE: Tommy came in today and told me his daughter is having to return from her holiday due to illness. She is to go for an immediate operation. They have all been through the mill but this is a good move for her and should give her a much better quality of life.

Met with a group of people from Lanarkshire today to talk about health and social care. They were scathing about Alex Neil's involvement in a number of health and social care issues in the area.

Spent the afternoon and evening canvassing in Livingston – pretty good response, and there doesn't appear to be any real Yes surge.

Two very different, but interesting, conversations today with SNP voters who will vote No. One said she worked with an English company and feared they would relocate if there was a Yes vote, while the other was an older man who said, 'We aren't getting to use the pound no matter what Salmond says. The rules of the EU are that if you join, then you use the Euro – and I am not voting for that!' It was very interesting.

17 JUNE: The mesh women were in parliament today for Alex Neil's session before the Petitions Committee. I spoke to them before they went in and told them not to be at all surprised it he announces a suspension of mesh – and sure enough he did. On the face of it, this looks like a fantastic victory for our campaign and the determined work of Elaine Holmes and Olive McIlroy. Neil is a political fixer and has delivered a suspension, but we will have to look at what this means in practice as it may be a case of smoke and mirrors. It also took him over a year to make this call and meanwhile 1,800 more women have undergone the operation. But today is a day for celebration and the women are rightly delighted.

Lord Bonomy's report into the baby ashes scandal has published. It really is disturbing and shows a complete disregard for human dignity. The campaigners have been resolute, determined and totally committed to ensuring the right thing is done in the name of their late daughters and sons. A very emotional day for many families.

Tommy's daughter had her operation today and all seems to have gone well. We are now all praying for her recovery.

Chloe is off on holiday to Magaluf with 10 pals – every parent's worst nightmare. She has endured months of warnings and lectures!

18 JUNE: To London for a series of meetings and had time to call into the Scottish Affairs committee evidence session on independence. Ed Balls was giving evidence and was unequivocal in saying that Scotland would not be able to use sterling if there was a Yes vote.

We had a few beers on the terrace of the House of Commons with Graeme Morrice, Michael Sharpe, Frank Toner, Dave Shaw, my brother John, David Hamilton MP, Tom Clarke MP, Elaine Smith MSP, Lesley Dobbin, Jim Sheridan, Katy Clark and Manuel Cortes from the TSSA. We were joined by Dennis Skinner, who is in his 80s and hasn't lost one bit of his spark of humour. He was on top form ripping into the Tories and the SNP.

That night it was off to the RMT offices at Clapham for the annual RMT Cuba garden party. What a fantastic event. It is held in the beautiful gardens at Maritime House and around 500 were in attendance. Great food and cocktails with the brilliant Alabama 3 playing live. Elaine Smith and I were guest speakers along with John McDonnell MP, George Galloway, Matt Wrack of the FBU, Alicia Castro of the Argentine Embassy and Mick Cash, the new RMT General Secretary. It was a brilliant, vibrant occasion celebrating the music, food, politics and culture of Cuba.

19 JUNE: Round table dinner to discuss technology in health care. It was interesting to hear of the developments that are coming down the line. Technology really is moving into areas that are mind blowing.

20 JUNE: In Govan with Johann Lamont and Ian Davidson MP to meet nurses and NHS staff for an NHS poster launch, then to UNISON HQ for a meeting of the Social Care Commission working group. David Kelly is doing brilliant work on this and I am really optimistic about what it can achieve.

Back home and the house is really quiet without Chloe. So far, all seems well with the Magaluf holiday.

22 JUNE: Fiona and I took part in a local mini triathlon, with Stephen

Brown making up our team. The weather was fantastic and I did the bike ride. Around 100 people were involved and the atmosphere was first class. I don't do anywhere near enough exercise and need a real kick up the arse to do more. Afterwards I spoke to mates who were reminiscing that today, 24 years ago, we were heading off to Italy for the World Cup – almost a quarter of a century ago! Can't believe how quickly the time has passed.

23 JUNE: Visited PCS picket line at Bathgate today. The Tories really are hell bent on destroying HMRC. The young PCS reps at the site are great and I always try to support them whenever they are taking action to save jobs and improve conditions.

Canvassing in Chapleton area of Polbeth, which isn't a great area for us, but we are still ahead of Yes.

The last 900 doors we canvassed has No at 66 per cent, and Yes at 27 per cent, but I suspect it is much closer than this.

24 JUNE: The Shadow Cabinet had a long discussion on post-referendum tactics and the need for Labour to take the initiative. We cannot allow the SNP to claim a victory in defeat. This is absolutely vital – if Labour fails on this we are in real trouble.

Today the British Medical Association gave a blistering critique of the SNP's handling of the NHS, saying it has been a five-year long car crash. They reckon the SNP is fiddling while Rome burns.

25 JUNE: Spent the day tidying up the office before breaking up for the recess.

26 JUNE: Picked Chloe up from the airport at 3am. Thankfully they are all back safe and sound and the holiday seems to have gone okay.

Into parliament for the final FMQs, where the BMA comments on the NHS dominate. Afterwards Alex Neil gave a statement on mesh. I asked why it had taken him a year to act and why he previously said he had no powers to do anything when clearly he had.

27 JUNE: Off to Copenhagen for family wedding. Great to meet my Scouse cousins and their sons and daughters who, like us, are over for Faye and Patrick's big day. The city is fantastic. It is so relaxed and well run; there are lots of bikes and the entire place seems clean. After a nice meal we

went up to the hotel room with Alistair and his pals who sing and play instruments – it was brilliant.

28 JUNE: Up early for a walk into town with all the family – Fiona, Mum, Anna, Jim, John and Sharron. We walked around the city centre, saw the changing of the guard, and headed along the canal before going back for the wedding. The ceremony was in the gardens of a city park and thankfully the weather was kind. We had fantastic food barbecued by a local chef and then enjoyed a full day of music from Ali's wide collection of pals playing fiddle, double bass, guitars and banjo. It was a brilliant international event and totally laid back. Afterwards, the guys in the band went into the town centre and played outside a homeless hostel for hours and the residents loved the free gig.

29 JUNE: Up early and took a walk down to see the Little Mermaid, before heading to an old fisherman's shack that has been turned into a restaurant. We had a beautiful Danish buffet of fish, vegetables and salad before moving on to the pub to watch some of the World Cup on TV.

30 JUNE: Today we visited Christiania, an area of Copenhagen set up as a social experiment. It is a green and car-free neighbourhood established in 1971 by a group of hippies who occupied some abandoned military barracks on the site and developed their own set of society rules, completely independent of the Danish government.

Christiania existed under special conditions for 40 years with conflicts and clashes between the local Christianites and the Danish state. After many years of uncertainty over the future of Christiania, an agreement was entered into in 2011, which meant that on 1 July 2012, the Foundation Freetown Christiania was inaugurated. The foundation now owns the entire part of Christiania located outside the protected ramparts, and leases buildings and land on the ramparts, which are still owned by the state. Part of the money is raised by selling the symbolic Christiania shares. Freetown Christiania is a mix of homemade houses, workshops, art galleries, music venues, cheap and organic eateries, and beautiful nature. It is still a society within a society. For example, you cannot buy a house in Christiania. You have to apply for one, and if successful, it is given to you. The area is open to the public – even with guided tours, run by the local Christianites.

It's quite a place, with lots of recycling, small enterprises and cooperatives. Drugs are sold in the street at small stalls and it has an eclectic, liberal feel to it. It was really worth seeing.

During the course of the referendum many references have been made to Scotland becoming like a Scandinavian country. The culture and history of Denmark is completely different of course but at a very basic cost level a lunch is around £25, a small family car £30,000 (subject to around 140 per cent tax) and a pint of beer £7. Not sure Scotland is quite ready for such prices yet!

8

Referendum Diary: July 2014

1 JULY: Home from Copenhagen and day off to recover. Spoke to Frank Toner, who said Miliband's weekend visit to Livingston shopping centre was a great success, with a lot of people wanting to speak to him and get selfies taken.

3 JULY: Out all day leafleting in Bents – and really pleased to see the old flats being knocked down. I have been lobbying the council for years to do this and now it is finally happening. It will make a real difference to the area. Bumped into Robert Nisbet, a good guy who is active in the community. He was updating me on all the work the Future Vision community group are doing in the village. It is brilliant. I worked with and encouraged them since I was on the council and it is great to see their efforts bear fruit so impressively.

Dennis Skinner was voted off the NEC today by MPs. He is 82 and has served many years within the organisation – and they have just dumped him. It's a sad day, but he is still a legend.

4 JULY: To the Gyle shopping centre to take part in a walkabout with Ed Miliband. I hate this kind of thing but it will be interesting to observe him in action. I was full of trepidation and thought something like this could go badly wrong, with the Yes camp organising a 'welcome committee' to give him dog's abuse, as that seems to be their tactic of choice. I met Kezia Dugdale and Cammy Day, PPC for Edinburgh West, at the entrance and we welcomed Ed and Johann Lamont before going into the centre. The reception he received was pretty remarkable; no hostility, and lots of people wanting to talk to him and get a selfie. Many folk told us they would be voting No, which was heartening. There was no abuse and he was relaxed, personable and quite impressive all round. It is my first time observing him

doing this at close quarters – he was natural and likeable and not at all the weird and wooden caricature of the media. Strangely, Johann kept her distance from Miliband, and wasn't up front meeting people. She appeared uncomfortable and to the casual observer it could look as though her heart isn't in it, and that her relationship with Miliband is strained, or may even have broken down completely. Maybe I'm wide of the mark but this is how it looked to me.

Back home for a quick bite to eat and then out with Fiona and the gang to see The Underground Jam in my local pub – the Grange. They played every classic track spot on. It was a fantastic night with all the old Mods belting out every song.

5 JULY: At the Renfield Centre in Glasgow for a Scottish CND event. Last year, the organisation, wrongly in my opinion, took a view on the referendum and supported independence because of the Yes campaign's opposition to Trident. I think they should have avoided expressing an opinion and tried to maintain and expand its broad base.

The meeting started with UK chair Kate Hudson discussing the after-effects of World War One. Jenny Clegg then spoke about the emergence of China as a global power to take on the US. I was there to speak about Venezuela and the forces at play there just now, which are trying to undermine the democratically elected government. I referred to my experience as an election observer and the social and economic progress it has made. I joked at the start that I welcomed the opportunity to speak about something other than the UK constitution and the referendum. At the Q&A afterwards, Malky Burns, the *Morning Star*'s Scottish reporter of all people, raised the independence question! I deflected his point saying I would prefer to talk about Venezuela for just one day, but a guy from the Yes camp jumped up and shouted that he was here as a Scottish patriot and I must address the issue of nuclear weapons and independence as that was why he was in attendance. He failed to mention that the meeting had nothing to do with that topic. Anyway he ranted and huffed and puffed and led a one-man walk out in his kilt! He couldn't help himself – everything, and I mean everything, to the likes of him HAS to be about independence.

Afterwards, I went to the Pot Still pub for a pint with Vince Mills and Pauline Bryan, two friends and great comrades. They are long standing stalwarts and organisers on the Scottish left and a very committed, intelligent couple who have worked like Trojans over the years to keep the Campaign for Socialism group alive and functioning. They said speculation suggested Johann would step down after the referendum. They think Jim

Murphy and Anas Sarwar are being lined up along with other potential candidates, such as Kezia Dugdale, Drew Smith, Jenny Marra and me, to succeed Johann!

Murphy has been trailing round Scotland standing on an Irn Bru crate shouting at passers-by and goading the madder elements of the Yes campaign into abusing him. It is clearly a blatant PR stunt and leadership bid in the making. Their view is that the left would expect and want me to stand and that I should be ready in the eventuality. We went through a list of possible others from the broad left – Katy Clark, Ian Davidson, Alex Rowley etc. I made it clear I didn't want to do it; I have no burning ambition to run (I'm not a personally ambitious type) but if it was Murphy and a coronation or coup by New Labour, I would see the left as having a duty to respond with a candidate. We all agree that Murphy would be a disaster. Anas is a much more likeable person, while Drew won't stand and it may be too early for Kezia, who will undoubtedly put her name forward at some point. There is an article on the Better Nation website fuelling this speculation. We live in interesting times – the next few weeks and months could be tumultuous.

8 JULY: Surgery this morning – housing, the environment and jobs were the issues raised. Later, canvassed Uphall Station – weather glorious and lots of people outside enjoying the sunshine, and we had a decent response.

9 JULY: Off to Greenburn Golf Club, in Fauldhouse, to meet committee members to discuss the club's future. Like many clubs across the country, they are struggling with falling membership and lost revenue. It's not simply a cost issue, although membership isn't cheap at around £500 per year, but also about cultural change with people having more choice in their leisure time and men playing a greater role in bringing up the family with less leisure time. I am committed to helping them, and any other club in the area, in any way I can to ensure their survival.

10 JULY: Went for a walk around Glasgow Green with Chloe and the place is buzzing for the Commonwealth Games. Even the weather was good. It was then up to the Radisson Hotel for a debate hosted by the Scottish Association for Mental Health (SAMH) on the referendum. 60 people attended, which was a mixture of professionals working in mental health and patients. I spoke alongside UNISON's Katrina Murray, and we were up against Michael Matheson and Sarah-Jane Walls from Yes Scotland. It was a decent, civilised and good-natured event.

11 JULY: With Graeme Morrice, David Cleghorn and David Dodds leafleting Fauldhouse in the glorious sunshine.

12 JULY: Should be in Durham for the Miners' Gala today but at the Policy Forum instead to discuss what we will include in the manifesto for 2015. A lot of charity, trade union and civic group representatives are present. A good debate and discussion.

15 JULY: Oban – prior to the recess. Neil Bibby, Drew Smith, Michael Sharp, Gregor Scotland and I had agreed to help in their council by-election. I suggested we source a tent and camp as it would be great fun and a bit of a change. We had an afternoon canvassing along with Johann Lamont, and a lovely evening door-knocking in Oban, before going for a meal with the candidate Keiron Green. We enjoyed a few beers before a nightcap at the campsite. Great fun.

16 JULY: Leafleted Oban town centre. There is a Yes campaign shop in Oban so it gives the impression it is a Yes town but the canvassing was pretty good – a lot of No voters and quite a decent Labour vote in an area that isn't at all a strong place for us. On the way home we stopped at Inverary and had a go on the dodgems. Who says politics is boring? Drove home in the worst downpour I have seen in years, but a great couple of days. Politics shouldn't always be a grind.

19 JULY: Watched The Open golf tournament on TV, and enjoyed seeing Rory McIlroy take the course apart.

20 JULY: More golf... and was thrilled to see McIlroy hold on to edge Sergio Garcia. He is some talent.

21–27 JULY: On holiday for a week. Med cruise. Bliss!

28 JULY: Back from holiday and straight to East Calder for canvassing. Phenomenal response. We 'chapped' 700 doors and got fewer than 100 Yes voters.

Into the office to deal with hundreds of emails, with many raising the appalling situation in Gaza, where the Israeli army are butchering thousands of innocent people and bringing the place to its knees. Dreadful stuff.

Today the Yes campaign are claiming that unless there is a Yes vote, the NHS will be privatised. God, they are getting desperate – the NHS in Scotland is wholly devolved. It can only be privatised if the Scottish Government decide to do so. The budget can only be cut if you accept the private sector is cheaper than the public sector. It never is, so this will not cut the budget, and if you look at the evidence, use of the private sector under the SNP is rising according to Audit Scotland. This is desperate stuff, and on every count they are wrong.

To Addiewell Miners Welfare for a referendum meeting with Pauline Bryan, from the Red Paper Collective, and a No voter; Jim Sillars and Angela Constance MSP. About 60 people turned up. Sillars is 76 and still sharp, speaking well and fluently, but his argument isn't great. Lots of assumptions and generalisations about everything being better with independence. Angela Constance is woeful – she is completely non-political and says lots of words, none of which amount to much. Pauline and I argued that it was in the interest of the trade unions and the Scottish working class to remain united with working class people across the UK. We spoke of being involved in the same struggles and that what we don't want is a low-taxed, neo-liberal Scotland with a race to the bottom on wages and conditions. We got a fair hearing and a good bit of support from the audience, but the Yes campaign had organised their people to be there. The Addiewell club is a brilliant place with great folk involved, always political and at the heart of the community.

29 JULY: To the blood donor centre in Glasgow where I met Andy Burnham. Gave blood and spoke to the staff about the service. They were excellent and it was interesting to hear about how it operates, but they are in need of donations.

30 JULY: Met solicitor Mike Dailly at the Govan Law Centre about a housing case involving a couple from Blackburn who have had 16 years of hell because they don't have the proper title to their property. It's no fault of their own as it was a lawyer's mistake, yet they have no comeback. Outrageous. Mike was helpful and will advise us on the case. He is a really impressive guy who does some groundbreaking community legal work.

31 JULY: At the regional office in West Calder where I met Jackson Cullinane of Unite to discuss TTIP, NHS, the referendum and a whole range of other things. I like Jackson a lot. He is vastly experienced, smart and committed. I always try and help the trade unions on a whole range of

things and am a member of EIS and Unite. I work closely with most unions and take pride in this work. When I came into parliament I saw it as my duty to work in tandem with them and have followed through on that commitment. I am also a member of the Unite, RMT and PCS parliamentary groups.

9

Referendum Diary: August 2014

2 AUGUST: To the Hydro in Glasgow for the Commonwealth Games boxing finals with my brother-in-law Jim. What a crowd and what an atmosphere. We saw Nicola Adams, who was lucky, and should probably have lost to a Northern Irish boxer, but the big event was the last two bouts with Charlie Flynn and Josh Taylor both winning. The place went absolutely bonkers – it was amazing.

We managed to get on a rammed last train home. Glasgow is bursting at the seams and the pubs and restaurants are doing a roaring trade. What a brilliant day.

4 AUGUST: St John the Baptist Chapel, Fauldhouse for the funeral of Peter Lynch, a stalwart of the local community. He was a family man, local trade union leader (UCATT), community activist, on the committee of the junior football club, compere at the children's gala day and served on the miners' welfare committee for 47 years. A Fauldhouse man to his boots – and a great loss!

5 AUGUST: Parliament back today due to the referendum recess having changed. Speaking to other Labour MSPs, they appear buoyant about the referendum – the SNP seem a bit down and lacking in confidence. After parliament I was straight out leafleting in Polbeth.

Big debate on TV tonight between Alex Salmond and Alistair Darling. Salmond was really poor, talking about trivial issues such as driving on the right hand side of the road! Darling destroyed him on the currency issue – asking what the plan B was. Social media response is that Darling won. Big boost to the No campaign but makes me feel no more positive about Better bloody Together.

6 AUGUST: Canvassing in Moredun, Edinburgh, for council by-election. 12 of us out door knocking, all with our tales up after last night's debate. Papers and TV all saying Salmond was poor and Darling won. Even Tom Gordon in the *Herald* scathing, with the headline to his piece 'Death of a salesman'. No matter how much spin the SNP put on it, he was gubbed. I bet he will be better next time – well, it shouldn't be too hard.

Spoke in the Trident debate today and nailed my colours to the mast, making it crystal clear I am anti-nuclear, anti-Trident and a member of CND. As a front bencher, I expected one of the whips might say something to me about my speech, but no one did. They knew my position before I was appointed. It's non-negotiable!

7 AUGUST: Salmond mocked on currency at FMQs, as he still can't give a plan B answer. This is damaging to the Yes campaign. They insist they can use the pound but why would they want the currency of an independent Scotland to be controlled by the Chancellor of a foreign country? The alternative would be the Euro, so good luck with that. Within the Yes camp the SSP, Greens and Dennis Canavan all reject using the pound in a sterling zone but they are bit-part players – it's the SNPs show and they will brass it out.

Attended a Gaza protest outside Holyrood – big attendance and lots of anger about what is going on.

8 AUGUST: Gilded Balloon, Edinburgh – went to see Blofeld and Baxter – two old duffers from Test Match Special talking about cricket and their exploits following England for the BBC. It was a hilarious show and a must for any cricket fan.

10 AUGUST: Mathew Hilferty started today on a paid internship sponsored by Crohn's and Colitis UK. He will be with us for three months. The charity want him to show how people with the condition can thrive in different jobs. He is a quiet guy who has gone through a lot, but we will ensure he has a good experience that will hopefully help him get a job.

Did a photoshoot outside a local bank with Councillors David Dodds and Cathy Muldoon, and Graeme Morrice. RBS have announced the closure of branches in Fauldhouse, Armadale and Harthill despite the fact they have a policy to keep the last bank in town open. We have launched a postcard campaign to get people to oppose the closures and are getting a great response.

12 AUGUST: Met representatives from the Campaign Against the Care Tax. They are calling for charges for alarms, aids and care to be funded via taxation and not through charges to people. The group have walked out of the COSLA working group on the issue. I asked whether they would speak out about the council tax freeze and its impact on services, but they won't. Some of the organisations that make up the coalition are afraid their budgets will be cut by central government if they do.

To the Shadow Cabinet where Ian Price advised that private polling shows good support for a No vote. Afterwards, I met with Norman Murray, the former leader of East Lothian Council, and Vince and Pauline to discuss regional list reselection – they are all willing to help.

I then spoke in an economy debate where the SNP contributions were pretty flat. Afterwards, there was a members' debate on Gaza hosted by Sandra White. Very good contributions condemning the actions of Netanyahu's government. Ken McIntosh gave the pro-Israeli line.

13 AUGUST: To Livingston Crematorium for the funeral of Joanne Burns, wife of Bobby, who worked with my da and I. All the old brickies were present, including Ronnie, wee Tommy, Martin Dirkie and the whole Burns clan. Good to see everyone there paying their respects.

On to Dalkeith for a public meeting on the referendum with Councillor Bryan Pottinger arguing with me for a No vote. On the other side was Owen Thomson, SNP leader of Midlothian Council, and Pat Smith of the Socialist Workers Party. The SWP position on independence in unbelievable. Only a few years ago, they were arguing that independence would divide the working class and the trade unions, and that it was a neo-liberal idea they as revolutionary socialists couldn't support, but now they are amongst the most aggressive and pro-independence groups lining up beside the corporate tax-cutting SNP. It's clear to me this is nothing to do with support for independence itself, but simply that the central committee of the party has seen the Yes campaign as a chance to recruit members to its cause, and therefore it is a tactic and another opportunity to attack the Labour Party, who they ultimately want to destroy.

Went into the Tun (BBC in Edinburgh) to do Scotland 2014 and discuss the NHS 'privatisation' claim. Think I did okay. Afterwards I went into parliament to pick up my bag. As I was leaving, I bumped into Tricia Marwick, who had been in the bar, and wanted to tell me all about her plans for 'playing a major role in bringing people together and healing our divisions after the referendum'! She clearly sees herself as some sort of Mother Theresa figure using her 'soothing words' to end hostilities. Good luck with that sister!

14 AUGUST: Met Henry Simmons from Alzheimer's Scotland and Matt Forde of the NSPCC to discuss health and social care issues. I then headed to Cathcart Old Parish Church for the Constituency Labour Party-led debate and discussion on health and social care policy. It was encouraging to hear members agree with my view that health inequalities and social care are some of the biggest issues facing the health sector. Some really good suggestions put forward.

15 AUGUST: Canvassing all day in Longridge. Tiring work, but hopefully worth it.

16 AUGUST: The NHS privatisation story is hogging the media headlines. The Yes focus groups must be showing it has traction. It is the biggest lie of the campaign to date. Here is why: 1 – No party in Scotland (not even the Scottish bloody Tories) support privatisation of our NHS. 2 – What happens to the NHS in England has no impact on Scotland because it is fully devolved. 3 – The private sector always comes out more expensive than the public sector. 4 – It is the SNP who are increasing the use of the private sector in Scotland – this is really cynical stuff.

17 AUGUST: Earlier this year, the Red Paper Collective offered to organise a short tour with George Galloway in key areas where we have good left speakers; the first is today. Fauldhouse Miners Welfare Club: Public meeting on the referendum chaired by Councillor David Dodds. The club was packed; more than 220 people in on a Sunday afternoon. Great to see it full for the biggest political meeting in Fauldhouse since the Poll Tax era. I spoke first and was really up for it in front of a home audience.

Galloway was next, and he was brilliant. His searing analysis of the case for independence was fantastic. He ripped apart the claim that oil could fund the services we all rely on, and also destroyed the currency argument. Tam and Kathleen Dalyell came along, but were a wee bit late, and when George saw him coming in he said Tam was one of the greatest parliamentarians he had ever met. Tam got a huge ovation from the audience. We did a Q&A session and the people present took it seriously with good, fair questions. There was no nonsense or aggravation. It was a great meeting with many people staying behind to talk and offer congratulations – even the Yes voters said they enjoyed it. A good day's work.

18 AUGUST: I popped into Labour Party HQ in Bath Street, Glasgow to collect referendum materials. The atmosphere in that place is awful. It should be lively and welcoming but it isn't.

It was then over to Adelaide's (also in Bath Street) for the second of the Galloway meetings with John Foster (Communist Party), Agnes Tolmie (Unite), Pauline McNeil (ex-MSP Glasgow Kelvin) and Galloway himself. The CP clearly had a three line whip and many people there were CP activists. It was an odd atmosphere at the meeting but it went okay.

Salmond gave his 'Arbroath declaration of opportunity' speech today. He really does think he is Mel Gibson! He also upped the rhetoric on the NHS.

19 AUGUST: In parliament, the SNP have gone nuclear on the NHS to take the focus away from Salmond's poor TV performance and the currency debacle. They are screaming about privatisation if there is a No vote and this is supposed to be the 'positive campaign'; the positive case for Yes and they call Better Together 'Project Fear!' Alex Neil gave a statement to parliament on this today. He really doesn't believe a word of it but goes through the motions because they think it is working.

In my reply I wanted to tell him they were the biggest bunch of shameless, cynical liars I have ever come across, but that would have been unparliamentary, so I found an alternative way.

The debate in the chamber then went like this...

Neil Findlay: 'At the SNP conference in 2014, Nicola Sturgeon said, "I can stand here proudly and say this: for as long as we are in government, there will be no privatisation of the NHS in Scotland." Yesterday and today, however, the First Minister and the Cabinet Secretary contradicted that position. In 2011, the SNP manifesto said: "The Scottish Parliament has responsibility for the health service and that means we can protect NHS budgets." The white paper says: "Without devolution, the NHS would have been repeatedly re-organised and exposed to private competition." I am not allowed to call anyone in the chamber a liar, but was Nicola Sturgeon not telling the truth at her conference? Did the SNP not tell the truth in its manifesto?' [Interruption.]
Presiding Officer: 'Order.'

Neil Findlay: 'Or is the Cabinet Secretary not telling the truth now? I am not allowed to call the Cabinet Secretary and the First Minister liars, but will they condemn a campaign that claims that private healthcare is cheaper and more efficient than public healthcare? I am not allowed to call the Cabinet Secretary and the First Minister liars...'

Presiding Officer: 'Your time is up, Mr Findlay. Do you have a question?'

Neil Findlay: 'Do they accept that the greatest threat to the NHS in Scotland is the £6 billion of cuts in public spending that would occur under their plans to break up the country? Will the Cabinet Secretary focus on his day job and sort out waiting lists, huge problems in accident and emergency, staffing and bed cuts, a social care crisis and a lack of general practitioners, instead of supporting the most scandalous deceit of the referendum campaign to date?'

Alex Neil: 'In the spirit of Mr Findlay's remarks, I thank him for the compliment at the start of his question. I do not think Mr Findlay understands what devolution means. Let me remind him that Enoch Powell said many years ago that power devolved is power retained. We must look at not only today and tomorrow but at five and 10 years' time. With a constitution that embeds and enshrines the basic principles of the NHS, Scotland will never ever have a privatised health service. Our powers in a devolved Parliament are not enshrined and can be overruled at any time by any future Westminster Government.'

Three times I said it – just to make sure everyone got the message, and hopefully they did!

Off to Auchinleck in Ayrshire for a meeting with Labour Party supporters in Cathy Jamieson's constituency. With me was MP for Wansbeck, and former miner and NUM president, Ian Lavery. He was fantastic and talked about class politics, the miners' strike, solidarity and the needs of people in his area being the same as people in Cathy's. Ian speaks with a brilliant, broad Geordie accent with passion and commitment – I like him a lot. I gave my standard Red Paper speech sprinkled with local issues and repeated arguments about solidarity and class justice.

Back to do *Scotland 2014* at STV; subject, the NHS. Prior to going on air, John McKay, the presenter, and the cameraman were discussing food, so when I walked onto the studio floor, he asked me, 'Sausage roll or bridie?'

'Oh no,' I replied. 'definitely a pie.'

'Oh, a pie man,' he said, turning to the cameraman, who shrugged his shoulders.

'But it depends what you mean,' I said. 'If it's Gregg's, then definitively a pie, but it must be on a Gregg's buttered roll. It's a perfect fit – made for each other!'

'Eh, whit,' says John and the cameraman, looking at each other in disbelief. 'A pie on a roll – no!'

'Aye,' says I, 'and with broon sauce tae. That's a must.'

We then got into the classic debate about chips and whether you have just salt, salt and vinegar or salt, vinegar and sauce – or as it's commonly known in West Lothian, 'everything!'

I then explained the Scottish writer Irvine Welsh's classic description of the region of Scotland that runs from Ratho, on the western outskirts of Edinburgh, to Harthill on the Eastern border of North Lanarkshire. According to Welsh, it's not West Lothian – it's 'the broon sauce corridor'! A place where in chippies you are automatically offered salt, vinegar and broon sauce (which is sauce diluted with vinegar), dispensed from a Barr's juice bottle with a hole pierced in the lid. None of your shitey wee sachets here. Bottles of said sauce are usually on sale in said chippy for £1 behind the counter!

John McKay and his cameraman chum were aghast at these revelations and we had a good laugh about it just before going on air. I thought one of us was going to burst out laughing during the interview.

Afterwards, he told me he was really pleased I had come in, and added, 'We will need to get you in as a food critic or cultural commentator next time!' It was all good fun.

20 AUGUST: Had my mum and her friend, and a great friend of our family, Maureen Byrne, in for lunch at the parliament restaurant. It was a lovely hour and a half.

Then over to Edinburgh's Royal College of Physicians for a referendum debate with Alex Neil. I was a bit anxious about this but it was a good debate in a beautiful building. I called out Neil on the NHS privatisation claim and he wasn't comfortable dealing with it because this audience knew it was mince. Their argument has now changed to 'if there is a No vote, then charges will be introduced to Scotland's NHS'. An even bigger lie. It was desperate, cyclical stuff.

It was announced today that Tricia Marwick will do 'time for reflection' in parliament after the referendum. This must be the Mother Theresa moment she spoke about a week or two ago. Hopefully her soothing words will heal the nation's divisions. The country waits with bated breath.

21 AUGUST: Last day before the recess for the referendum. Prominent doctor and cancer specialist, Anna Gregor has dismissed the NHS privatisation charges claim as 'complete and utter lies'. At FMQs, Salmond was asked about his 'Arbroath Declaration', public spending and the NHS. He really is full of himself with an ego beyond compare.

In the afternoon debate on the future of Scotland, Johann gave an excellent speech – thoughtful, dignified and principled – a complete contrast to Salmond's bombast. At the end, Johann walked across the chamber to shake Salmond's hand; he didn't know where to look or what to do – it really threw him but I'm not sure many folk realised it had happened, although it was a fine gesture after months and years of fierce debate. I wonder if the press will pick up on it. Johann is a thoroughly decent, straightforward person. I don't always agree with her, and believe her 'something for nothing' speech was a bad idea, but I have huge respect for her and always enjoy our chats.

22 AUGUST: Day off with Fiona in Edinburgh so we went to the theatre to see a youth production of *Blood Brothers*. After that, *The Confessions of Gordon Brown*. It was funny but could have been better. Afterwards, we went to the Doric for a drink and then home. It was good to have a day away from the referendum.

23 AUGUST: A leafleting session in West Calder and we got a lot done. I bumped into a guy I used to work with at the council who is a lifelong Labour voter, but told me he will vote Yes. This depressed me, but my mood was lightened a bit when he told me why. 'I don't want Maurice Johnston to be the next Prime Minister!' (I think he meant Boris Johnston and not Maurice, the controversial footballer who became the first high-profile Catholic to sign for Rangers, having previously played for arch rivals Celtic). Mind you, maybe wee Mo would make a better job of it than that buffoon Boris!

25 AUGUST: Howden, Livingston – best canvassing session for a while, with three-to-one expressing their intention to vote No.

Evening meeting at Loanhead with Cathy Jamieson, Davie Hamilton and George Galloway. About 80 people there and it was worthwhile. I have enjoyed doing these events with Galloway, observing and listening to one of the best orators in politics. He is a master communicator and it has been interesting to watch him at work. His performance at the senate a few years back is etched in my memory – it was utterly brilliant.

Tonight was the second referendum meeting between Salmond and Darling. As predicted Salmond came out fighting and was much, much better. He was aggressive, arrogant, and scrapping, but very effective. The polls afterward says it was 71 per cent to Salmond, and 29 for Darling. Thank God the TV debates are over – they were pretty awful, with people shouting over each other and the audience acting like a football crowd. But such is life with a long and increasingly polarised debate.

26 AUGUST: Out canvassing in Livingston and it is 60 to 40 in favour of No.

27 AUGUST: Armadale Community Centre for a meeting with RBS. MPs Graeme Morrice and Michael Connarty are also there. Michael Crow, former Tory Spin doctor, and now RBS press chief, is present along with two of their managers from retail banking. We gave them a torrid time and refused to accept the closures. We said we had huge public support and that they had a responsibility to loyal customers who they have made money off for years. They want to replace the branch with a visiting mobile service for two half hours a week. They said they had to get value for shareholders from selling the building. They didn't like it when I pointed out that WE are the shareholders, since the bank is owned by the government. Michael went ballistic at them. I summed up, saying we were formally asking them to withdraw the plans to close the branches and that they had a duty to undertake a full consultation with customers. I asked them to come to a public meeting about it, and they refused! They really are a shower of careless chancers who have ripped people off for decades.

To Whitburn for West Lothian Trades Council referendum public debate where I was up against Fiona Hyslop MSP (I have always got on pretty well with her). Fiona got a torrid time and didn't really know what to do as she was not used to it. She tried to claim Police Scotland was more effective and democratic than before the merger of the forces. She got ripped to bits for that. I enjoyed tonight.

28 AUGUST: It has been revealed that while on his Irn Bru crate 'world' tour, Jim Murphy was pelted with eggs by Yes supporters in Dundee. He is of course milking this for all its worth. These events are getting worse

and worse and the Yes mob who turn up are doing exactly what Murphy wants. He wants them to behave like a rowdy mob so undecided voters will be turned off by it. Salmond is saying very little about it with no real condemnation of their behaviour. Social media is in overdrive and some of the abuse and infantile stuff being thrown around is awful. Sometimes it's hard not be drawn into it.

In the afternoon, I headed to the Marriott Hotel for a UNISON nursing conference to debate the referendum with Christina McKelvie MSP. She acts left but does little to follow through on it – full of rhetoric. I could sense a number of the shop stewards were sympathetic to the Yes camp, based on the nonsense about privatisation of the NHS, and no matter how well or often this is rebutted, they want to believe it!

Spoke to a Norwegian trade union magazine journalist about the SNP plan to have Scandinavian social services whilst levying Texan taxes. They found this incredible, and of course it is!

29 AUGUST: George Galloway was attacked in London today and had his jaw broken by someone shouting about Israel.

Spent the day campaigning in Knightsridge, Livingston, before going for a curry with Fiona, Jimmy and Kathleen. It was a relief to get out and speak about things other than politics.

30 AUGUST: Otherwise sensible commentators like Mandy Rhodes, McWhirter and others are brushing off the aggression in the campaign as a bit of rough and tumble – it is more than that with the atmosphere getting pretty heated and ugly at times.

31 AUGUST: Salmond on TV today claiming he would have a sovereign mandate to negotiate a currency union in the event of a Yes vote. What utter nonsense – he would have a vote for independence and nothing else.

Sunday Herald claiming they have evidence from Dr Alyson Pollock that there will be NHS privatisation with a No vote. They have nothing of the sort, and what she says is that privatisation is less efficient than the public sector. This is exactly my argument, as it would actually cost more with privatisation, so if it is imposed in England then spending in Scotland would subsequently INCREASE not decrease. But hey ho, they won't let the facts get in the way of a good story.

Went to Thompson's Solicitors' fireworks event at the festival. It was brilliant and I spoke to lots of good friends. Patrick McGuire looking much better after his illness – big relief for his wife and young family.

10

Referendum Diary: September 2014

1 SEPTEMBER: Poll out today has the gap between Yes and No at just six per cent. I think it is a bit bigger than this, but not too much. Conference call with Shadow Cabinet and MPs, and lots of concerns raised about the message we're putting out; the NHS, momentum for the Yes campaign etc. Jemma Doyle MP, Hugh Henry and Brian Donohoe all saying things are okay in their patch. Frank Roy MP reckons people shouldn't panic. They must have private polling showing a bigger lead if he is saying that.

Evening canvass in Pumpherston resulted in a three-to-one vote for No. I knocked on the door of my granny's old house in the south village (she moved to a home about 10 years ago). The woman who bought the house from my granny still lives there and we had a lovely chat about her and the house. The woman then disappeared inside, before returning and handing me a large piece of plywood about 20 inches square. She said it was an end bath panel that was removed when they fitted a new bathroom suite. On the other side of it my granda, who was a great writer, had written his life story. All about growing up, his family, his jobs, village life etc. It was amazing and very moving to read. The woman then went back inside to get her husband and we had another long chat. It was lovely. As I handed it back they insisted I keep it, as it belonged to our family and not theirs. I was choked by their kind gesture. I took it straight to my mum's, where we sat and read the whole thing. It was brilliant and I will get it mounted.

2 SEPTEMBER: Canvassing in Ladywell, Livingston. This is an SNP stronghold, and the vote is 70 per cent Yes. No surprises here.

Into parliament for a visit from the pupils of Westfield School. A wee guy in primary six asked the best question ever. He said, 'If a bad guy comes in here, have all the MSPs been taught karate to stop him stealing stuff?' I promised to raise his very sensible suggestion with the Presiding Officer.

TV debate tonight with Douglas Alexander, Kezia Dugdale and Ruth Davidson up against Nicola Sturgeon, Patrick Harvie and Elaine C Smith. It was a pretty decent debate, with Kez doing well, but Labour MPs and MSPs on a platform with the Tory leader is not good.

3 SEPTEMBER: Leafleting in Knightsridge, Livingston with Councillor Danny Logue. His wife is really ill with cancer; I feel for him and the kids.

In the afternoon, it was over to Linburn Centre for War Blinded to debate with Councillor Greg McCarra of the SNP. He was a councillor in my ward when I was on the council and he and I have never got on. He is an intelligent guy but one of the most patronising people you are ever likely to meet. The veterans were real characters and a pleasure to speak to, asking about pensions, the NHS, jobs, oil etc. There was an even split between Yes and No voters.

Today the RMT released results of their survey of members on the referendum. Only 30 per cent replied, with 1,000 voting Yes, 900 voting No and 300 who don't know which way they will vote. Phil McGarry called to say the executive would make no recommendation to members. This is a good result as I thought they would be coming out clearly for Yes.

ISIS have decapitated a journalist and posted footage online – horrendous and very worrying developments across the globe.

The papers report that Thomas Doherty MP has said he will resign if there is a Yes vote – well if there is anything to give me a shaky hand in the polling station it's that announcement. Doherty is awful. How he became a Labour MP is beyond belief. I've never heard any of our MPs say a good word about him.

4 SEPTEMBER: To South Lanarkshire Council where I met with Jackie Burns and UNISON's Stephen Smillie, Katrina Murray and Lizanne Handibode. We discussed social care, low pay, 15-minute care and much more. It was a really worthwhile meeting. Stephen is now a pro-independence campaigner and there is a bit of tension between us as we have had fiery exchanges on social media, but I like Stephen and think he's a good guy and a very committed socialist.

During an evening canvass in Bents, we covered 200 houses. The result was; 140 No voters, 38 Yes with the rest undecided. Brilliant response but I fear many of the 'don't knows' will vote Yes. No evidence of this, just a gut feeling that people aren't all telling the truth on the doorsteps.

5 SEPTEMBER: With Tommy and Diane to Liverpool for the GMB justice conference. I have a lot of relatives in Liverpool and it's one of my favourite cities. It's very like Glasgow in its outlook, humour and some of its history (slave trade, tobacco, Irish immigration) and its obsession with football and music. We took a bus tour and visited the fantastic Catholic cathedral (beautiful inside), the Hard Days Night Hotel, Mathew Street – home of the famous Cavern Club – and the magnificent Philharmonic Pub, before meeting up with my cousin Mike and his wife Pam, who are among my closest relatives and great company. We had a lovely night with them. The town was buzzing and has changed so much over the 45 years I have been going down there.

6 SEPTEMBER: To John Moores University for the justice conference. I had approached Paul Kenny, GMB General Secretary, a year ago to see if he would help in sponsoring an event to bring together all the major justice campaigns across the country to discuss and learn from each other. Paul agreed it was a great idea and asked Paul McCarthy, the North West organiser, to get on the case. 'Yesterday and Today' is the culmination of that work. The conference was fantastic and heard from a range of campaigners including the amazing Margaret Aspinall, of the Hillsborough campaign; Andy Burnham; actor Ricky Tomlinson, who was jailed and went on hunger strike after being framed during the building trade strike in the '70s (my da was also on strike in that one); blacklisted construction workers; Tom Watson MP, who spoke about phone hacking; Davie Hopper on miners justice and Orgreave; the Cammell Laird workers and the Justice for Daniel campaign. I spoke on the Scottish campaign against blacklisting and the situation with the Scottish miners and repeated my calls for an inquiry.

There is a real political earthquake tonight. One poll puts Yes on 51 per cent and No on 49 per cent. Bloody hell!

7 SEPTEMBER: The Labour Party are clearly panicking over yesterday's poll, while trying to claim they aren't. They asked us to call 50 undecided voters over the next few days, along with door knocking, leafleting and everything else.

8 SEPTEMBER: There is a media frenzy over the first poll showing a Yes lead. There's no doubt Cameron will be 'filling his Huggies'. He is toast if Yes win. Salmond is gloating like a big fat cat who has just downed a gallon of cream. A sober and considered approach may have been more appropriate. In response, Gordon Brown has come up with a timetable for more powers to be devolved to Scotland – at this stage! If they had listened to the Labour left, Unite and the people behind the Red Paper Collective, we would have been offering a federal solution with a range of devolved powers ages ago. The Lib Dems, with Menzies Campbell's report, also had a road map towards achieving it, and at the last minute we have a panicked response and the Yes camp are loving it.

Canvassed Craigshill, in Livingston, which is a difficult area for Labour. We had all 16 councillors out canvassing, which is a miracle, as some haven't been seen during the entire campaign, while others have been putting in a huge effort. We canvassed 300 doors and were 10 ahead – this is going to be really, really close. That night I urged Fiona to book a holiday for October as we all need it. She has put up with a lot over the last year.

9 SEPTEMBER: Edinburgh is abuzz with the news of the joint declaration on powers and a timetable from Labour, The Lib Dems and Tories. Prime Minister's Questions has been cancelled to allow Cameron, Clegg and Miliband to come to Scotland to campaign – as if that's going to help! The hated Tory leader, the discredited Lib Dem leader and the weird Labour leader. That'll get them running to the polls to slap their big 'X' in the No column!

To Edinburgh College for a debate with Tommy Sheridan in front of students and staff. Sheridan is an attention-seeker extraordinaire. He is of course a fine old fashioned orator but in a small lecture theatre he roared at the top of his voice at the students, who wondered why this man (who very few of them knew) was shouting at them. I felt good about my performance and was encouraged and surprised by the number of students who stayed behind to say they would be voting No; and even more surprising were the many students from Poland and Lithuania who were totally opposed to independence. Seumas Milne from the *Guardian* was up to watch the debate and we had a good long chat afterwards about the Scottish Labour and the No-voting left, and what might happen afterwards. Seumas is very smart. I will keep in touch with him especially on issues relating to miners' justice.

We canvassed in Eliburn, Livingston, usually a strong SNP area, but the returns showed No with 150 votes, and Yes with 100. There were 30 don't knows.

10 SEPTEMBER: Had a lie in until nine, then to Glasgow to collect material for the last week of the campaign. Spoke to Frank Roy, who says their polling is good. Later chatted with Hugh Henry, who also felt their returns are decent. Home to collect 'A' boards for polling day before hitting the streets of my home village for canvassing. Not a bad response.

Today, Standard Life said they would relocate if there is a No vote. Labour attack leaflet out calling Salmond a liar. He may well be, but maybe not the best tactic.

11 SEPTEMBER: Standard Life, BP and Shell call for a No vote and Salmond has a pop at them all. He attacked Nick Robinson for asking questions about the potential loss of jobs and has now got his warriors on full attack on the BBC and Robinson himself.

To Glasgow where 100 Labour MPs are to arrive to help us campaign in the final week. They were met by a guy on a mobility scooter and a loud hailer playing the Star Wars theme and shouting about the arrival of 'our imperial masters'. Very funny actually. We then stood on the steps at the Royal Concert Hall for what felt like an eternity, certainly enough time for the Yes campaign's wilder elements to gather and start shouting, pushing and giving us dogs' abuse. Sean Clerkin and his band of zoomers were there. It got really, really ugly. We then spilt up and went to different constituencies to campaign. I went to Coatbridge.

Astonishingly George Galloway has been given a place in the Better Together line-up for tomorrow's youth debate at the Hydro. Should be 'interesting!'

Canvassed Fauldhouse tonight: 118 No, 33 Yes.

12 SEPTEMBER: Went for a meal with Fiona in Leith and the place is covered with Yes posters. I didn't see the debate tonight but heard Galloway was awful. I suspected he might be as this is not his type of format.

13 SEPTEMBER: To Livingston shopping centre for street stall. We were there an hour before someone contacted the Yes campaign, who soon

appeared with their stall. Local MSP and Cabinet Minister Angela Constance was with them and they were giving out 'The wee blue book' to passers' by. This is a book of fantasy about independence, produced by the vile blogger Stuart Campbell on his Wings over Scotland website. It is quite unbelievable that a Government minister is handing out such tripe from such a cretin. He has written some dreadful stuff, especially about the Hillsborough campaign and the victims.

Spoke to Alex Bennett, retired miner and NUM official, who told me he had Dennis Skinner up at the mining museum in Newtongrange to talk to a group of retired miners about the referendum and the need for solidarity and unity across the UK. Apparently a group of Yes campaigners turned up to heckle him and were shouting that he was a 'red Tory!' Dennis Skinner, a man totally committed to class politics, who has supported workers on strike and in struggle, all his life, who gave up his wages for the miners for a year during the strike and who has always been a left wing socialist, being called a 'red Tory' by folk whose political commitment consists of abusing others online or on their way into meetings. It is laughable.

There was a huge Yes campaign rally in Glasgow tonight.

14 SEPTEMBER: Tam Dalyell called to see how things were going. He has been asked three times to go on Newsnight and Panorama but has refused as he doesn't want to cause any problems. He expressed his anger at Gordon Brown fronting the campaign (he really doesn't like Brown).

Went to Auchingeich for the annual memorial service to the 47 miners who died in a pit accident in 1959. The service was excellent and included songs by a group of talented school pupils, speeches and afterwards great crack and reminiscing. I love the folk that go to these events. They are honest, committed, funny, clever working people. Just like the folk I was brought up with and who have taught me everything I know.

The Yes campaign picketed the BBC with effigies of Nick Robinson calling for him to be sacked. What a state of affairs! Some of these folk are capable of anything – God knows what they'll do if they lose.

15 SEPTEMBER: Blair Jenkins, leader of the Yes camp, is refusing to criticise those who are taking his cause too far. Anyone and everyone who is Labour is getting abuse heaped on them simply for being Labour. People who have given their lives to class politics, have supported workers in struggle and

represented people all their lives are being abused and called red Tories by folk who have been in politics a few months and have never lifted a hand in a progressive campaign in their lives. It is a scandal. If they lose it won't surprise me if they topple the Donald Dewar statue and hit it with an old Adidas samba trainer à la the guy in Baghdad!

Canvassed with Labour councillors in Armadale tonight. The outcome was a two-to-one for No. An excellent response.

NHS story has been leaked. £450 million of SNP cuts planned. So much for the NHS being their biggest issue.

16 SEPTEMBER: Preparing for polling day. 'A' boards ready, polling station rotas sorted. Today Gordon Brown made a blistering speech on the case for the UK, calling out the SNP on their claim to steal our culture, our flag and our nation. The *Daily Record* front page carries 'The Vow' from the party leaders: a commitment to introducing new powers and a timetable for doing so if there is a No vote. If this doesn't have an impact nothing will.

To the BBC as a guest on *Scotland Tonight*. Main topic is SNP cuts to the NHS. I met Ian McWhirter, who said No had a six per cent lead, but I reckon it's more like 10 per cent.

I did the interview along with Alex Neil, accusing him of misleading parliament and the public about the extent of his planned cuts. He mentioned that I had tried to get him sacked, which is true as I moved a vote of no confidence in him as he misled parliament. It clearly still niggles him.

Tennis star Andy Murray has come out for Yes.

17 SEPTEMBER: All preparations now complete after three years and tomorrow will determine the future of Scotland. I love my country but I love my class and community too. Working people across the UK have the same needs, wants and ambitions. We benefit from the Barnett formula and its loss would have huge negative implications for our public services and jobs. The big social developments across the years have come from working people and the Labour movement; NHS, free education, the national minimum wage and the welfare state etc. We should not divide the UK trade union movement, which is one of the greatest forces for progressive change we have. Tomorrow I hope my friends, relatives and

constituents agree and vote No; but vote No for change that will see Scotland assume more powers in a federal UK.

18 SEPTEMBER: Up at 6 o'clock putting out our 'A' boards at polling stations. Lots of people out volunteering. Great to see people young and old coming forward to help, especially those who have never been involved before. From very early the polls were busy and the atmosphere was generally good humoured. We had a couple of local incidents with aggression towards us and towards polling staff, and one couple who appeared in full highland dress playing the bagpipes all the way into picking up their ballot paper. It was both mad and funny but for many nationalists this is the day they have dreamed of all their lives. For others on both sides of the debate this is their first foray into politics. Without a shadow of a doubt, one of the biggest days in Scotland's history.

After the polls closed, I do as I always do at the end of polling day – go off for a pint with party workers, then to West Lothian College for the count. The news stations pointed to a 54-46 win for No. The body language of Yes activists at the count is not good – they look deflated. Our vote sampling points to a 4,000–5,000 majority across West Lothian, a bit close for my liking but it will do. To be honest, we knew we had won when the West Lothian Council SNP group leader Peter Johnston left the hall at around 2am – long before the declaration – with a face of deep crimson. He really is a bad loser.

As the results from other areas come in, Clackmannan has voted 54 to 46 for No, Shetland 2 to 1 for No, Orkney the same, Inverclyde voted No by just 86 votes; Dundee voted Yes as did North Lanarkshire. Both West Dunbartonshire and the big one, Glasgow, also voted Yes.

Everywhere else voted No and in West Lothian we voted almost exactly in line with the national result 55.2 per cent to 44.8 per cent. The No majority was 12,000. A very good result for us locally after years of hard work by lots of people. The result of this huge democratic event was a clear majority of around 400,000 votes across the country for No. Turnout was an astonishing 85 per cent.

Following photographs for the media I went home for an hour's sleep before heading to the Emirates Arena in Glasgow for a media event hosted by Johann Lamont, Ed Miliband and Alistair Darling. It was fairly subdued with little celebration. Everyone is completely knackered.

19 SEPTEMBER: Up at 4pm to see Salmond has resigned. He looks shattered but is putting on his bullish, arrogant face and saying it is now over to Westminster to deliver. Meanwhile, social media is full of poison, accusations and insults. Words like 'traitors', 'scum', 'quislings' etc are being thrown around like rancid confetti.

So, where do we go to from here? Labour must move to the left and offer a radical agenda for change. Communities have felt left behind and are desperate for change, any change, and Labour are seen, rightly or wrongly, as part of an establishment that is unwilling to offer a radical alternative. The fact that independence would be financially disastrous for our public services seems neither here nor there. Populist rhetoric did cut through and no matter how much the veracity of this was challenged and exposed, and the fantasy claims of the White Paper identified as complete fabrication, some people wanted to believe it and did. There will of course be political fall-out for all parties but I fear the decision by Labour to join the dreadful Better Together project will damage us badly and for some time.

For the SNP, Sturgeon will probably get in unopposed as no one will dare challenge her and they will continue to build on the result and call another referendum when they think they can win. There will be huge pressure from the ranks of the Yes camp to go for another one, and their clever strategists will have a job trying to hold this back.

The Tories, with Ruth Davidson at the helm, have enjoyed a good referendum and she is a more capable performer than I initially credited her with. Cameron's job is safe for now but he is venturing into dangerous territory talking today about the West Lothian Question and English Votes for English Laws. If he reneges on commitments given there will be a political storm.

As for Salmond, he is undoubtedly a very clever and skilled politician with a skip-load of arrogance and self-belief thrown in. Ultimately though his lifelong ambition, his project, has failed.

Farage is now writing to Scottish MPs asking them not to vote on issues relating to England.

Needed a break so went to the pictures with Fiona to see *Pride*, the film about the lesbian and gay community's support for the miners during the strike. What a fantastically emotional and uplifting true story. A film reinforcing my belief in solidarity is just what I needed.

Came home to see on the news that there were clashes between hooligans in Glasgow. Some are linking it to the referendum but it seems more like people taking advantage of the situation to get involved in sectarian or racist violence, or even violence just for the hell of it.

20 SEPTEMBER: Up at 8.30am for the Shadow Cabinet meeting in Glasgow. Despite winning, it felt like a wake with members quiet, down and sombre. The post-mortem began with statements from Johann Lamont and Anas Sarwar. Johann thanked people for their huge efforts and reminded us we had won, and by more than 10 per cent, that Salmond was gone and our task was to get us back to the everyday issues that matter to people, such as the NHS, jobs, low pay and public services. She also said Scotland and Britain have changed and there would be new powers coming to parliament.

Jackie Baillie spoke next and was understandably very emotional. She had been a board member of Better Together and had invested a huge amount of personal effort in the campaign. Jenny Marra talked about jobs, housing and hope and the need for an effective Labour response. Paul Martin, Sarah Boyack and Kezia Dugdale then spoke. Kez's main point was poor organisation and the loss of working class support in her target seat of Edinburgh East.

When it was my turn I spoke about the appalling idea that was Better Together, the failure of the Labour Party to embrace new powers and argue for federalism, and the timidity of the Devolution Commission's proposals. We also failed to promote a radical Labour alternative and route map. I called for a return to class politics with a radical agenda that puts clear red water between ourselves and the SNP. The problem we have is No won in SNP areas like Aberdeenshire, yet we lost traditional Labour areas like Glasgow. We have huge political and organisational problems. The UK Labour conference starts tomorrow – I am definitely not going!

Social media poison still in full flow.

21 SEPTEMBER: Sunday papers full of analysis and commentary: young people voted Yes in big numbers, older people No in big numbers. Women voted No too. Some on social media saying once the older generation die independence will come – what a charming bunch!

The SNP are being flooded with new membership applications as are the Greens. Even the SSP are claiming an increase – that'll be them up to a dozen then!

Salmond is claiming the SNP will declare independence if they gain a majority of MPs at the UK election – he is losing the plot! Sturgeon is the clear front runner for SNP leader but Humza Yousaf, Derek McKay and others are keeping their powder dry. Alex Neil has ruled himself out.

22 SEPTEMBER: The conspiracy theories are in full flow with the Yes campaign claiming the vote was rigged, ballots weren't counted and votes were rubbed out by a yeti flying over the Bermuda Triangle looking for the Loch Ness monster!

On day one of the Labour Party conference Ed Balls announces a two-year freeze of one per cent on child benefit – well, that's a vote winner if ever there was one! Bloody hell, people need hope and a vision of change not middle of the road crap.

23 SEPTEMBER: Back to parliament today with some trepidation. It is strange in that the No vote won, yet it feels like a defeat.

To the Shadow Cabinet for discussions on the way forward. We need big policies on housing, full employment, social care etc. I spoke at length to Hugh Henry, Alex Rowley and Patricia Ferguson. All extremely concerned.

To the chamber for the debate. Salmond is clearly still fuming at the result but was his smug, arrogant self. He really can't take defeat or being seen to be on the losing side. He was not at all dignified. Johann Lamont gave a speech full of humility and said we would reach out to Yes voters. Ruth Davidson called Salmond out on his Unilateral Declaration of Independence for Scotland (UDI) proposal, as did Willie Rennie. In speeches, Christina McKelvie and Christine Grahame were bitter and spiteful, while Marco Biagi gave a pretty good speech.

On the way home I learned that John Wilson had resigned from the SNP. John is a decent guy. He is an ex-Labour councillor and someone I have always got on with. I often meet him on the train home and we have a good chat about a whole range of issues. The SNP have ostracised him for years for having a mind of his own. His wife left the party a few years ago over Trident.

It looks like Sturgeon will become leader unopposed with, possibly, Stewart Hosie as her deputy. Their party membership has reportedly grown by 25,000 in the last few days.

Chloe's first day back at university after five months off for summer. I can't help feel that universities could condense courses into a year less if they wanted to.

24 SEPTEMBER: Sturgeon announced her leadership bid today. Lots of speculation about a challenge from Humza Yousaf (no chance), Stewart Hosie (no chance), Keith Brown (she would eat him for breakfast) and Angela Constance (whoever suggested that has been at the cooking sherry).

Around mid-morning, Hazel McIver, who works for Johann Lamont, came to see me. There is a move on against Johann and Hazel was asking my thoughts. I said she should stay where she is and not allow Jim Murphy and his gang to force her out, but she needs to make radical changes and remove Paul Sinclair as her advisor, and build a better and more capable team around her. I believe Frank Roy MP and Ross McRae have been briefing anyone and everyone at the UK conference saying Johann must go. It is reprehensible.

Went to the cross party group on disabled people to hear Ian Hood, of the Campaign Against the Care Tax, talk about hidden charges for services like alarms, aids and adaptations. This is a big issue.

Lynn McMath from our press team came in for a chat. She is leaving today after a few years. She was treated very badly by Sinclair and has had enough. She is a cracking worker and has a good rapport with the journalists but can't take any more of being treated abysmally. She will be a real loss.

25 SEPTEMBER: Spoke to the local representatives of a major charity for older people with mental health problems about social care. They spoke of the terrible state of social care and how the care staff are being ripped off with low pay and poor conditions. Many of them are bailing out to work in supermarkets etc as they pay better and value their staff more. They are all frightened to speak up, as are their managers, because they have been warned their organisation will have their funding cut. It is a disgrace.

Met the chair of NHS Highland to talk about the problems in the NHS – they are absolutely huge and major funding is required.

Spotted close allies of Murphy walking the corridors and going into each MSPs office asking them to support Jim if he runs for leader. This is an outrage. I hate the way these folk skulk about behind the scenes scheming and plotting against people they have been close to and worked with for years. They don't have the bottle to approach Johann and tell her to her face that she should go. They are also trying to get rid of Ian Price and are piling the pressure on him.

Sadly, I don't think Johann will last the weekend. The briefings from 'Team Murphy' in the press will finish her off. God, I can't stand this.

Off to the Ryder Cup at Gleneagles tomorrow. Can't wait, it should be something special.

26 SEPTEMBER: Up early and off to Gleneagles with John Pentland. The organisation was fantastic with a superbly efficient park and ride system in place at Stirling. The weather was good and the Strathearn looked magnificent with its beautiful autumn colours. The foreign visitors were blown away by its beauty.

On the first tee, the atmosphere was amazing, with lots of singing, players having banter with the crowd and a deer running up the middle of the fairway with around 30,000 looking on. It was fantastic. The pressure on players teeing off must have been unbearable. In fact, it must be the highlight of their career. At the first, we tried to follow the Rory McIlroy match from tee to green but it was impossible. Mind you, we saw his putt dropping in from around 150 yards away, and the roar was deafening. We sat for ages at the 7th grandstand and watched the games coming through. Noticed Martin McGuiness and Peter Robinson following McIlroy's match. Looks like the peace process extends to the golf course. After lunch we returned to our perch on the 7th and watched the four-balls and enjoyed some great crack with folk from Ireland and America. They were loving the location and atmosphere. What a brilliant day and a privilege to be there.

Overnight score: Europe 5 USA 3.

27 SEPTEMBER: At our John's all day to watch the golf. Poulter's chip in at 15th an obvious highlight. Europe won the foursomes 3.5 to .5 and are in very good position going into the singles.

Overnight score: Europe 10 USA 6.

28 SEPTEMBER: Pitched up at John's for the final day of the Ryder Cup. Sat and drank beers all day and loved every minute of such an iconic sporting occasion. Kaymer chipping in, McIlroy on fire, Rose 4 down getting it back to half, Poulter half, Gallacher 4 under and still lost but played well. The standard of golf was brilliant and the atmosphere and spirit electric. Mickelson and Watson at each other's throat over selections and results, and to end it all Salmond was booed by the crowd! What a brilliant event showing Scotland as the best golf setting in the world.

Final score: Europe 16.5 USA 11.5 (Europe win the Ryder Cup for third successive time)

29 SEPTEMBER: Met with Patrick McGuire of Thompson's Solicitors. He is totally committed to working with the Labour movement. Thompson's represent a number of trade unions and campaigning organisations and of course as a commercial company make money but they also give a lot back in terms of time, effort and support. We discussed a whole range of issues including possible support for members' legislation, the future of the Labour Party and what we should do about the issue of employment rights and devolution. He is in favour of devolving employment rights, but I am torn between seeing the possible advantage of doing so and the solidarity argument of wanting improvements for workers across the UK, regardless of where they come from. I need to give this much more thought.

Met Jim Swan to discuss an event to mark the 30th anniversary of the miners' strike in West Lothian. Jim Neilson, former pit delegate at Polkemmet, has agreed to come and speak.

Weekly surgery tonight dominated by housing and cuts to bus services.

30 SEPTEMBER: To Shadow Cabinet meeting. I really think some of my colleagues are not fully comprehending the enormity of what has just happened. The good news is Paul Sinclair has gone, now hopefully we can now bring in a top quality backroom team. They are looking at options. We discussed the work being done on carers issues – it really is good stuff.

Took part in a members' business debate on wind farms where I gave my scathing critique of Scottish Government policy, which is the biggest missed opportunity in decades. We could have had community and public sector ownership, and a decent spread of projects, but instead we have sites owned and run by foreign multinationals and venture capital firms with the profits fluttering off to the boardrooms of Paris, Madrid and Milan instead of into local communities and public services. It is a scandal and very few people seem to give a damn.

1 OCTOBER: News is my selection process to stand in the Almond Valley seat will start on Friday. I need to properly prepare for it.

After two health related meetings with students and occupational therapists I met with Francie Graham and Stuart Merchant to discuss the contracts that have been awarded to notorious blacklisters, McAlpine's for the regeneration of the Dundee waterfront. So much for the SNP dealing with blacklisting in public contracts. Nothing has changed.

Hosted the Age Scotland awards – very inspiring and moving.

3 OCTOBER: Emailed all local party members to advise them I would be putting my name forward to stand in the parliamentary seat in Almond Valley.

11

Leadership Declaration: October 2014

THIS IS SET to be another important month in the history of the Labour Party in Scotland, although I seem to be saying that a lot these days. The tale of Ian Price's sacking precipitated a crisis in our party, which resulted in the resignation of leader, Johann Lamont. Ian was the general secretary of the Scottish Labour Party – our chief official. A quiet, polite man who had all the charisma of a breeze block, but he worked hard for the party for a few years under Johann's leadership, and his record was pretty good. We won council and parliamentary by-elections in Dunfermline, where Cara Hilton took the seat from convicted domestic abuser Bill Walker, and in Cowdenbeath where Alex Rowley, who would become Labour deputy leader, won the seat following the death of Helen Eadie, whose passing shocked me in its speed. She was a lovely woman.

After the referendum, Labour Party General Secretary, Iain McNicol, based in London, and with the support of Ed Miliband, sacked Price without any consultation whatsoever. Why they did this I don't know but this 'backstage' humiliation was clearly aimed at undermining Johann's role and authority. I have no doubt the fingerprints of Jim Murphy and his Better Together gang were all over the silver revolver, but Johann is a good and decent woman and this could prove the final straw.

22 OCTOBER: I wrote an article for the *Morning Star*, suggesting there was only one way we could take on a post-referendum SNP, and that was to come at them from the left. Anything else and it would be a waste of time. I made a few policy suggestions in the column, and these were:

- Committing in principle to a policy of full employment. It is the most basic need of human beings to have the wherewithal to provide for themselves and their family

- Establishing a national house-building programme to build council houses and social housing on a grand scale
- Setting up a living wage unit in the Scottish Government that would use grants, procurement and every lever of government to raise the minimum wage to the living wage
- Re-democratise local government, financing services and freeing councils to set their own taxes again and be held to account for doing so – and begin reversing the 40,000 job losses across our councils
- End the social care scandal by making it a rewarding, fairly-paid career and ending the indignity of short-timed care visits – following the best practice in the sector
- Create quality apprenticeships and new college places that set young people up for life – 130,000 places have been lost under the SNP
- An industrial policy that promotes manufacturing and new sustainable jobs
- A wholesale review of our NHS – recruiting enough staff and rewarding them to ensure we have an NHS fit for the 21st century; ending the increasing spend on the private sector
- Build a charter of workers' rights with new legislation on the fatal accident inquiries and strict liability, devolved health and safety, new legislation on equalities, the living wage and blacklisting, and a commitment to an inquiry into the miners' strike.

These are policies that will have an impact on people and communities across Scotland – especially those who have been victims of the Tory class war on the poor, and those who have been left behind as the SNP try yet again to be all things to all people.

24 OCTOBER: Received a text about 9am this morning saying Johann had resigned and had given a blistering interview to the *Daily Record* for tomorrow's edition. As soon as I got this, social media went mad. One thing is for sure, life as a member of the Scottish Labour Party is never dull. Let's see what tomorrow brings but Saturday's Campaign for Socialism post-referendum conference promises to be interesting, that's for sure.

25 OCTOBER: Glasgow STUC – Campaign for Socialism conference. The CFS had arranged this weeks ago to discuss the fall-out from the referendum, win lose or draw. On the way in I read Johann's article where she attacked the UK party for running Scotland like a 'branch office!' This is dynamite and clearly the relationship with London and Miliband was awful and

the sacking of Ian Price, without her knowledge, the final straw. I know she had been scrapping with Ian McNicol for more resources to fight the referendum, but didn't get anything.

The following extract from the *Daily Record* report opens with a quote from Johann Lamont:

'I am proud of what we have achieved over the last three years. The Scottish Labour Party had never been at a lower point than 2011 – but we became competitive again. We won well in Glasgow in the 2012 council elections and did well in a series of by-elections, and I believe we held Alex Salmond to account. And those were vital elements in the Scottish Labour Party being the foundation of the referendum campaign which thankfully we won decisively. That was the best possible result for ordinary working people.'

Lamont then started to lay out her vision for the future. Frustrated that the demands of the referendum campaign had stalled the pace of party reform, she opened up the review of Labour structures in Scotland – and that is when the problems started. A senior colleague began lobbying members of the Scottish Labour Executive to ask Lamont to go, while never doing so to her face. Westminster MPs threatened to leak critical letters to the press. And worst of all, Ed Miliband's office replaced Scottish Labour General Secretary Ian Price with their own candidate without even the courtesy of a phone call, a move current Labour rules meant Lamont could not stop.

Having remained loyally quiet during the fiasco of the Falkirk Labour selection in 2014, this was too much to bear. It was clear the Labour leadership at Westminster wouldn't say anything to her face but were planning her political death by a thousand cuts.

Lamont said: 'This has been orchestrated by people who do not understand the politics they are facing. Scotland has changed forever after the referendum. Party members up and down the country, as well as voters on the doors, have spoken to me about the change they want – and that's a Scottish Labour Party which reflects their views. That's what I've been trying to build. However, some wanted me to become the issue. Scottish Labour and its renewal are far more important than me. That is why I am standing down – so that the debate our country demands can take place.'

She concluded: 'And just as the SNP must embrace that devolution is the settled will of the Scottish people, the Labour Party must recognise that the Scottish party has to be autonomous and not just a branch office of a party based in London.'

So, what happens now? Well, Murphy has been planning this for years. If he thinks he is the big beast who can ride in and sort things out he is completely deluded. I think he will run with Kezia as deputy. If this happens, there is no place for Anas, who I think wanted it too but wouldn't go up against Murphy. There will be huge pressure for a left challenge, which is understandable. We cannot let Murphy have a free run. Other contenders named in the press are Alex Rowley, Jenny Marra, Drew Smith, Ken McIntosh, Douglas Alexander – and me. Such is the state we are now in and the fact that since the referendum everybody and their dog has joined the SNP, I think we should approach Gordon Brown to come in and lend some weight. I know this might be seen as a backward move but we are in a desperate place!

When I turned up at the CFS meeting there were around 130 people there. Many were asking if I would stand or if the left would challenge. I had a chat with Elaine Smith MSP and John McDonnell MP, who was one of the speakers at the event. They both urged me to throw my hat into the ring. In his speech, John said, 'The left has a duty to stand and put forward an alternative to austerity and more of the same.' He went on to say that, 'if necessary, he would get down on his knees to plead with the left to put up a candidate'. John is a highly principled and straightforward politician. I really like and respect him.

Katy Clark, Jackson Cullinane and I spoke at the event. I set out the agenda I believed Labour had to put forward to win again in Scotland and across the UK. At the end, Pauline Bryan put forward a motion recommending the left put up a candidate and this was supported unanimously. The pressure is now on.

I went home and spoke to Fiona about why I don't want to stand. I already work a huge amount of hours and enjoy my time with family and friends and doing normal things occasionally. I don't want to become a political bore with nothing else in my life. I pride myself on being 'normal-ish' and would hate to lose that. I also don't want Chloe and Fiona put under any pressure. As expected both told me they will support me 100 per cent if I want to go for it. I knew they would, as they always have. Much to think about but I am pretty sure it's a no from me...

26 OCTOBER: Sunday papers full of speculation about who will run. Johann's leaving and the crisis in Labour with yet another leadership election splashed all over the front pages. Whoever takes it on has a mountain to climb and a great big one at that! I take several phone calls from journalists asking when I will declare. I fend them off for the time being but by not saying no, speculation will only increase.

Then it was down to party headquarters in Bath Street for the Shadow Cabinet meeting. Press were all there and shouting out questions to try and get me to respond, but I have no comment to make at this moment in time.

27 OCTOBER: Phone calls, texts and emails all day from people across the party, the trade unions and out-with the Labour Party urging me to stand. Murphy is lying low but my understanding is that he is putting in place his team and strategy that he has been working on for years.

Around 11am there was a surprise announcement – Sarah Boyack MSP is standing for leader. Well no one, and I mean no one, saw that coming. She is not a serious challenger, but at least she has had the bottle to put herself out there. I can never place Sarah's politics – she is neither right nor left nor even centre! I just don't know where she is, but she is a decent person and we get on fine.

Just had yet another discussion in the office with Tommy. He has been brilliant. Politically he wants me to stand, but understands the personal pressures it would bring. He will support whatever I choose to do.

Anyway, I decided I would try to persuade Gordon Brown to stand and approached Alex Rowley about this. Alex is adamant Gordon won't stand (but urged me to) and sure enough a statement came out to that effect.

At 6.15 pm, just before leaving my parliamentary office for home, I typed up a press release stating I would not be standing, but just as I was about to press send, I stopped, hovered above it for what seemed like an eternity and left it on my screen. I stared at it one last time before heading out to catch the train…

When I got home, Fiona, in her no nonsense tone, said, 'Right, what's happening?'

When I told her I wasn't going to stand she called up to Chloe, who was in her room, 'Chloe, down here now – family conference.'

Chloe trudged downstairs wondering what she had done.

After a very brief chat I was told by both, 'You have to do it. You can't give Murphy a free run,' and that, 'you will get 100 per cent support from everyone in the family!'

So that was that – my mind has been made up for me!

Inside I was very apprehensive, but equally, I was quietly pleased. I knew I had to do it and Fiona and Chloe were just the people to ensure I did.

28 OCTOBER: I was in the office early this morning – I had a press release to get out. I hadn't even thought about what I should wear or what I would say or any of that crap. My thought was that Murphy had been planning

his leadership assault for years. Me? I had been planning mine for five minutes. When Tommy came into the office, he immediately launched into why I should stand. I let him rattle on for a few minutes before saying, 'I decided last night that I would stand!'

He seemed confused at first, before a broad smile broke out across his face: it was game on. We both agreed we would wait until 11am before putting out media. I tinkered with the press release on my screen and pressed the send button at the agreed time.

'Bloody hell,' I thought, 'what have I done?'

The media went into overdrive. BBC, STV, *Daily Record*, *The Sun*, *The Scotsman*, *The Times*, *Daily Mail* – they all wanted interviews. With no team in place, Tommy and I did our best; an exercise in firefighting. It was crazy, but we got through it.

I got home around 9.30pm. When I eventually went to bed, I just lay there, staring at the ceiling. My mind was still racing and I didn't sleep a wink.

29 OCTOBER: Jim Murphy officially declares his intention to run for Scottish Labour Party leader.

Me, I spent the day speaking to colleagues to try and secure support. I don't really like doing that as I get along with most on a personal level and want that to continue after this election. I didn't want to put anyone in a position, but those who have confirmed they will support me so far include MSPs Elaine Smith, Alex Rowley, Jayne Baxter, Cara Hilton and Elaine Murray. I have asked Ian Davidson and Michael Connarty to work the Westminster group, but I should get Katy Clark, who is running for deputy (we have agreed to work very closely but not as a ticket), Jim Sheridan, Cathy Jamieson and Graeme Morrice, and, I hope, David Hamilton, although I have my doubts. Hugh Henry thinks I should stand for deputy but there is no way I could work under Murphy.

It was with genuine trepidation that I went to the Labour gala dinner at the Grand Central Hotel. Serial protestor Sean Clerkin and his merry band were outside screaming and shouting about something or other. Prior to the event, the Scottish Labour group had requested a meeting with Miliband to discuss our problems north of the border, and have a cards-on-the-table discussion. Miliband was awful. He sat there like a lost puppy and was savaged by member after member. He could not reply to the points raised. Margaret McDougall ripped him to pieces!

Going into the dinner, the atmosphere was pretty awful. People who were long-standing friends either couldn't look me in the eye or avoided me like the plague. Margaret Curran came up and offered the most insincere congratulations I have ever heard. She has some brass neck – having just been partly responsible for ending the leadership of her lifelong friend, Johann Lamont. She then got up and gave a glowing tribute to her. It was enough to make a pig vomit!

After Curran, the stand-in leader Anas Sarwar gave his speech and in the middle of the main party fundraiser of the year, with many guests and donors in attendance, he resigned as deputy leader. What the hell is going on in this party? I was furious; the Murphy coup was now complete.

I called over Dave Watson, Alex Rowley and Tommy for a quick chat. I was seething and very, very tempted to there and then withdraw from the leadership race, and let the rest get on with it. Miliband was then being ushered round the tables to meet people. When he came to me he said, 'Neil, congratulations on putting your name forward. I hope we can look forward to a good clean contest where we debate all the big issues.'

I said to him calmly, 'You are having a laugh, aren't you? We are at a major fundraising event and the deputy leader resigns in the middle of his speech. It's a sick joke!' His response was to look at me vacantly with those big panda eyes.

I sat back down at the table with some of the Unite officials and Jim Sheridan - they are the real good guys of our movement - but left halfway through the dinner as I couldn't stomach staying any longer.

Throughout the evening, Murphy sat at the GMB table. He is clearly pulling out all the stops to win their support. The reality is he hates the trade unions but it would be a real blow to him if he did not get the GMB on board, as he is a member.

30 OCTOBER: Poll out today has Labour on 23 per cent and winning only four Scottish seats at the general election. Wow! Why would anyone want to lead this party right now?

I did GMS and the *Today* programme with John Humphries, and received a phone call from Tam Dalyell afterwards to say I did very well against Humphries, who is a difficult interviewer. That was a real boost. We are however still drowning in phone calls etc. I need to get a team together ASAP.

Received a call from Kevin Lindsay, Scottish Organiser for ASLEF, the train drivers' union. They have come out in support of me. A good early hit. Things are warming up.

The following article appeared in today's *Daily Mail*. It was written by the Scottish Political Editor, Alan Roden, and sat alongside an article saying that electing me would take Labour back to the 1980s. It was clearly designed to damage my chances, but when my campaign supporters saw it, they loved it, and were convinced it would boost our chances! Under the headline 'The Wit and Wisdom of Comrade Neil', it went as follows:

ON HIS HOBBIES: 'Going for a pint.'

ON NICOLA STURGEON'S FASHION SENSE: 'Nicola, change the red dress.'

ON FOOTBALL: 'We stood on terraces, frozen to the bone, and had to use toilets that were knee deep in – well, something. In my view, in those days the game was a bit more honest and a bit more grass roots.'

AFTER TORY MSP MURDO FRASER POINTED OUT THAT LABOUR CLOSED MORE COAL MINES THAN MRS THATCHER: 'Presiding Officer, you will have to excuse me as I wipe the vomit from my chin having listened to Murdo Fraser's rewriting of history.'

ON THE RYDER CUP: 'The Ryder Cup had everything: the noise of an Old Firm game, humour, song, sportsmanship and dreadful clothing – and even a deer running up the first fairway in front of 20,000 spectators, wondering what the hell we were all doing in its front room.'

AFTER QUITTING FOLLOWING ONE DAY WORKING FOR FORMER MP JIM DEVINE: 'I have no desire whatsoever to give up a professional teaching career only to become involved in what can only be described as a bizarre nightmare situation.'

ON HIS FAVOURITE NEWSPAPER: 'You know you are in a quality pub when the newspapers they have include the *Morning Star*.'

ON BED-BLOCKING: 'The Cabinet Secretary is living in cloud-cuckoo land if he does not think that this is the biggest issue in health and social care at the moment.'

ON ALEX SALMOND AND NICOLA STURGEON: 'I am not allowed to call the Cabinet Secretary and the First Minister liars.'

With UNITE the union and Blacklist support group members on one of the many events at Parliament during the campaign exposing the scandal of blacklisting in the construction industry.

Campaigning with women injured by transvaginal mesh – they are an inspiration.

At the Liverpool Labour conference, the Jam exhibition was taking place nearby –
I just had to visit.

On a chilly picket line with PCS members at the Bathgate tax office defending public services and
opposing austerity.

With my great friend the late Tam Dalyell and Nicky Wilson NUM President – at the unveiling of the new miners' memorial in Whitburn.

During the referendum I took part in over 65 public debates with leading political figures, including Gordon Brown, Nicola Sturgeon, Dennis Canavan, Jim Sillars and George Galloway, who is pictured with me above.

The 'Battle of Buchanan Galleries' – when 200 Labour MPs appeared off a train from London to 'help' in campaigning in the final days of the referendum.

With some of the campaign team during the 2016 Scottish election.

My wife Fiona, daughter Chloe and the gang raising funds for Breast Cancer UK.

My sister-in-law Sharron, Fiona, Mum, sister Anna and brother John in Copenhagen.

A day at the races for my pal's 50th birthday. Left to right: Kathleen Swift, me, Norrie Dixon, Jimmy Swift, Phyllis Dixon and my wife, Fiona.

During the Scottish leadership campaign Labour women members gave me a very warm welcome at the annual Scottish women's conference.

With leadership contenders Jim Murphy and Sarah Boyack at one of the many hustings – this one in Dundee. (Photo courtesy of Jimmy Thompson)

With family and friends just after taking the oath in 2016.
(Photo courtesy Katielee Arrowsmith)

Corbyn looking out over Glasgow – we started to win back seats in Scotland under his leadership. Inset: The *Daily Record* front page announcing its support for Jeremy Corbyn.

AFTER PUBLISHING A MOCKED-UP VIDEO OF HOLYROOD'S POLITICAL REPORTERS DRESSED AS ELVES: 'Instead of my usual predictable socialist festive greetings I got my daughter to make up something that I hope provides you with some festive amusement.'

ON THE SNP'S FAVOURED POLLSTERS, PANELBASE: 'Panelbase poll out today sees Berti Vogts named Scotland's greatest ever football manager.'

ON EDUCATION SECRETARY MIKE RUSSELL: 'I think he has been locked in a cupboard till after the referendum.'

TO NATIONALIST MSP STEWART MAXWELL DURING A LENGTHY DEBATE ON THE REFERENDUM: 'I wish I had missed your speech.'

I texted my sincere thanks to 'Comrade Roden' and his *Daily Mail* chums.

12

Leadership Race: November 2014

1 NOVEMBER: To UNISON in Glasgow for the Labour Link hustings, while Murphy launches his campaign in an Edinburgh hotel. Sarah (Boyack) and I spoke, and then took questions. This was the first hustings of the campaign. I didn't speak too well and will need to sort out a slick, punchy speech, but that will come. I fared better in the questions addressing the need for us to become the LABOUR Party again, building houses, creating jobs, having a living wage and fairness at work. Afterwards the vote was taken and I won unanimously, with the other two failing to register a single vote. Delighted with this and the offer of assistance from UNISON, especially Dave Watson and Stephen Low – both are very clever and will be of great help. I have asked Alex Rowley to be my campaign manager as a lot of Elaine Smith's time is taken up with her Deputy Presiding Officer role, but I will still lean on Elaine.

As expected, Murphy's launch was slick and polished. He apologised for Labour's poor recent performance, spoke of his patriotism and the need for Labour to take on the SNP. He said:

> If I am elected leader of Scottish Labour, I will have three priorities.
> The first is to unite our country after the referendum. There is nothing that the people of Scotland can't do to solve our problems when we work together.
> Secondly, I want to increase prosperity. I want successful businesses and young people from working-class backgrounds like my own to get on in life and do better for themselves than their parents did.
> Thirdly, I want to reduce poverty, and that includes for those in work. Too many families in Scotland are one wage packet away from serious trouble. That's just not right.

2 NOVEMBER: The Labour-supporting *Sunday Mail* has come out for Murphy despite not bothering to speak to me or look at any of my policy or organisational proposals. Lots of glowing press and spin about Murphy's launch.

I went to UNISON offices in Glasgow for a campaign planning session. We asked a lot of people who we think can contribute to turn up and around 50 appeared. Alex Rowley spoke first about the need to organise and how we were in this to win. When it was my turn to speak, the first thing I said was, 'If anyone wants this to be a personal campaign against Jim Murphy, or the unions against Jim Murphy, they should leave now!' I spoke about hope and a vision for a fairer Scotland where people have a decent home, a secure place of work and a health and education system that supports them and their family. I spoke about how we would need to use the skills of everyone in the room if we were to win – and that we could win!'

Afterwards I met with a small group of key people who have pledged to help. Anneliese Midgely, from Unite, is one of the group. I don't know her personally but she is well rated, having worked with Ken Livingstone at the Greater London Authority, and she is a Scouser, which definitely helps!

So, the team will be – Alex Rowley as campaign chair; Annaliese (organiser); Stephen Low (press); Kevin Lindsay (fundraiser); Tommy Kane (advisor); Dave Watson (treasurer); Ian Davidson (Westminster liaison); Vince Mills and Pauline Bryan (organise activists); Jackson Cullinane (trade union liaison), and Elaine Smith (Holyrood liaison).

Patrick McGuire from Thomson's has offered his Edinburgh office for use as a base. The offers of help are much appreciated and the campaign starts in earnest today!

3 NOVEMBER: I have decided to hold my campaign launch in the Fauldhouse Miners' Welfare Social Club. It is a place of huge importance to me and provides an excellent contrast to Murphy's shiny and slick stuff. It is the right place to have it but I worry it could go wrong and the contest could be over before it begins. All it would need is a few of the Yes campaign wreckers to come in. I need to have a good think about how we do this.

Lots of people making contact to volunteer, while donations are coming in thick and fast. The website is being set up, texts going out, photos taken – although it has been a nightmare trying to set up a bank account!

4 NOVEMBER: To the House of Commons – Ian Davidson had set me up a series of meetings with 'undeclared' MPs. I spoke to Russell Brown, Ann McKechin, Jim McGovern, Ian McKenzie, Brian Donohoe, Sheila

Gilmore, Lindsay Roy, Ian Murray and Sandra Osborne amongst many others. I honestly believe they had all made their minds up already and none were voting for me. They kept saying, 'Oh, we like you, but Jim's a winner and the public know him!' My response was, 'Yes, but it depends what you know him for.'

Went for a meal with Cathy Jamieson, Michael Connarty, Jim Sheridan and Ian Davidson – and enjoyed the crack. Stayed at Michael's flat afterwards. He was very hospitable.

5 NOVEMBER: Up early to go to the parliamentary trade union group to hear about the plight of migrant tobacco workers In the US – horrendous exploitation by the tobacco multi nationals. Met Ian Lavery, John McDonnell and Kevin McGuire, of the Mirror, afterwards. Then off for a chat with Katy Clark, who is running for deputy. We discussed where we could work together and how we can help each other. The Transport Salaried Staffs' Association union are supporting her, which is good.

Went to PMQS – a complete rabble and a totally different atmosphere from our FMQS. After a horrendous battle through London traffic to Stansted, Tommy and I got the flight home. London is a great place to visit but I couldn't imagine myself living or working there. It's chaotic, very expensive and God knows how people make friends outside work. It's the complete opposite of where I live and the close culture of the West Lothian community. Tommy and I stayed in Edinburgh as we were late into the airport and have to be up early.

Alex Rowley has been on the phone all day wanting to see the speech Stephen is writing for the launch. I have told him repeatedly he will get it but he clearly likes to get his own way. I don't work that way. The working relationship between us isn't running as smoothly as it should be.

6 NOVEMBER: Press interest is huge and now that Anneliese is in town we are getting properly organised. Stephen Wright, a friend who has a theatre company, is working on the launch. We have decided to make Saturday an 'open doors' event, despite the obvious associated risks. It's my call and if it all goes tits up there will be no one else to blame. Mind you, I haven't eaten a thing in three days through worrying about it. We have to get it right and it isn't helping that Alex is becoming quite demanding!

7 NOVEMBER: I met with Alex this morning as he wanted to rewrite huge sections of the speech and make it all about business. He also made a few

comments I didn't really like so we agreed it would be better if I continue with another campaign manager. He would still support me but wouldn't take part in the campaign. We shook hands on this. On one hand it is obviously a huge blow to lose your campaign chief on the eve of the launch (an understatement I know) but on the other I am relieved as we simply had different ways of working and I have enough pressures to contend with. I think the fact it hasn't got out that Alex and I have parted company before we even launched the campaign proper is testament to how tight and united our team is.

To the GMB offices in Glasgow, where I was interviewed by their seven-person political committee, including Scottish secretary Harry Donaldson, for their nomination. I spoke about blacklisting, the work I did with their ambulance staff, my wider trade union work and pride in being a union member and supporter. It is one of the best interviews I have ever given. If I don't get their nomination I will be gobsmacked.

On the drive home I was able to clear my head and am now much happier about tomorrow's launch, and how it will be presented. Fiona is on nightshift and Chloe is at her boyfriend's, so I fell asleep on the couch at 8.30pm and didn't wake up until 1am, when I staggered to bed. I had missed a call from Harry Donaldson, but he left a message saying I had won the nomination unanimously. Murphy will be gutted, but I slept much better tonight and am actually looking forward to the launch now.

8 NOVEMBER: To the miners' welfare with Fiona, who has just come off a 12-hour night shift at the hospital, and Chloe. Stephen has the hall set up superbly with large pop-up banners and lectern against the backdrop of the miners' mural painted by Tommy Shelley. He had chosen Primal Scream's 'Movin' On Up' as the campaign music, which was a great choice. I was amazed by the turn out. The hall was packed with family, my oldest friends, ex-workmates, councillors, MSPs, MPs, students, trade unionists, children, comrades from Dundee, Ayrshire, Glasgow, Fife, Edinburgh, Midlothian, Lanarkshire, Renfrewshire and all over Scotland.

Cara Hilton MSP welcomed everyone to the event, and the atmosphere in the hall was fantastic.

She then introduced Elaine Holmes from the Scottish Mesh Survivors group who spoke very powerfully and emotionally about the work we have done together on behalf of the mesh injured women. She also paid tribute to Tommy for his outstanding work and set the scene in a non-partisan way.

We then had Jimmy Gordon, a lifelong Labour man who voted Yes at the referendum. Jimmy is 75 and was in my mum's class at school. He is a stalwart of the Catholic Church and a hugely respected figure in the Bathgate community. Jimmy spoke about being Labour all his life, but how the Blair Government and Iraq had made him reject the party, although how the type of Labour I represented would bring him back. He was fantastic – straightforward, no nonsense, no spin, totally genuine. My niece Eleana then introduced me (Chloe understandably didn't want to do it and I would never have pushed her). That was my cue to move to the lectern. This was my pitch to the Scottish Labour Party and the wider public...

Good morning ladies and gentlemen and thank for you for coming along in such big numbers this morning to the launch of my campaign to become the leader of the Scottish Labour Party. Today I want to set out my vision for the future of Scotland; a Scotland based on timeless Labour values of community solidarity, fairness and justice. These are the values I was taught and had instilled in me by my parents and the people I grew up with in this great community here in Fauldhouse. And I'd like to tell you a bit about why I believe only the Scottish Labour Party, with these values running through everything we do, can lead Scotland and why I am the person best placed to lead our party.

I never sought to have a career in politics. I am not a career politician, nor a machine politician. The modern day conventional political career is school to university to working for a politician then into parliament – not for me. Like many people here I left school at 16 without many qualifications. I started my working life as a YTS trainee, then an apprenticeship with my dad. For the next 10 years I worked as a bricklayer and met some of most intelligent, funny and entrepreneurial people you will ever find. But with the encouragement of my family I returned to education, first at college then university. I got a second chance and I took it.

And working as a housing officer I saw how good-quality housing changed people's lives and provided a secure environment for their children to grow up.

As a teacher I saw the power of education but I also saw many pupils failing to reach their potential and denied opportunities.

And as an MSP I've worked tirelessly to deliver for people in this community and beyond, whether it be women injured by faulty medical products or workers blacklisted for standing up for their workmates – I have been on their side campaigning for justice. Where given the chance, I've tried to make a difference – and I know that Labour, the party of social justice, the party of devolution and the party of fairness, has made a difference for Scotland and can do so again. We have to use the powers we have and the powers we will get to make a difference in every community to transform Scotland and improve the lives of all our people.

And to achieve that, tackling poverty and health and wealth inequality must be at the heart of all we do. Waging war on the poverty that blights communities and ends lives prematurely will be my priority. It is to our great shame that families in our country cannot afford to feed their children or heat their homes and have to rely on foodbanks. A national strategy to end poverty in Scotland will be at the heart of our 2016 manifesto if I am Labour leader. Central to that will be a pledge to put an end to youth unemployment – no young person should be left behind. Training, skills and new jobs, opportunities for all, must be our ambition and Labour will deliver that.

And in education I will ensure that vocational education has the same priority as academic education so that we can prepare our young people to take up these new opportunities in the world of work.

And when people are in work they have to have a sense of security and feel valued. Nelson Mandela said that, 'Poverty is not an accident, it is man-made and like apartheid and slavery it can be eradicated by the action of human beings.' The zero hours, low pay insecure culture we see now is not just bad for people, it is bad for our economy. The most successful economies are also the most equal societies so it will be my aim to end exploitation and insecurity in the workplace and replace the national minimum wage with a living wage. It is unacceptable that in 2014 over 400,000 Scots earn under £7.85 per hour. Tackling poverty pay is a political choice and it is one that I will make.

The great John Smith said, 'Governments are not impotent. They have the power at their disposal to shape events, bring about change, to improve the lives of the people whose trust they carry. That is why it is unacceptable, so unbearable to see the injustice in our country, the waste of human talent, the lack of hope, the loss of pride, because it is not inevitable.'

And he was right. Where we have the power to act, we must do so. Now let me tell you about one of the greatest scandals of our time – social care. 500,000 bed days lost to the NHS because people are stuck in hospital costing £4,000 per week and can't get home because our social care system doesn't work for them. More and more care homes failing to provide an acceptable standard of care for our older people. Our mums and dads, grannies and grandads subjected to 15-minute care visits from carers who want to care but can't do their job because of the way contracts are determined. I will put an end to the social care scandal and will make social care a rewarding and fairly paid career – this is about the wellbeing of our elderly people not about the profit margins of the company shareholders.

And in our NHS, the greatest social policy of the 20th century, and still the envy of the world, there is pressure like never before. GP's closing waiting lists, A&E departments bursting at the seams, delayed discharges in every area, patients boarded out in wards not designed for their condition, staff shortages up and use of the private sector up. It is for these reasons I will bring forward a wholescale review of the NHS in Scotland to ensure it is fit to meet the demands of the 21st century. But let me be clear – there will be no privatisation of Scotland's NHS under my leadership.

And there is one other issue where there is so much need that I could not leave here today without highlighting it. That is the growing housing crisis in Scotland. Poor housing impacts on health, educational attainment, access to employment and poverty. Over 150,000 people are on council waiting lists today – more than the entire population of the city of Dundee, and the equivalent of the number of folk in West Lothian.

This can't go on. Labour can, and under my leadership will, tackle this head on.

As leader of Labour in Scotland I will bring forward a national house-building programme to be included in our 2016 manifesto.

As the next Labour First Minister of Scotland I will roll out that programme, building 50,000 new homes for rent over the term of that Labour government.

Not only will this provide much needed homes but it will also create skilled jobs, training places and put demand into the local economy. But fundamentally this is about realising that politics as usual is not enough when there are thousands of families in need of somewhere decent to live.

We must give people hope; we must act to end the housing crisis and we must move beyond sympathetic rhetoric and deliver decent homes for every child, for every family, for every person.

In my Scotland, a Labour Scotland, our Scotland, having a roof over your head will be a basic fundamental right.

And on the question of further powers for the Scottish Parliament, Labour delivered the Scottish Parliament. We initiated the powers that will come from the Scotland Act and we support further devolution now. But unlike the nationalists I have never confused constitutional change with social change. It's not devolving more powers that makes a difference, but having the political will to use them that matters. And under my leadership Labour will use the new powers that come to change Scotland.

That is the sort of leadership that Labour needs to show and that's the sort of leadership I'll bring.

Let us once again be the 'Labour' party – the clue is in the name; the party that stands up for working people, the party that challenges poverty, homelessness and inequality.

Taking Labour forward, taking Scotland forward.

Our ambitions for Scotland must be big enough to match Scotland's needs.

Labour values for a Labour Scotland.

That's the challenge we face – let's rise to it.

Despite the importance of the event I was calm, and felt I spoke well. We then asked everyone to stand up and hold aloft the Vote Neil posters and leaflets, which made for a brilliant photo. The hall was truly buzzing – it looked great.

I did a number of press interviews afterwards, and while they are desperate to paint me as a far left winger, I wouldn't let them, as this would play right into Murphy's hands. I keep saying my views (the views I have always had) are mainstream Scottish opinion today. The campaign will focus on policy and not personality with jobs, security at work, the living wage, social housing, social care and tax justice some of the key themes.

It was a fantastic day and a brilliant launch. The campaign team were delighted with how it went and so was I. It couldn't have gone any better, and the fact a lot of my mates (not political animals) turned up made it even better. Not one to blow my own trumpet but I felt proud of myself today!

9 NOVEMBER: More than 1,000 people have offered to help with my leadership campaign, which I find astonishing. The media coverage of the launch is generally very positive. Great footage on the BBC and STV.

The *Sunday Mail*, *Sunday Post*, *Observer* etc all very good, although the Sunday *Herald* is typically snidey.

I was at Murieston Village Hall, in Livingston, for my own Constituency Labour Party (CLP) nomination event. I spoke and took questions – the other candidates were invited but didn't attend. I won the vote almost unanimously but not quite – with five supporting Murphy. I could name them, but I won't! Katy lost by just six votes, which was unlucky, but I am very pleased. The CLP also donated £1,000 towards my campaign.

I found out tonight that Glasgow Kelvin, the biggest CLP in Scotland, has also supported my nomination – fantastic.

10 NOVEMBER: Meeting with the team at our office in Edinburgh. Niall Sokoo and Colin Stuart from Unite are now involved along with Stephen, Tommy and Anneliese. We ran through all the things we have to do and everything is falling into place. It is hectic but Anneliese is brilliant and is going to pull in some GMB friends to assist.

11 NOVEMBER: Went to the Scottish Parliament with the Scottish Mesh Survivors group to speak at the petitions committee, and it went very well. They are doing fantastic and we have worked superbly as a team on this issue.

I then did an interview for the Unite magazine which will go out to all members prior to the ballot.

In the evening I fulfilled a long-standing engagement by hosting an event for Pancreatic Cancer UK.

12 NOVEMBER: The Musicians Union and RMT have come out in support of my candidacy. Jackson Cullinane is doing a great job with the nominations. The MU are affiliated while RMT aren't, but this is important as it shows I can extend my appeal beyond the party.

To Kirkcaldy CLP for nomination meeting event. Sarah and I were there but Murphy wasn't. Given this is Gordon Brown's constituency I expected it to go against me but I won pretty convincingly – very good result.

13 NOVEMBER: Picked up by Jimmy Thompson who is going to act as my driver during the campaign. Jimmy is an ex-miner from Musselburgh. He used to be the driver for Michael (Mick) McGahey and Arthur Scargill

during the miners' strike. He has a fantastic big people carrier with all mod cons and great comfort and loves driving so has agreed to be at our disposal for the duration. It's such a help as I hate driving and will be able to prepare better if I can read in the back of the car.

First port of call is the Scottish Hazards conference where I was a speaker along with the SNP's Clare Adamson. Clare spoke first and didn't really say anything of substance. I spoke about the work of the hazards movement, advances in health and safety and threats to it from the election of a Tory government. There were a lot of Yes voters and former Labour people there so I was pleased to get a good reception from them – these are the people we need to win back!

Next it was up to the north east, where I met George Ramsay, the Dundee UCATT organiser. I have a lot of time for George. The *Herald* and *Dundee Courier* were there and I used this as an opportunity to launch my policy to build 50,000 social houses using bonds and new borrowing powers.

Then to the Dunfermline CLP nomination meeting at the town's Our Lady's Church. Sarah Boyack and I turned up. The meeting took place in the actual church, which was interesting and it felt pretty good. This is the CLP of Thomas Doherty MP, who is the most right wing Labour MP in Scotland – no one knows why he joined the Labour Party. There is a great story about Doherty and his burning ambition to be speaker of the House of Commons. He is one of those people who knows the rules inside out but only uses them to try and show how clever he is. Most of the Scottish Labour MPs think he is an arse and really can't be bothered with him. Ex-miner and Scottish whip Davie Hamilton had been receiving complaint after complaint about Doherty's annoying and self-promoting behaviour, so decided to call him in for 'a wee chat!' Picture the scene, gruff, straight-talking Davie and spoffy, wet Thomas...

Hamilton, 'Right, Thomas son... aw the Scottish MPs are scunnered wi' yer cairry oan!'

Doherty, 'But David, David...'

Hamilton, 'Shut up son and listen... now all yer colleagues think you're a c**t! ... and I have investigated these allegations and found out that you are a c**t, so start behaving yersel!'

Chat finished!

After the speech and questions I had to head home but asked Cara Hilton to text me the result. I was exceptionally pleased to win this CLP – apparently Doherty stormed out afterwards without speaking to anyone. Made my week that!

A lot of social media traffic tonight, with the top story Len McCluskey's attack on Murphy in a blog piece. I would prefer them to talk positively about my campaign than to have a go at Murphy, but his analysis is spot on. Murphy won Shettleston and Cathcart tonight, whereas I won Clydebank, Leith, Edinburgh West, Dunfermline, Dundee and Maryhill. Patricia Ferguson MSP has come out in support of me.

Fiona received a call at home tonight from Murphy's team, asking her to support him. Of course, she said she would!

14 NOVEMBER: Off to Thompson's office in Bath Street, Glasgow for training with one of their media team. It was very helpful. I haven't done too much media training so it opened my eyes, although I don't want to lose my authenticity and come over all false. I will leave that to Jim and his soft spoken, jokey, 'I'm everyone's pal' act!

The McCluskey piece is attracting a lot of attention and Murphy is loving it. It's in all the papers.

Lisa Johnston is up from the GMB to offer help – she seems really switched on.

Nominations closed today: Murphy leads with 24 MPs, 17 MSPs, 2 MEPs, 100 Councillors, 34 CLPs and four affiliates.

I have six MPs, six MSPs, 75 Councillors, 18 CLPs and 10 affiliates.

Sarah Boyack has seven MSPs, three MPs, 13 Councillors, one CLP and one affiliate.

For deputy; Kezia Dugdale has 21 MPs, 32 MSPs, two MEPS, 149 Councillors, 48 CLPs and seven affiliates.

Katy Clark has eight MPs, three MSPs, 42 Councillors, seven CLPs and nine affiliates.

It's clear the party machine, Ian McNicol (who is Murphy's pal) and the appointment of Fiona Stanton as stand-in General Secretary for Scotland, means they are prepared to do anything to ensure Jim and Kez win, but we have them scared. They are wheeling the injured, the lame, the disinterested and the payroll vote out. Students are being intimidated and warned of career prospects, or lack of them, if they vote 'the wrong way'.

15 NOVEMBER: Over to Glasgow for the STUC Scottish Labour women's conference. I was met at the door by around 30 women comrades with a large banner and t-shirts saying Neil4leader! Great reception – our team really are up on how to handle these events and make the best of them.

Deputy candidates first – Katy is strong, confident and principled, while

Kez tries to come across as the friendly, smiley girl next door.

I was up first in our debate and felt relaxed; I'm gaining in confidence. I spoke about housing, low pay, job insecurity etc being women's issues, but also everyone's issues. Murphy spoke without notes or using the lectern. He wants to show he is the statesmen and is smooth and relaxed. He doesn't have much substance and is clearly moving left onto my territory to try and win votes.

The vibe in the room was positive and feedback was good.

Afterwards, Murphy asked Sarah and I if we could stick to a line on taxation, what with the Smith Commission at a critical point in their deliberations. I said I had no problem with this and that we need to let the Commission do its work, as did Sarah.

The post mortem in the pub concluded that we need to put clear red water between me and the rest on tuition fees, Trident, railways, PFI etc. as these are places Murphy cannot go.

16 NOVEMBER: This morning I was at BBC Scotland's Pacific Quay base in Glasgow for *The Andrew Marr Show*. I have decided to 'press the nuclear button'. Marr played a bit of Nicola Sturgeon's speech about Trident and I said I agreed with her on it and that Trident should not be replaced, and that I have always been opposed to nuclear weapons. I also mentioned tuition fees, PFI, rail nationalisation etc. The pressure is now on Murphy to address these issues.

Stephen then drove me the short distance to Caledonian University where I took part in a youth and student conference debate. I was met outside by a group of students with the Neil4leader banner. Did a lot of photos and press.

At the Deputy hustings, Kez was doing the 'I'm the students' pal' stuff, having worked for the NUS and come through the University-NUS-Labour students-researcher route. She should be at home here. Katy, as she does, spoke well on policy and showed she has real substance. She needs to be a wee bit lighter at times to make her seem more human, but she is doing well at these events.

My speech went well. I got in Iraq and said the war was a disaster which I had opposed from the beginning. I also raised Trident and tuition fees. In response, Murphy is now saying if he had known then what he knows now about Iraq he would have voted against it. This is utter bollocks. He was one of the most gung-ho for the war and also wanted to bomb Syria when Miliband opposed it. He really will say anything, and I suppose he will be opposed to tuition fees next! Or maybe that's a step too far even for him.

Sarah gave a good speech and in it she spoke about list MSPs who ended up in parliament against all expectations. At that I raised my hand and got quite a laugh – it's true though, as I had expected to be weeded out by party vetting as a dangerous socialist, never mind win a seat!

Trident stuff is going to be the issue in the news tomorrow – plan has worked great!

Someone told me the bookies have me at around 7/2 to win the contest, which is about right I'd say.

17 NOVEMBER: At The Tun in Edinburgh for Good Morning Scotland with Gary Robertson. He is a very robust and excellent interviewer and kept asking how things would be paid for. He was very aggressive, so this means they must be taking me seriously.

The Scotsman today has a cartoon of me depicted as Che Geuvara and an editorial saying I won't appeal to voters if Labour are on the fringes. Looks like the establishment piling in behind Jim. I heard today that the GMB political committee overruled Harry Donaldson's recommendation in relation to the nomination last week. Very interesting!

I headed south to London, to the Red Lion in Westminster, where I met Owen Jones, who has offered to help me in any way he can. His mum and dad live in Falkirk and voted Yes but re-joined the party to support me. He is well connected and will do some supportive articles. He has done well as a left commentator. His books are very good and well researched.

It was then into Committee Room 13 in the House of Commons for a hustings with Scottish MPs. Well, if this isn't hostile territory I don't know what is. I had managed some really good prep with Neil Foster of the GMB (very clever and switched-on guy) and this really helped. The group is chaired by Michael McCann, who is very right wing and has a reputation as a bit of a bully. Murphy was all smooth and pally on his home patch and had clearly primed his supporters, such as Anne McGuire (who sat and glared at me the whole time), Gemma Doyle, a long time Murphy ally and member of Progress, and Ann McKechin, who is to the right of Osborne on taxation. Irrespective of the hostility, I perversely enjoyed it and didn't allow them the opportunity to paint me as some sort of Marxist, militant, revolutionary nut job, which I'm sure displeased many of them.

Afterwards, I went into the House of Commons bar with a few colleagues. I ended up speaking to Graham Jones, an MP from Manchester, who started lecturing me on how to take on the SNP and said we just had to do what they were doing in his patch with UKIP (clueless). He didn't know who I was and said, 'I hear they are worried in Scotland as Findlay's closing in on Murph!' Well that made my day. I smiled and said nothing.

From our canvassing, Stephen has put out a press release saying we are only two per cent behind – now the Murphy camp WILL be getting very nervous!

18 NOVEMBER: Train to Edinburgh – got a text from Kevin Lindsay saying some of his members have reported how Murphy's canvassers are saying to party members when they phone, 'Oh, we don't know how Neil voted in the referendum!' Shameful. The reality is apart from Jim touring the country on an Irn Bru crate and shouting at people, I did more referendum public meetings than any other Labour politician (65 in total). I did many trade union events and public events in hostile territory arguing for a No vote, not on the basis of Better Together, but on the basis of solidarity and class interests; concepts completely alien to Murphy and his Better Together entourage.

A *Daily Record* survation action poll has Labour on 23 per cent for the General Election!

My train arrived in at Waverley Station a little late so just missed Salmond's resignation statement but heard the end of Jackie Baillie's speech (she is deputising in the absence of a Labour leader). She got the tone completely wrong. Ruth Davidson and Willie Rennie were good, while Stewart Stevenson spouted awful, sycophantic guff as only he could!

Scotland playing England at football tonight but will miss it because we are doing a TV debate for *Scotland 2014*.

Met Tommy and Stephen Low for a quick bite to eat before heading over to the TSSA offices to meet all the people who have been doing such brilliant work on the phones for us. The place was buzzing with around 40 people young and old working away and speaking to members. I thanked them all for their help and gave them encouragement to continue their great work. It was fantastic and very humbling to see the effort being put in on my behalf by students and young trade unionists – many of whom have a bright future.

No rest for the wicked as it was over to Pacific Quay for the Scotland 2014 debate with Sarah Smith. The audience comprised supporters from all three campaigns and I spotted many friends. I felt pretty relaxed and seemed to do quite well. I raised the issues I have been concentrating on and also mentioned I had 1,000 volunteers working on our campaign, which I think genuinely shocked Murphy – it was intended to!

19 NOVEMBER: Colleagues at parliament, and social media, very complementary about last night's performance. I am beginning to enjoy this and feel much more at ease. Magnus Linklater came in today to do an interview. No doubt he will do me in as he is Establishment through and through. I enjoyed the joust, and raised TTIP and why Labour should be totally opposed.

Nicola Sturgeon sworn in today – she is the epitome of a career politician, having worked almost all her life for the top job, so it must be a real sense of achievement for her to get there. She is very capable but also very cold and will have to work on that if she is to be a success. The team around her will be critical but they are at the top of their game and streets ahead of the people we have. If I win I will clear the decks and bring in the best strategists, advisors, press folk etc. I will also use the really intelligent people we have in the movement in Scotland like Dave Watson, Richard Leonard, Jackson Cullinane and students such as Iona Baker and Ewan Gibbs as well as young trade unionists Jamie Caldwell and Sam Ritchie. These people are very capable but instead of being viewed as an asset, they have been seen as a threat, which is just plain daft.

Last night on Twitter I joked about whether I should wear a shirt and tie for the debate or my usual preference of a Fred Perry. Today I spoke to a group of fifth year pupils from Broxburn Academy who were visiting parliament. When it came to questions, one of them asked, 'So, did you wear the Fred Perry on TV last night?' I enjoyed that.

After that, I headed up to the Serenity Café on the Royal Mile for an MSP hustings. There were about 15 colleagues there, and it was pretty poor all round – all have already made up their mind.

Murphy's side are being dragged left every single day. He is now talking about poverty, social housing, low pay etc. These are things he has never spoken about in his political life. He did say he didn't want to raise council tax, so there is a real opportunity to ask how councils will be funded and jobs preserved. The reality is the council tax freeze is a disaster for jobs (40,000 have been lost), for services being cut across the board and for local democracy, as it is centrally imposed. Labour MUST reject this democratic outrage.

20 NOVEMBER: I was in at the Scottish Parliament early this morning, and spoke to Neil Foster of the GMB on the phone, before doing some more hustings prep. It was very helpful. Then it was into the chamber for Nicola Sturgeon's first FMQs. She was trying far too hard to be all consensual. 'I will listen, we will work together, I am a caring cuddly person.' Dull, dull, dull – let's see how long it lasts.

To the Dundee Marriott Hotel for hustings. Over 100 people there, and lots of support in Dundee from some great people. It was one of the best hustings yet. I felt I performed well. Murphy isn't impressing people, despite his experience and a life in politics and having been a cabinet minister etc. He has surprisingly little to say about key basic issues and sounds false and vacuous. We bolted down to Edinburgh for the latter half of the Scottish Politician of the Year event. Sturgeon won the award again (yawn)! Hugh Henry got a committee award but the highlight of the night was the award given to Gordon Aikman for his outstanding campaign following his diagnosis with MND. His speech was magnificent. He really is a very dignified and humble guy who has captured everyone's imagination. The award for the Who Cares Scotland team, for their work on care leavers, was also fully merited. I dealt with them a lot when I sat on the education committee and Neil Bibby and I forced the committee to meet them during our inquiry into the care system. A number of SNP members, including the convener Stewart Maxwell, were not keen but we embarrassed them into it.

21 NOVEMBER: Renfrewshire CLP hustings – this is the neighbouring CLP to Murphy and I expected it to be packed out with his people but it was evenly split. Stephen McCabe, Inverclyde council leader and Murphy cheerleader, was there. When it came to the questions he asked, 'How would you vote if there was another referendum?' I replied, 'Given I did 65 meetings campaigning for a No vote, probably more than almost all other MPs and MSPs, I think my position was and is very clear!' I also congratulated him on the most ridiculous question of the campaign! Mind you, at least he said out loud and to my face what Murphy's team are saying on the phones to members. Pretty desperate stuff.

22 NOVEMBER: Met Katy Clark and her team for a canvassing session in Mayfield, Edinburgh, with by-election candidate Kenny Young. Over 20 in the team – decent response and he might just nick it as there is a strong

local independent candidate who will split the vote.

The SNP held an event at the Hydro today where 12,000 turned up – bloody hell, 12,000! It was like a US convention with all the glitz and razzmatazz. Sturgeon treated like a rock star, which is quite bizarre but also something unseen in Scottish or even UK politics.

Spoke to Elaine Smith tonight. The party hierarchy are clearly having to invest in nappies as they see my campaign continue to build momentum. They are now pulling every trick in the book. Fiona Stanton is just obeying orders from McNicol and is pulling all the strokes. In the booklet to go out to candidates, the names of MPs, MSPs and MEPs who have nominated each candidate will be listed, but the names of CLPs and trade unions won't so this will show a large number of nominations for Murphy and Dugdale and very little for Katy and I. Outrageous. On top of that there will be no secret ballot for MPs, MSPs and MEPs, so their vote will be published. This again is clearly designed to intimidate people into voting for the establishment candidate. Unite and ASLEF have complained. I spoke to Fiona Stanton and Anas Sarwar about it, but nothing will be done. We will be raising this in the media tomorrow. The party machine is in full flow to stop us having any chance of victory.

23 NOVEMBER: To the BBC's Pacific Quay studios where I met Stephen Low and Tommy to prepare beforehand, then went on to do an interview with Gordon Brewer. All three of us were on with him. It was a really poor interview with little to get our teeth into. Very disappointing. Still, it is good to see the row over the candidate booklet making the headlines.

To Glasgow City Halls for hustings. They booked a pretty small room holding approximately 150, so many people couldn't attend. There were lots of Murphy people there. Not a great atmosphere or much oomph to proceedings.

Newspapers full of Sturgeon at the Hydro and the radical Independence campaign's 3,000 strong event, at which the self-important Alan Bissett read a 'people's vow'. Who the people are and what authority he has to make this vow I have no idea but he seemed awfully pleased with himself, so that's good then!

Tom Watson MP, an old foe of Murphy from their NUS days, has done an article on why a Murphy win would be bad for Labour in Scotland. This is very helpful, even though I didn't know he was doing it. Ivan Lewis MP has attacked Tom for this on Twitter.

24 NOVEMBER: Off to the Royal College of Nursing in Glasgow to hear the public inquiry report into Vale of Leven hospital deaths. Judge Lord McLean said families were justified in their calls for an inquiry – major issues for the NHS, government and practitioners. A moving day for all families associated with this.

I then popped into Glasgow City Chambers for a Labour councillors' hustings. A fantastic honour to speak in such a beautiful building and dramatic chamber. I felt I put in one of my best performances and rose to the occasion. I enjoyed it a lot. Matt Kerr, John Kelly – who has since tragically died from MND – Bill Butler, Jonathan Findlay, Emma Swift and many others were there supporting me, which was very encouraging.

Picked up by Jimmy Thompson and then down to Dumfries for the hustings. All three candidates did an interview with Borders TV beforehand and I said, 'I think we need an MSP in parliament ready to take on Sturgeon right away,' which was intended in a not-so-subtle-way to say to Sarah's supporters, 'Vote for me with your second preference and for mine to vote for Sarah with theirs.' Murphy tried to laugh this off but was clearly taken aback and unhappy as he mentioned it afterwards. The usual questions came up in debate, like how to get us back into power, economic policy, austerity, council tax freeze etc. but afterwards a number of people, including councillors I didn't know, came up offering their support. Elaine Murray MSP, who is supporting me, said I performed best, which gave me a boost. I really like Elaine, she is an honest person with good politics. Jimmy Thompson offered to give Sarah a lift home as the alternative was a very late train to Edinburgh. When we got into the car he opened up a cool box and passed Tommy and me a couple of ice cold beers – luxury!

25 NOVEMBER: Fight about the candidate's booklet goes on.

To Shadow Cabinet for discussion on Smith Commission. After agreeing a line between the three leadership candidates on taxation prior to the Smith report, Murphy has today broken ranks and said he will introduce a 50 per cent tax rate – this is just a re-heat of Ed Balls' policy and nothing new at all. MPs are furious about this – he was totally against this a year ago and now champions it as his policy. This after he had approached Sarah and I to stick to an agreed line on taxation. Utterly shameless and duplicitous. He is also talking about poverty, inequality and fairness. We have hauled him to the left on policy. The problem is he is completely lacking in credibility on many of these issues but some people have bought the idea that he is a winner.

Into the debating chamber for Shona Robison's statement on Vale of Leven Hospital. She seems very cold and lacking in empathy.

To STV for interview with *Scotland Tonight*. Murphy claimed he didn't have an inside line on the Smith Commission, which is utter bollocks, because I have no doubt Iain Gray and Greg McClymont MP will have been keeping him fully informed all the way through.

26 NOVEMBER: The Smith Commission reported today with ALL parties signing up to the package of measures. The following are just some of what will be devolved; all income tax, quite a bit of welfare, housing benefit, attendance allowance, railways etc. It is a significant package of measures. The SNP, despite John Swinney signing up in full, are now rubbishing it before their signature dries on the agreement. They look bitter and grudging.

27 NOVEMBER: Papers full of the Smith Commission. Sturgeon's statement in the chamber critical of what they have just supported.

To a packed Apex Hotel, in Edinburgh's Grassmarket. First question was the best so far, 'I don't want to know about your policies, can you just tell me about your favourite band or music.' Well that was easy, with The Jam, the Specials and punk and new wave getting an airing! Good question.

28 NOVEMBER: Up north to a hustings in the Kingsmill Hotel, Inverness. Fiona and Diane came with Tommy and I. The hustings was dull, with very little atmosphere and not a lot of audience reaction or participation; perhaps the worst yet. We all felt really flat afterwards.

29 NOVEMBER: Attended a councillor conference hustings in Glasgow, before going to Govanhill Baths, on the south side of the city, where community worker Jim Monaghan arranged for us to meet a group of BME community reps. The baths are amazing and were saved following a long sit-in by activists. The building is superb and there are plans to reinstate it, but it will cost millions. It could be a tremendous community hub for one of the most deprived and diverse neighbourhoods in Scotland (over

50 languages are spoken in Govanhill). I spoke to representatives of the Irish, Roma, Caribbean, French, Arabic, Pakistani and black communities to discuss the issues and challenges they face – it was a hugely interesting and educational meeting and made a real mark on me. Housing, poverty, exploitation in employment and access to services were the big issues raised.

30 NOVEMBER: Up to see my mum for her birthday then to Bathgate Partnership Centre for a Linlithgow CLP hustings. The party here is in a poor state and needs new blood and an overhaul. Murphy and Kez didn't appear and it was good to get my old CLPs nomination.

Following the death of Tony Benn earlier this year I approached comrades on the left to organise an event to celebrate and commemorate his life. Stephen Wright duly obliged with a fabulous concert at the Mitchell Theatre tonight. Tony's granddaughter Emily Benn was in attendance to receive a presentation of a gold badge to recognise the 40th anniversary of the UCS work, and I was privileged to present it to her. We had brilliant performances from James Grant, Rab Noakes, Arthur Johnston, Alistair McDonald, Sheena Wellington and others.

What a fantastic night with lots of friendly people on the left offering great support.

13

Leadership Race: December 2014

1 DECEMBER: Up to Aberdeen on the train with Colin Stewart of Unite, and had a meeting with Katy before taking part in a pre-hustings event with left activists, which was hosted by Councillor Nathan Morrison. Around 25 activists turned up and were hugely supportive. Then to a neighbouring hotel for a packed hustings – the best one yet. The atmosphere was good and there was plenty of humour and an excellent debate; I enjoyed it immensely.

Spoke to Tommy. So as not to be left completely flatfooted if I win, I will have to give some thought to who I appoint to the many political and key advisory roles. My key Shadow Cabinet appointments would be Hugh Henry, Drew Smith, Alex Rowley, Patricia Ferguson, Elaine Murray and others who didn't support me but who I respect, such as Graeme Pearson, Neil Bibby, Mary Fee, Richard Simpson and Rhoda Grant. I won't appoint any of the crew who did the dirty on Johann Lamont.

Today, a video of three Renfrewshire SNP councillors has been released showing them burning copies of the Smith Commission. One of them works for Derek McKay, the Transport Minister. The image of nationalists burning books is not a particularly pleasant one.

3 DECEMBER: To Thompson's in Edinburgh for a team meeting to discuss PFI buy-out policy proposal. This is looking really good. By using new borrowing powers we could look at each PFI contract and, where beneficial, refinance it and save money. We would move from interest rates at eight per cent on average to around two per cent, potentially saving hundreds of millions of pounds. It's a no brainer and would end the great PFI/NPD rip-off. This will have quite an impact when we launch it.

Labour business today included the NHS. I led for us in the debate and spoke about the huge pressures on general practices, the crisis in social care, delayed discharge, waiting times, boarding out etc. and repeated our call for a wholescale review of the Scottish NHS to make it meet the demands of our times and ageing population. There are problems from the front door to the back. The government of course deny all of this and use their usual patronising get out, saying Labour is talking down our NHS and its staff, but they are in denial.

Went to a round table meeting on lobbying, but it was awful. Stewart Stevenson MSP, John Downie of SCVO and lobbyist, and ex-Tory MP, Peter Duncan were the speakers. A complete waste of time.

Sturgeon suspended the Paisley book burners today.

4 DECEMBER: After hosting a tour of the Scottish Parliament for pupils from Whitburn Academy I went to the chamber for FMQs. Jackie Baillie led for us and spoke about the NHS. She is doing well at FMQs. Sturgeon's tactic appears to be acting all consensual when she gets a difficult question – won't last!

I asked a question on TTIP, urging unity and asking everyone to join together to write to Cameron opposing this appalling proposal, which threatens our public services.

It was then off to Kilsyth for the Lanarkshire hustings. Deputies first and Katy received hostile questions about Trident from a Better Together Tory type, no doubt a new recruit after the referendum! Of the leadership candidates, I was up first. Given this was the last one, I was determined to go out on a high and enjoy it – and I did.

Afterwards, I headed straight to BBC Scotland to appear on the *Scotland 2014* programme. The topic was the policy on PFI. They had put up right wing economist Jo Armstrong against me in an attempt to rubbish the policy, but she couldn't as it's sound and as long as we take each NPD/ PFI project on a case-by-case basis we could save hundreds of millions of pounds. We should set up a debt reduction unit in the Scottish Government to do this. I was very pleased with the interview.

5 DECEMBER: Enjoyed a rare long lie – luxury, and then to Glasgow for STV online Facebook interview with Stephen Daisley. Going in I sought out John McKay and gave him a presentation gift bag (he obviously thought

it was a bottle of wine), and said, 'Oh thank you very much.' Of course, when he opened it, it was a Barr's bottle of chippie sauce. There were sincere thanks all round for such a wonderful and culturally sound gift!

I did the online interview which was great fun. Once we got through the mad people ranting about every subject under the sun, and offering the full dictionary of profanity (some of it very funny, mind you), I was able to answer lots of questions. Afterwards, I did a one-to-one interview for the website.

From STV it was over to the STUC for a campaign rally and Christmas party for the team. Beforehand we had a meeting with a few key allies and some of the campaign team. We have fought a great campaign, even though we know we won't win, but we all agree this is the start of a new lease of life for the left and we must build on it. The event itself was fantastic. We had Stephen Wright, Fraser Spiers, Vince Mills and Eddie McGuire playing some great music. All the young people involved in the campaign were there, as well as my family, including Fiona and Chloe. Lots of my oldest mates, and trade unionists, MSPs, MPs, councillors and many of my Campaign for Socialism pals showed up. It was great fun. There was a tremendous atmosphere, and a feeling that whatever happens with the result, we have rebuilt the left and gave people their confidence back. That, if used and developed properly, is the greatest legacy of the campaign.

6 DECEMBER: For the first time in ages I had a quiet day and then went to my brother John's 50th birthday bash in the local pub, the Grange. Brilliant to see so many old school friends.

7 DECEMBER: To Pacific Quay to participate in the Crossfire programme with the other candidates. After the interview, Murphy asked me, 'What will Unite [the union] do if I win? How should I approach them? Not that I am taking it for granted that I will win of course.' What a bizarre thing to say. 'Well,' I said, 'I don't know, but I could make a suggestion. Why don't you do something unique and go and meet Len McCluskey and sit down and have a chat rather than engage in gunboat diplomacy through the newspapers?' Don't think my advice went down too well!

8 DECEMBER: At Stoneyburn Community Centre for the annual pensioners' party. It's a great event run by community nurse Doreen and her team. She is a hero in the community, and organises holidays, day trips and a lunch club for pensioners in addition to her job as a nurse. She is magnificent. I knew lots of people there, and many are Fiona's relatives and people her mum knows.

9 DECEMBER: At the Scottish Parliament for a Shadow Cabinet meeting to discuss local government finance, as this had been raised by both Alex Rowley and Hugh Henry at the group meeting. The discussion was dreadful, summarised as 'well, we can't call for more money for councils because that is not popular.' This despite social care being in crisis and council services and jobs being lost on an unprecedented scale. So we will end up arguing for more money for the NHS to keep more people stuck in hospital at £3,000 per week as opposed to getting them looked after in their own home at a cost of £350 per week, and in a place where people want to be. This is so awful and short sighted – completely conservative. It is the SNPs line and we just repeat it.

MP Margaret Curran came out in favour of Murphy today, despite saying she would remain neutral. I couldn't be less surprised.

Met Johann Lamont for a chat. She was scathing about former close colleagues who had put the boot in, and so she should be. She also gave an interesting insight into Miliband and his main weakness, which is a complete lack of confidence.

Curran said she was supporting Murphy 'because he is good on women's issues', which is utter crap! Johann is going to support Katy and me, which is a huge boost.

Did an interview with Gary Gibbon of Channel 4. He said he had spoken to 100 people at an SNP branch meeting and in the street, most of them Labour voters or former Labour voters, and they said Labour doesn't represent them anymore. He was genuinely shocked at the extent of defection, which I think is very real and very worrying. We are heading for an electoral nightmare.

10 DECEMBER: After our health team meeting I took Elaine Smith, Louise from her office, Annaliese, Stephen Low, Tommy and Colin Stuart to lunch to thank them for their hard work. After the vote we went to the Café Royal where we had a nice night. Voting closes today, and there is relief all round.

11 DECEMBER: At the Scottish Parliament there are lots of good wishes from Jim Hume and Tavish Scott, both Lib Dems, Patrick Harvie and Alison Johnston of the Greens, Cameron Buchanan, a Tory, and a number of others.

Just a fortnight till Christmas and I'm home early. This is what I call luxury!
12 DECEMBER: I was at the office in West Calder this morning. My first job

was to write and send out all our Christmas cards, and it took hours. I then headed home and penned a speech just in case of victory (which our phone canvassing shows is increasingly unlikely). The Murphy camp have really upped their game in the last fortnight and it is showing in our returns.

I went over to the Fauldhouse Miners' Welfare Club for the pensioners' Christmas party. All my pals' mums and dads were there, as was my own mum. Christine Cook, who does an amazing job organising the over-50s club, took the mic and asked everyone to wish me well tomorrow, which was nice but embarrassing. Then over to Tommy's for his daughter's 21st birthday party. If anyone deserves a celebration after what she has been through it is her. Lovely to see her healthy, well and enjoying herself.

13 DECEMBER: It's D-Day. Well, R-Day. Results day at the Emirates Arena in the east end of Glasgow. I headed there with Fiona and Jimmy Thompson. As we pulled into the car park, Sean Clerkin (mad as a hatter, and serial abuser of Labour politicians) was walking beside Murphy, shouting in his face and trying to provoke him. It was a certainty he would be there.

When we walked in the front door, I had a wee peek into the room and it was packed. It was great to see so many friendly faces, but it was tense as we awaited the results. Party officials announced, privately to us in a back room, the deputy leadership result first, which Kezia won with just under 63 per cent of the vote. Katy received 37 per cent.

Then it was time for the leadership results. I won the trade union affiliated vote, but not as comfortably as I would have liked. I polled 17.34 while Murphy took 13.26.

Then the overall result, which Murphy won with just over 55 per cent. I scored 35 per cent, while Sarah Boyack received a little over nine.

My first emotion was one of relief that it was over. We fought the best campaign by a long shot, we had innovative policies and managed to remain positive throughout, staying clear of public acrimony. The team we assembled was superb and there is no doubt at one point we had the Murphy camp reeling. However, the party machine then clicked into gear. They pulled every trick in the book to ensure their man won! Fiona Stanton and Ian McNicol, as officials, and Davie Hamilton and James Kelly as politicians, delivered for Murphy.

I don't regret standing one bit, and feel proud of what we achieved, but the reality is we were well beaten. We now have to ensure we organise the left and make it an organisation with much broader appeal than just the Campaign for Socialism (although it is an organisation I am extremely proud to be a member of).

Afterwards Murphy and Kez were all smiles and he gave his speech, which was all about patriotism and social justice (we dragged him into social justice territory). It was pretty flat to be honest, and that's not sour grapes. Later, we all went into a pub in town for a party. It was great just to relax with the team. Then who should phone to commiserate – Ed Miliband. To be honest, I couldn't get him off the line quickly enough. Murphy also phoned, but I didn't take it. I will speak to him tomorrow.

14 DECEMBER: TV this morning is full of Jim's election, showing him in a Scotland football top running along the banks of the Clyde. It's just so contrived – 'look at me and how Scottish I am!'

No time to feel sorry for myself as I headed for Stirling County Hotel, and a meeting between MPs and MSPs. A number of colleagues avoided eye contact. We had a presentation from a party pollster, then one from Murphy and another from Kezia. The polling is dreadful – we are in very deep shit but some of them really don't get it and believe it's merely a temporary blip. Clearly given the length and content of Jim and Kez's speeches, they had been tipped off they had won – either that or they were up all night writing lengthy and detailed presentations!

15 DECEMBER: To Dynamic Earth in Edinburgh to hear Murphy's speech about his plans for the party and country. He then announces – straight out of Tony Blair and Peter Mandelson's 1997 manual – that he is going to rewrite Clause IV and make it reflect Labour's patriotism. Pass the sick bucket! This is the guy who toured the country shouting 'Better Together', and now he's screaming 'hoots mon, we're a' Jock Tamson's bairns and there's a moose loose aboot the hoose' whilst wearing a Scotland top and drinking Irn Bru! It is utter, utter bollocks. Who advises these folk? Well, of course, the answer is the world's worst political strategist, John 'the serial loser' McTernan. I despair. Before the leadership election I was under the impression the likes of Murphy and McTernan were some sort of political clever clogs, master tacticians who could win over the people we previously couldn't reach, but the reality is very, very different.

Back to the sanity of my office to answer hundreds of emails, texts, phone calls and good wishes etc. from party members, family and friends. Spoke to Murphy who says he wants me on board in his team. I would rather pull my own teeth out with pliers but I know the people I rely on for advice, and who are rarely wrong, will tell me I have to be in there arguing the case for sanity and a leftward approach to tackle the SNP. Joy!

16 DECEMBER: At the parliament, there are kind words and commiserations from people across the political spectrum, from the posties Alan and Jimmy, Jim Hume, Tavish Scott, Jackson Carlaw etc. I met with Murphy at 11. He is appointing his team and wants me to do the Shadow Fair Work and Skills job – which is logical, given my interest in these issues. He is moving everyone. Jenny Marra will replace me at Health. Drew Smith looked like someone had just pissed on his bonfire as he is being made Murphy's PPS. What a shame, you wouldn't do that to your worst enemy. I really do feel for him. Jackie Baillie is running about like the cat who got the cream – she really thinks she is the fixer. Hugh Henry is back at Justice, which is good. All Murphy's supporters have been rewarded – Kez, Clare Baker, Ken McIntosh, Iain Gray, Mary Fee, and Sarah Boyack, who is also back in.

In the backroom team it is the Better Together tribute act with Blair McDougall on lead vocals.

17 DECEMBER: Met with Rhoda Grant and Richard Simpson – they are remaining at Health which is good. I thanked them and their staff for their help over the last year or so and urged them to continue with the health inequality and social care work I began, as this is crucial. It emerged that Siobhan McMahon will work with me on the employment portfolio, which is good as Siobhan and I get on well and she is a straight talker, which I like.

Chloe got her tonsils out today – she is fine, but very sore. Afterwards, I went to the annual Labour group Christmas party. It was good fun and turned into a late night.

18 DECEMBER: Met Patients First to talk through a whole range of NHS issues they are concerned about. Jane Hamilton was there. She has been told she will have her contract terminated and will be paid a significant amount to go away. The treatment of her has been outrageous. She doesn't want the money; she wants her life and career back. Sadly many other NHS staff have been treated the same way. She has done nothing wrong but has been treated as though she has.

To FMQ's for Kezia Dugdale's first offering. She did well on falling oil prices, job losses and the crisis in the North Sea, as a result of oil selling at less than $48 per barrel. Sturgeon not confident and trying to be consensual – it doesn't suit her.

It was then over to Edinburgh University, to their 'grand room', for the Shadow Cabinet meeting. All of this is part of Murphy's spin to make us look like 'the Cabinet in waiting'. Every single thing they do is about spin and presentation and nothing to do with policy or people in the communities we represent. The reality is the people in Fauldhouse, Addiewell or Craigshill don't give a toss about whether or not we look good on *Reporting Scotland*, sitting in some ornate and opulent room, but do care if we can make their lives better.

We had a presentation on polling and focus groups, which said, 'The voters can't wait to give us a kicking!' Sounds ominous. Murphy said Shadow Cabinet meetings would be business-like and last an hour, as this worked well under Tony Blair. Oh well, we must follow.

Heard today that Murphy is set to dump my Beveridge 21 proposal for a full review of the NHS that my health team developed. The reason given is that it doesn't allow us to attack the SNP on health. This is just ridiculous. We must look at health care in the 21st century and ensure it is fully fit for purpose and not just look at how we attack our opponents.

Just spoke to Chloe and she is still in agony after her operation.

19 DECEMBER: Went for a lovely lunch with my mum, John and Sharron, Anna and Jim and Fiona – great time had by all. Ah, normality!

20 DECEMBER: Murphy on *Off the Ball*, the irreverent radio football show, where he said he wanted a return to drinking at football matches. Where on earth did that come from – just what we need in Scotland!

22 DECEMBER: Had planned to go to Glasgow with Chloe to do some Christmas shopping, but decided to go to Braehead instead of the town. We then heard there had been a big accident with an out-of-control bin lorry mowing down people near George Square. This is absolutely awful. Six people are feared dead; students, a primary teacher, and members of the same family. Just terrible.

23 DECEMBER: Survation poll shows a negative 'bounce' for Labour following Murphy's election – he seems to be very unpopular. The poll suggests Labour would win only four seats at the election, which I think is pretty accurate. Scottish Labour MPs will now be incredibly nervous. I don't think Murphy will be leader for long. The election will probably see him off if the polls are right.

14

Business as Usual: January–May 2015

ONE OF MY first commitments of 2015 meant a trip to Edinburgh's Dynamic Earth. There were around 250 folk there for Jim Murphy's New Year speech, but before we got underway, someone suggested that losing to Murphy might just have been a godsend. I agree – I think I dodged a very painful bullet.

He started with a commentary on the global economy and the challenges that accompany it – oil price fluctuation, Russia in turmoil, Greek crisis etc. – then returned to Scotland and announced his '1,000 nurses more' pledge. He said that an incoming Labour Government would recruit 1,000 more nurses into the NHS than the SNP. So if the SNP announce a million nurses we would recruit one million and 1,000. It is nonsense. After the speech, all those who put the boot into Johann (Lamont) for making policy on the hoof congratulated Murphy for doing exactly the same. Pretty astonishing. He also said he will bring back chartered teachers, but again there was no discussion with anyone who happened to be, or had been, a teacher; just an announcement. I believe the announcement regarding the nurses typifies their approach to politics: made because it sounded good rather than because it was the right thing to do. I think people are increasingly rejecting this type of approach.

This is shaping up to be quite a year. Oh, and we have a general election to 'look forward' to!

6 JANUARY: Scottish Parliament – met Michael Hogg and stewards from the RMT about the City Link group going bust. The company continually told workers all was okay before pulling the plug on Christmas Eve, leaving 450 staff high and dry. Many were self-employed, having bought their own vans, and some now have as much as £27,000 of debt. I called Katy Clark to see if the Business, Innovation and Skills committee at Westminster would haul the directors in for a grilling. She said she would try but

doubtful the Tories would do it. I asked Ian Davidson MP if his Scottish affairs select committee could do it. He was keen and promised to look into it immediately. Within an hour, he'd called back to say they will begin a short inquiry on Monday. Great result; Ian doesn't mess about. Michael Hogg and Gordon Martin from the RMT are delighted. Here is the clearest example of aggressive venture capitalism ripping money out of a business and letting it go bust with no regard for workers.

7 JANUARY: Spoke in a parliamentary debate on health inequality. The Scottish Government talk a good game on this stuff but do little as redistribution is key to tackling it. You could fill the parliament several times with reports written on health inequality but it just gets worse. Experts say the living wage is the most important policy to tackle this.

8 JANUARY: At Crichton House in Edinburgh for a Shadow Cabinet meeting. Murphy gives details of his new Clause IV. It's all fluff that no one could really disagree with, except where he says, 'We will work in the "patriotic" interest of the people of Scotland.' I spoke out against the inclusion of 'patriotism' and said you don't need to tell people you are patriotic to show you love your country and its people. I was joined by fellow MSPs Hugh Henry and Ken McIntosh. I was surprised Ken agreed as he is in the same constituency as Murphy, and they are close. If Murphy thinks this will win over Yes voters he is deluded. It is nothing to do with principle or belief, just sheer opportunism and misguided at that. This is the guy who along with folk like Michael McCann, savaged Johann for wanting more autonomy and for wanting to take a different policy direction in Scotland. The hypocrisy is unbelievable. Murphy then drops the bombshell that serial loser, and the world's worst political adviser and tactician, John McTernan is coming in as his chief of staff! It's a disaster waiting to happen. He worked for Henry McLeish, then polished Blair's shoes before advising Australian PM Julia Gillard, who lasted a year after his appointment. Now he's working for us. Oh well, if his magic touch continues, another leadership election will be along shortly!

9 JANUARY: Into the West Calder office where I met Graeme Morrice to discuss forthcoming local campaign. We need to up the profile across the Almond Valley constituency and work with Graeme to get him re-elected. He is sitting on an 11,000 majority but is rightly worried.

10 JANUARY: Spoke to Richard Leonard, Jackson Cullinane and Dave Watson on their return from the Scottish Executive committee where

Murphy's Clause IV passed 14 to 8. Apparently he was all over the place when he spoke, and was even trying to rewrite it mid-meeting!

The policy forum meeting was quite messy despite there being many decent policies. I was in Ann McKechin's group, but all she wanted to discuss was business competitiveness, increasing profit, private sector tax relief etc. She was completely ambivalent to the workers' rights agenda I've been working on. It won't matter for her anyway as she's sitting on a majority of just a few thousand and won't return after the election.

Later that night, Fiona and I went to see Paolo Nutini at the Hydro. It was an excellent concert, but we were forced to travel home in a blizzard, which was really scary at times.

12 JANUARY: West Lothian College – met Mhairi Laughlin, the Principal, to discuss the consequences of cuts to the college sector. I love the college and what it does for people. I have been a student there three times.

13 JANUARY: Shadow Cabinet meeting and Murphy has made an energetic start on the oil slump, NHS etc. He has been proactive and the back room is better organised. He wants us to meet on Mondays across the country starting next week in Dundee. We have to arrange visits to groups when we are there and do press each time. Time will tell if this has any impact.

Just heard parliament staff will be on strike on Thursday. Last time I refused to cross the picket line, and was joined by Drew Smith, Patricia Ferguson and Elaine Smith, and I won't be in this time either. Neil Bibby, our whip, came to see me about the strike and I told him my feelings. The first law of trade unionism – you don't cross picket lines!

Spoke in today's debate on public services. The government's hypocrisy is unreal. They talk about the contribution of public servants, and the great work they do, but not a word about the job losses, pay freeze, council tax freeze etc. I quoted John Stevenson of UNISON who said, 'If 40,000 jobs were lost in any other sector, politicians would be calling for a task force, an inquiry and urgent action.' Councils are key to tackling poverty and inequality. All parties think standing up for council services isn't popular, but not me.

14 JANUARY: Visited Doosan Babcock in Renfrewshire where I met the plant director and one of their head engineers, an impressive young Swedish woman. She was practically evangelical about engineering. We were talking

about the company's excellent investment in its staff, apprenticeships etc. I asked about their corporate social responsibility policy and how it was applied. Like others they do community work, such as gardening or DIY at a local old folks home. I suggested they get their engineers into schools and colleges, where they can encourage young people, especially women, into the industry. They seemed keen. There is real potential in developing an industry ambassadors' programme to expose school pupils to different trades and careers in a more systematic and inclusive way.

At the Scottish Parliament I met Murphy's policy man, Blair McDougall. I gave him the charter of workers' rights, my housing policy from the leadership election and the PFI buy-out policy – probably the last I'll hear of them! On a personal level, I quite like Blair. He is an approachable guy, but politically we couldn't be more different.

15 JANUARY: Spoke in the Holyrood debate on low pay before hosting 10 members of the German IG Metal Union, in Scotland on an English language course. We had an enjoyable tour and discussed devolved power, trade unions, the referendum, etc.

It was then off to meet Fiona and Chloe to go for a meal for Chloe's birthday – really nice evening.

16 JANUARY: St Mary's Church, Bathgate for BBC Big Debate with Lib Dem Mike Crockhart, journalists Ruth Wishart and Alex Massie, and SNP MSP, Fiona Hyslop. Quite a few SNP members in the audience, but Hyslop was all over the place on fracking and said she couldn't give a view because she was a minister and may be involved in planning application appeals – total nonsense! Last week at Westminster, Tom Greatrex MP played a blinder getting all fracking licences devolved so the SNP will soon have power over these issues and there will be no escape. The show was largely mundane and uninspiring – my best contribution was about the poorest communities being burdened with intrusive and damaging environmental projects.

17 JANUARY: Full house tonight of Chloe's pals – including cousins Eleana and Eva – for a very noisy birthday party!

19 JANUARY: Shadow Cabinet meeting in Dundee and Murphy has recruited Gregor Poynton, Jenny Duncan and Susan Dalgety – the New Labour takeover is complete. A small group of protestors gave Murphy a hard time as we entered the building for our meeting. I fear this will continue as the Yes side hate the guy with a passion. We visited a training

project for disengaged young people and spoke about issues such as training and apprenticeships. Afterwards we went canvassing – not a good response at all.

West Calder High School public meeting about new school. Great news for the community but opposition from residents.

Tonight I heard that the SNP had 27 canvassers out in East Calder – 27!

20 JANUARY: Refused to cross the picket line at parliament, so went to help at the Kirkcaldy by-election. We have a good candidate, Liz Nicolson, who works at the local YWCA. It was a beautiful day, although not for me. I got shat on by a seagull, then stood at a polling station, frozen – and there were few voters out. To top it all off I locked my car keys in the boot and had to get Fiona to come for me – NOT a good day!

On the way home I took part in a conference call with Murphy. Labour is 15 points behind in the polls which would leave us with six seats. Shocking, but unsurprising. NHS, unemployment and benefits are the big issues, he said. Well you don't need a focus group to tell you that. We move into full election mode on Monday, which will just look like panic or a half-cocked reaction to bad polls.

Result came through from Kirkcaldy. There was a 23 per cent turnout, and in one of our safest Scottish seats held by Gordon Brown, we lost the council seat by 350 votes.

23 JANUARY: At UNISON in Glasgow to discuss my Charter of Workers Rights. This includes action on zero hours contracts, the living wage, fatal accident inquiries, corporate homicide, ending tribunal fees, equal opportunities, health and safety, blacklisting, miner justice, apprenticeships, procurement, violence at work legislation, collective bargaining, occupational health and workplace learning. A significant package we should be shouting from the rooftops. The challenge will be to get Murphy to grasp it and acknowledge its importance, but I'm not particularly confident. After the defeat in Kirkcaldy, and polls showing us poised to win a paltry six seats, there is panic in the air.

Just heard Midlothian MP Davie Hamilton is retiring. A former Communist, Davie entered parliament in 2001 and was the most rebellious of the new intake. Previously a miner, he was arrested and jailed during the strike. I like Davie and worked with him on the Miners Justice Campaign, but he went from being a rebel to whip and seemed to enjoy the Westminster scene too much, becoming a party enforcer and going back on many of the policy positions he once held. He got a lot of flack from many of his ex-mining colleagues for supporting Murphy, which put a strain on relationships going back decades. This saddened me, but I wish him well in retirement. Given the polls, I think it's a good choice, although rumours suggest he's going into the House of Lords. That really would be something. If it did happen, I think a lot of his former comrades would find it impossible to take. I hope for his sake this doesn't happen.

24 JANUARY: Watched Murphy on *Sunday Politics*, still ducking and diving about whether or not he will stand again for Westminster, insisting he will tell his constituents first. He is now in favour of a people's railway or a nationalised/not for profit railway. Murphy arguing for nationalisation – whatever next? He also said we were opposed to fracking unless a local referendum gave it the go ahead. I have always supported renationalising the railways and am opposed to fracking but none of this has been discussed with the Shadow Cabinet. He just makes random announcements and expects everyone to fall in behind. He will come a cropper with this approach – it's inevitable. The problem with this stuff is that having never spoken about these things in his political career, no one believes him. A complete lack of authenticity is his big problem. On one issue he remained consistent – Trident, where he said that not renewing it would be a mistake. I completely disagree.

Today the *Sunday Herald* reported on spending in the leadership election, saying the trade unions donated around £30k to my campaign, with the GMB donating cash to defeat one of their own members – Jim Murphy!

26 JANUARY: Up to Pittodrie Stadium in Aberdeen for a Shadow Cabinet meeting. Focus groups dominate our discussion – McTernan and Murphy seem obsessed with them. Apparently the NHS and youth employment are the big issues. Well, what a revelation. Who'd have thought jobs and the NHS would be the voters' big issues?

Back home for a surgery in Fauldhouse. I still like doing surgeries even though most people now email or call into the office. Tonight's issues were equal pay, housing repairs and housing allocations.

27 JANUARY: Scottish Parliament – to petitions committee for mesh evidence session with US attorney Adam Slater. Unfortunately the video

link was down due to heavy blizzards in the States. Around 60-70 of the women and their supporters turned up. I urged the committee to hold a chamber debate. John Scott MSP (Cons), Jackson Carlaw (Cons) and John Pentland MSP (Lab) all very supportive but they will hold a session with Slater before deciding what to do. The women were pleased with the outcome. They are an inspiring and very likeable group of people.

28 JANUARY: Scottish Parliament – there is a big rammy going on about fracking. Labour has proposed a triple lock with a local referendum before proceeding but our MPs abstained on the infrastructure bill which proposed a moratorium. The SNP are spinning like mad about this.

To the chamber to hear Fergus Ewing, who would frack under his own arse, squawk and squirm, and announce a moratorium until consultation has been carried out. He doesn't support a word of this, but why would that matter? Joan McAlpine sat at the back smiling away – she and Ewing have been having a battle about fracking. She's right on this issue.

At Education Questions, I asked Angela Constance about college cuts. Her reply was the usual mince. How can it be possible to say so many words that mean absolutely nothing?

29 JANUARY: Spoke to student leaders at Edinburgh College. The college applied for £1.3 million for student financial support but were awarded £300,000 – so much for supporting poorer students. How on earth are people not seeing through this government?

At First Minister's Questions, Kez, who has been taking the lead because Murphy sits in the UK parliament, skewered Sturgeon on the issue of school exam appeals that have fallen by 75 per cent as charges for appeals have landed with schools. So, state school appeals have fallen but there has been no change in private school appeals. Sturgeon was woeful and Tom Gordon of the *Herald* said in his parliamentary sketch that Kez had 'silenced the honking seals on the SNP backbenches'.

I read that Murphy had Ed Miliband and Margaret Curran at a training centre in Glasgow. Neither I, as youth employment spokesperson, nor Paul Martin, the local MSP, were informed or invited (what a relief).

2 FEBRUARY: To Armadale Primary School to meet the primary six pupils. They were excellent and well informed. Some great questions about parliament and my family life. One was hilarious, 'Do you like Nicola Stockton?' Another question I was asked, was 'What kind of pet did you

have when you were wee?' I said, 'We had a dog called Barry and a chicken that was eaten by a fox!'

3 FEBRUARY: Tomorrow's Ashcroft poll won't be kind. They have polled 1,000 people in 16 key seats and Labour would win only one. This would be Armageddon. The analogy with Rangers FC is obvious. A successful team, media-friendly owner and manager, well-known stars, but built on sand and when pressure is applied, everything falls apart. That is the reality of New Labour. No matter how energetic Murphy and Co. are, no one believes what he says. This project also has foundations of sand.

4 FEBRUARY: Met Tracy Murdoch of Kidzeko. She runs a social enterprise recycling baby clothes and equipment and trains young people to take classes for young mums and folk with mental health problems. She has two shops, in Bathgate and Livingston, and has done everything possible to keep the shops going but needs a little help with cash flow. We met with the Scottish Government to discuss the situation, but their response was dismal. There is no financial assistance for established social enterprises. I agreed to do all I could to assist and will look at all my contacts. We can't lose great projects like this.

Met with Unite and UCATT members at our lobby of parliament on the umbrella companies scam. This is the latest in a long line of tricks deployed by large construction companies to rip off workers. The employer acts as an agency who transfers the worker to an umbrella company where the worker has to pay for his own pay slip, as well as both employer and employee national insurance. They are paid the minimum wage and told to claim expenses to make up their wages. The Treasury loses huge amounts in tax via this scam. I compared these practices to employers in *The Ragged-Trousered Philanthropists* and *The Great Money Trick*. I attacked the employers and called on the UK and Scottish Governments to take immediate action on procurement. I hosted a meeting afterwards and the Scottish Government said they are doing everything they can, which is complete rubbish. They blame everything on Westminster, even though responsibility for contracts in Scotland is under their control.

Cara Hilton spoke well at the debate. She is a terrific speaker, and even right-wing Tory Alec Johnston condemned the use of umbrella companies.

5 FEBRUARY: Fallout from the polls is reverberating around the country. The SNP are cock-a-hoop. Apparently the Radical Independence Campaign are organising a march to demonstrate at Katy Clark's office, demanding

she is defeated at the election. A socialist woman who consistently votes against Trident, war, austerity, privatisation etc. but that doesn't matter to these people. They don't care about class issues – it's become all about nation and flags.

6 FEBRUARY: Good news today as the report from the standards and procedures committee on lobbying is positive – and the government now has to act. I was told Joe Fitzpatrick, the government's business manager, had all the lobbyists in the parliamentary bar buying them drinks to try and pacify them!

At FMQs today, Kez did well on the NHS. Sturgeon is quite clearly still struggling to find her feet.

7 FEBRUARY: And so to London with Fiona and my pals Jimmy and Kathleen for a few days break. We enjoyed a tour around the House of Commons, and were then shown the Lords. Who was there but none other than (Neil) Kinnock. My word, this is the same guy who used to sit with Skinner in the Commons during the Queen's Speech, protesting at the illegitimacy of the Lords. Now he sits there in ermine, picking up his £300 a day attendance allowance and fully aboard the gravy train. I always disliked Kinnock but nevertheless worked my arse off to get him elected.

Had a lovely dinner and a few beers at a restaurant in Covent Garden.

8 FEBRUARY: University of London for a Left Platform meeting. John McDonnell brought together people from across the left to discuss tactics and campaigns that we could prioritise should there be a Labour victory or a coalition. Over 100 people there including Michael Meacher MP, Jeremy Corbyn MP, Mick Cash RMT, Richard Murphy tax advisor and Professor Prim Sikka, an economist. A wide range of contributions were made by serious people. I spoke about the situation in Scotland post-referendum and the problems we face. People listened with interest.

Afterwards I met up with Fiona, Jimmy and Kate at Camden Market, which is a fantastic vibrant, buzzing place. We later saw The Commitments at the theatre.

Got a text from Murphy to say I was the only Shadow Cabinet member who hadn't submitted his campaign plan for this week. I told him I was on holiday and will advise him in due course. He clearly thinks I don't want to work for him. He is of course wrong, as I always put my heart and soul into the Labour Party whoever the leader is, but he simply wants to exert his authority and is watching my every move. He even has someone monitoring how many tweets I send!

9 FEBRUARY: Home from London to over 200 emails. Got a call from Kevin McKenna of the *Guardian*. He is a (former Labour) Nationalist Yes supporter, and he was interested in my miners' justice campaign. He thinks Sturgeon is left wing, and might support a review of the convictions. I think he must be on something if he thinks this but I will write to her and make the case again.

10 FEBRUARY: At West Lothian College for the opening of the new skills centre. It is an excellent initiative which will train more engineers, joiners, painters etc.

Met local developers of the Heartlands project at the former Polkemmet Colliery to hear plans for retail and industrial development at the site, and the latest housing plans. I will try to signpost partners to them who may be able to bring jobs, houses and services to the area.

Today, Sturgeon went to London for an anti-austerity speech, demanding additional spending and saying she would cut less. More smoke and mirrors. She is setting her stall out for a coalition with Labour and says she won't deal with the Tories. She wants a 'confidence and supply' deal with Labour – the party she hates so much and wants to destroy.

12 FEBRUARY: Met Tracy Murdoch of Kidzeco social enterprise, which works with mums and dads on parenting, play and children's wellbeing. It is a brilliant project. She has taken on a new property but has had major problems with the landlord. So I went along to his office unannounced and refused to leave until we had resolved the situation. Thankfully we managed to get it sorted out.

13 FEBRUARY: Met a constituent who has terminal cancer – very moving to hear her talk about her experiences of the NHS. Some of it excellent, other parts a bit chaotic. I will do all I can to support her and her family.

Big fall out from PMQs today with Miliband calling Lord Fink 'dodgy' because of his tax dealings. He is right, these folks are tax dodging on an industrial scale.

14 FEBRUARY: Morning door knock in West Calder before heading up to Fauldhouse for United's Scottish Cup last-16 match against Musselburgh. Really good crowd and great set up at Park View. Musselburgh won, but it was a good match.

TV reports that the film *50 Shades of Grey* is being released for Valentine's Day. We now have lots of middle class professionals and academics debating the cultural, political and sociological meaning and consequences of it. They assume people are completely stupid and don't realise it's just a very poor book (apparently) and will probably be a poorer film. You don't need a PhD in sociology to realise that. There are reports that B&Q have been giving staff tips and advice on the sale of gaffer tape and cable ties. Tory members of the House of Lords seem to be getting far too excited!

Today the Tories are saying that people who are overweight and on benefits will lose their entitlement if they don't lose weight. I look forward to Eric Pickles, Nicolas Soames and Kenneth Clarke arguing that policy on Question Time!

16 FEBRUARY: Shadow Cabinet meeting at Glasgow City Council, and Murphy reports they are engaging legendary US pollster Stan Greenberg to do more focus groups and polling – and it's costing fortunes. They continue to focus on the NHS but this is not landing a blow on the SNP. Blair McDougall spoke about the positive response on our workers' rights and fairness agenda. I have been urging them for months to focus on this stuff. It's a no brainer.

I got an email from Jimmy Gordon, a friend from Bathgate, about Murphy's tactics. He was scathing about him wearing the Scotland top after being elected and about him jumping on every bandwagon going, not to mention his cynical use of the media and false patriotism. If this is how Yes-voting Labour folk think then the election will be a major car crash – like we have never seen before.

In the 35–44 age group, polling shows we are 35 per cent behind the Nats.

Gordon Mathieson was then wheeled out to speak about the achievements in Glasgow and the success of the council. He is a gallus, proud Glaswegian and promotes the city whenever he can but he is clearly being pushed by Murphy as an MSP candidate for 2016.

During discussions, Jenny Marra, a Murphy ally, said she was against the alcohol at football policy. As health spokesperson, she clearly hadn't been consulted. Murphy said, 'Well, it's now policy so move on!' No debate, no discussion – awful. He said that because young working class men don't like us we had to do something. So the answer apparently is to get them all bevvied at the fitba'! He hasn't a principled bone in his body. This is the type of politics people are rejecting.

I emailed him about making an announcement on the miners' justice campaign – no reply yet.

Met with my old West Lothian Council pals Paddy McLaughlin, Alex McGuire and Martin Armstrong at the Glasgow Housing Association, where they now run the organisation. They have turned it around from a failing basket case to a successful and progressive entity. I was there to discuss their apprenticeship programme and other things.

Over to Glasgow East to campaign for Margaret Curran. I have no time for her. She conspired against Johann Lamont, said she wouldn't get involved in the leadership election, then came out for Murphy. She can't even look at me now, which is good. During our door knocking, pensioners were sticking with Labour but the rest weren't. The bold Margaret will soon be looking for another job I suspect.

17 FEBRUARY: Got a call from Tam Dalyell about the proposed meeting with Alicia Castro, the Argentine ambassador. He was on fine form and was scathing about the way the Scottish party is run, as well as its policy announcements, which appear to be coming out every five minutes. For the first time since 1964, he will not donate cash to the UK or Scottish campaigns, but will donate to local candidates. I love talking to Tam – he is clever, sharp, contrary and totally principled. A great man and everything you would want in a parliamentarian.

A journalist called advising that the POA, who had been threatening to go on strike, had been offered £2k per member to prevent it. This has been offered to officers only and NOT backroom staff. It is dressed up as 'professionalization' of the service. This amounts to a seven per cent increase. Good for them, but what are the other public service unions getting? What are PCS, Unite, GMB and UNISON getting – one per cent? Those who accept have to agree not to strike for two years. Hat's off to the POA for securing this deal but it's at a cost, regardless of how it's dressed up. It's a no strike deal and makes a mockery of public sector pay policy. I raised this at the Labour trade union group tonight.

20 FEBRUARY: When I got home after work, I cooked for the first time in

ages – made a paneer curry and homemade chapattis. Best thing I've made in a long time. Nice evening in with Fiona and Chloe.

21 FEBRUARY: Shettleston St Joseph's Church for a Labour event with Yes voters. Murphy and Margaret Curran trying to push the message that the referendum was last year's disagreement and that we should now agree to get rid of the Tories and only Labour can do this. This is fair enough but it is making no inroads.

23 FEBRUARY: The Channel 4 show Dispatches has snared Malcolm Rifkind and Jack Straw in a lobbying sting. There is now a press feeding frenzy as both said they could make speeches or get access to people for cash. Rifkind said he couldn't live on £650k per year and Straw said his speeches start at £5k a time. This is absolutely sickening when there are people out there trying to survive on £6.50 an hour, and queues at food banks lengthen by the day. No wonder people are cynical about politics.

24 FEBRUARY: Scottish Parliament petitions committee. Dr Neil McGuire for the Medicines and Healthcare Regulatory Authority (MHRA) gave evidence on mesh – and he was woeful. Despite all the evidence, he is still claiming the benefits outweigh the risks of mesh being implanted. There was a big turnout from the mesh survivors group. When I asked if he would allow his wife to be implanted by mesh, he said he would ensure a big list of things were in place beforehand and waffled on and on. Totally unconvincing and arrogant.

Adam Slater, an American attorney, was blistering in his evidence. Two million people worldwide have been fitted with mesh. Hundreds of thousands of lawsuits are waiting to be heard in court. He described mesh as a social cancer like asbestos (deemed a super product at first but with disastrous health consequences). He said the mesh industry was riddled with conflicts of interest and he had internal documents from companies showing serious malpractice. His evidence was explosive.

Rifkind has resigned as chair of the House of Commons security committee today and won't be a candidate at the election. Straw has had the whip withdrawn. Idiots. Two former foreign secretaries with over 60 years' experience between them in parliament getting themselves involved in a lobbying sting. Unbelievable. This is exactly the type of case that feeds public cynicism of the political process and the belief that all politicians are on the take. This is why we need a lobbying register.

25 FEBRUARY: Met again with Dr Jane Hamilton and her friend. Jane, a respected psychologist, has effectively been sacked by the NHS after a long period of suspension. She was suspended for raising concerns about dangerous practices and poor levels of service within the National Centre of Excellence for Perinatal Mental Health at St John's Hospital, Livingston. She says people have died and been badly injured because of poor service and bad management. She tried numerous times to raise concerns with management but was bullied, belittled and had her professionalism questioned. This is someone I find credible and who prior to this had an unblemished record in the NHS. After five years of suspension on full pay, she has now been told she has to accept a financial package and leave. She doesn't want to go and money is not the motivation. She wants her name cleared and the service made safe with all serious incidents investigated. There has been a review of the service but this was done by friends of the management and is seen by many staff as a whitewash. Each complaint she has made and the serious incidents she reported have not been fully investigated. It's clear we need a powerful, fully independent health care regulator with real powers and real teeth. At the moment anyone who raises concerns against the NHS is singled out, marginalised, has their professionalism questioned and is manoeuvred out the door.

At Justice Questions today I asked the new Minister Michael Matheson if he would hold an inquiry into the miners' strike and the miscarriages of justice related to it. Matheson parrots the line that McAskill gave – individuals should complain to the Scottish Criminal Cases Review Commission. The reality is they don't want to do anything to right these wrongs.

26 FEBRUARY: Dr Jane Hamilton has now been paid off and none of the issues raised have been addressed. There is still a poor culture in the NHS around whistleblowers, inadequate training for staff and many other related problems remain. She is adamant people have died because of these failings, and I believe her. This won't go away – neither Jane nor I will let it. It is too important.

27 FEBRUARY: I brought together the developers of the Heartlands project at Whitburn and the Wheatley Partnership, a social housing group, to discuss the potential for social housing on their site. We badly need more housing for rent in West Lothian and there is a possibility the abundance of land at Whitburn could be used for new homes for rent. A deal could be done to bring more much-needed social housing to the area. Fingers crossed.

To Blackburn leafleting with Graeme Morrice. It was good to be back in Ladeside Road where my Aunty Mary stayed and in the park where I played as a kid. The flats we stayed in are gone but I still have great memories and a real attachment to the place.

To Bathgate for my school reunion – 30 years after we left St Kent's. We met in David Stein's pub in Bathgate. David was one of my badminton partners and a pal at school. He now runs a bar and a couple of family butchers shops. Some of the folk I hadn't seen for decades but I still recognised them all. It was great fun meeting them again.

28 FEBRUARY: Great news today as my sister-in-law Gail had a baby – he is called Leo. This is her first child at the age of 44. Her and Louis have gone through a lot but this is fantastic news – a genuine miracle. Louis isn't a man who gives much away but he is the proudest dad I have ever seen – good on him. Great day!

29 FEBRUARY: In Glenrothes for Shadow Cabinet meeting. Murphy spoke about Clause IV, and will attempt to rush it through conference. He said he wanted me to talk to the unions to get behind it. He asked what I thought about it and wasn't happy when I said I wasn't 'exactly bursting with enthusiasm for it', and was sure some would oppose it. He then said he *wanted* us to be enthusiastic and show our support. I won't but will just stay quiet as there are things to die in a ditch for, but this is such bollocks and it's not worth it. No one really cares. Afterwards, as we were having a cup of tea and a sandwich, Murphy said very loudly, and in front of all colleagues, that UNISON Labour Link had voted against the new Clause IV, and that he wanted *me* to speak in support of the change and reference to 'patriotism' at the coming one-day conference. I said, 'Sorry I don't believe in it. I think it's unnecessary and divisive.' Looking me straight in the eye, he said, 'I am now asking you to speak in favour.' I looked him in the eye and replied, 'I wouldn't ask you to do something you didn't want to, so don't ask me to do the same!' He replied, 'Yes you would, it's called leadership! I need you to do it.'

I said, 'I can't and won't.' He was seething, and clearly expected me to roll over in front of everyone.

Jim won't let this lie, but how could I go out there and sell my soul for such nonsense? If the boot was on the other foot he would be nowhere to be seen. Over the last two years the Labour left fought nationalism, taking stick from the pro-Indy left in very tough community and trade union meetings throughout the country. We argued for economic solidarity and redistribution, common social and cultural class bonds and the need for a unified trade union movement across the UK. And now Murphy, one of the central characters in the Better Together fiasco, wants me to bail him out of his Clause IV mess, all because he ignored the advice of senior members in the Shadow Cabinet and senior members of the party's executive committee.

On the way home from campaigning in Fife, I took a beautiful photo of the winding wheel at the old Frances Colliery – tomorrow is the 30th anniversary of the miners' strike.

3 MARCH: Hugh Henry told me that CLPs in his region who generally support Jim don't like his Clause IV proposal. He said I was right not to speak in favour of it.

4 MARCH: Morning leafleting session in Fauldhouse. Freezing and feeling awful so home and straight to bed. A few minutes later Hugh Henry phoned to say Murphy had asked HIM to speak at conference in favour of his Clause IV. Hugh said his own CLP was opposed just as he was opposed and that he wouldn't do it. Good on him.

Ashcroft polls have the SNP on 53 seats, Labour one (Murphy by one per cent), Lib Dem one and Tory one. This is cataclysmic. I'm beginning to feel that every time Murphy appears on TV, every comment he gives or photo taken loses us more and more votes. When I ask people I know for an opinion on him, they say he is false, insincere, lacking in any substance and hasn't a principled bone in his body. Scotland is heading towards a one-party state!

Chloe started her second occupational therapy placement at the Royal Edinburgh Hospital dealing with people with acute mental health problems, schizophrenia, depression etc. She is loving it and taking it all in her stride. I am so proud of her attitude and quiet confidence.

5 MARCH: Met with a rep from Whitburn Community Development Trust frustrated at the lack of progress on town centre funding. Whitburn is a town of around 10,000 folk, many Glasgow overspill people who arrived in the '60s and '70s to work at British Leyland, Polkemmet pit, Levi's and Plessey. The town has a number of prominent abandoned or burnt out buildings, like the old Labour club, miners' welfare, British Legion etc. It badly needs a lift and investment in the main street. Many initiatives have

come to little but the latest is a community consultation called a 'charrette'. These type of things have been done time and again and bugger all happens. MSP Fiona Hyslop has an office in the town but has done nothing to move things forward. I will write to the council to find out what's happening with town centre budgets.

Met with Prison Officers Association chief Steve Gillan to discuss the no-strike deal. We had a friendly, frank and open chat. It appears that inter-union rivalry between the POA and PCS in the prison service is causing bad blood. He rejected the claim that it's a no-strike agreement, so we agreed to disagree.

Jackie Baillie led for us in today's debate on the economy. Swinney tried his best 'Honest John' routine, never mentioning corporation tax once. This was a central pledge of their economic case for independence, but not one of their MSPs mentioned it. In my speech I went for Swinney and Mark McDonald and have never seen Swinney so angry – he was mouthing a very clear expletive at me across the chamber! He likes to dish it out but can't take it back. McDonald is just a sycophant.

Tonight I was invited to the newspaper editor's event. Salmond was there. He has just entered into an agreement with Rupert Murdoch for his book – Harper Collins will publish and *The Sun* will serialise it. The editors who spoke don't think the election result will be as bad for Labour as the polls suggest but I'm not so sure. I fear the worst.

A strange thing happened at the event. I was one of the only Labour MSPs there and stood over at the right hand side of the room, watching proceedings. Salmond was on the other side, 20 yards away, but by the time the editors' panel started answering questions, he had edged his way over and was on my shoulder almost breathing down my neck! It was really odd behaviour. I ignored him but he was clearly trying to intimidate me. I think it may have been his response to me criticising him for doing a deal with Murdoch. He is a strange man.

6 MARCH: 46 today – 40-chuffing-6! Where has my life gone? I don't feel any different from when I was 26 or 16; I still have the same mates, laugh at the same rubbish and live in the same place but I can't get my head round 46. I see Chloe and my nieces Eilidh and Millie growing up and I'm stunned at the speed of time. Clichéd I know, but also true.

Met adult learners from the Ladies of Livingston group. They were brilliant and I enjoyed talking to them. These are women who for various reasons such as bringing up a family, having a poor school or family experience missed out on education but are now involved in learning through the local community centre. They have completed a community health course and are growing in confidence and taking a real interest in local issues and politics. We had a great debate and discussion on a whole range of issues. I told them about my return to education via evening classes, college and then university. I hope I have encouraged them to keep up their interest.

7 MARCH: Edinburgh International Conference Centre for Scottish Labour one-day conference. This is a crucial event as we are only two months from the election. The big issue is Murphy's Clause IV. Unite and UNISON are allegedly voting against and GMB may abstain. All week the leadership has been nervous, thinking they might lose. They won't because they never do – if necessary they will manipulate the debate to secure their victory. I went in for the debate and sat at the back of the hall. Jamie Glackin, the party chairman, duly obliged calling eight people in favour of Murphy's Clause IV, including the Community Union (shock horror), Bill Butler (he was clearly approached by Murphy to do this when Hugh and I refused), Davie (I am on a journey) Hamilton (how many journey's has Davie been on?), and the patriotic Anne McGuire. Vince Mills spoke against for Unite and was excellent, speaking about class not nation and quoting Keir Hardie on patriotism. It was easily the best and most substantial speech in the debate. I couldn't help but recall the 1994 Clause IV debate. Then, Jim Devine chaired superbly, calling 18 in favour of change and 17 against. All the serious players took part, it was electric and Blair's Clause IV was carried by a small majority with UNISON abstaining. Today's debate was a whimper by comparison, but we are all patriots now apparently.

Miliband's speech was okay but he doesn't excite or inspire. Some of the policy stuff is good, for example the living wage, zero hours and taxation policy, but he just can't connect with people.

Murphy's speech was impressive. He made new announcements about no tuition fees and £1,600 for all young people not in education or on an apprenticeship. Good policies, but the problem is he lacks authenticity. If you haven't mentioned nationalising the railways or redistribution for the last 20 years, then suddenly it's all you talk about, it's no surprise when no one believes you.

9 MARCH: Motherwell Shadow Cabinet meeting. General view is the conference was good and there were positives to build on. McTernan gave a presentation on the feedback from yet more focus groups. People are

telling them they think the parliament has done its job, protecting Scotland from the Tories. They want Labour to connect with them on Labour values. They want us to tell them how we will make life better for them and their families. They want credible people to put across our message and will use the phrase 'Scotland succeeds when working families succeed'.

We got a briefing from MP Frank Roy. He took 61 per cent of the vote in 2010 but his area voted Yes in the referendum and he's a worried man. We went canvassing in Craigneuk and time and again people raised Labour's Better Together pact with the Tories as the reason for their desertion. This is in the street that overlooked Ravenscraig – no wonder they are scathing.

10 MARCH: Leaflet run done by 7am then to the Dogs Trust at West Calder for a visit. They look after all sorts of abandoned dogs. They never put down a healthy animal and keep them for years if necessary. Great facilities and great staff.

I missed the Labour group today but apparently McTernan gave a presentation and took questions and when asked about Miliband's unpopularity and how it was coming up on the doorstep he said Miliband was very popular and his policies were hugely successful. When someone asked a similar question he refused to discuss it further. This guy is unbelievable – Labour members pay his wages but he thinks he can do and say whatever he likes to whoever he likes.

Hugh Henry said that Murphy is planning to open up the list process. This will be to get his pals in who lose their seats at the General Election. All the so called 'A team'!

11 MARCH: GERS figures out today show how Scotland would lose heavily with full fiscal autonomy. This would be devastating for the funding of public services. The STUC described it as 'a sobering reminder of the consequences of ending the Barnett formula'. UK-wide redistribution is central to creating a fairer society.

Received a phone call from a film company who had read my report into the miners' convictions. They are keen to make a film about someone seeking justice and overturning their conviction. I spoke to Bruce Shields at Thompson's Solicitors, but he was lying on the floor at the time with a bad back. He wants to help and I asked them to consider Alex Bennett's case.

Took part in economy debate. John Swinney did verbal and economic gymnastics to try and prove that a massive public spending deficit under

FFA is actually good news. In a throwaway line Swinney casually said the gap would be filled by increasing exports by 50 per cent. Just like that! Now why hasn't anyone else thought of that? Do folk really swallow this stuff? 50 per cent, really? Gil Paterson took to lying to defend his position, saying it was Labour who wanted to end the Barnett formula.

Tommy off today with the lurgy – everyone seems to have it. Awaiting my turn.

Got a PQ reply on blacklisting. Keith Brown now trying to say they cannot determine whether the companies involved now are the same legal entities as those who blacklisted in the first place. This is yet another attempt to wriggle out of doing anything. The rhetoric from government and their actions are miles apart. They really are duplicitous on this.

12 MARCH: Met with blacklisted sparks Stuart Merchant and Francie Graham, along with Jackson Cullinane from Unite. Both lads are real characters who have been working together for years, but have been denied work on numerous jobs because they were trade unionists. They are unhappy at the way the SNP have been dealing with blacklisting. Guidance issued to contractors is a waste of paper and is being ignored as blacklisting companies have secured contracts on the new Victoria & Albert, in Dundee, the Aberdeen by-pass and a Dumfries hospital. I will pursue these issues for them.

At FMQs, Kez led on the GERS figures and the black hole it would leave in Scotland's finances. Knowing she was on a hiding to nothing, Sturgeon reverted to 'Labour talking Scotland down' – utterly pathetic!

To Whitburn Labour Party to talk about the situation post-leadership election and where we go from here with preparations for the election. Apparently some SNP branches are getting 150 at a meeting. We had seven people there. That's the challenge we face.

13 MARCH: After work, Fiona and I went to see *The Slab Boys*. Brilliant play by John Byrne – working class humour that reflects real life. Right up my street.

14 MARCH: To Ferguslie Park, Paisley where I was asked to launch big Jim Sheridan's campaign. Jim is a solid working-class MP, a former printer and councillor and chair of the Unite group of MPs. He doesn't like Murphy

and nominated me in the leadership election. He should win his seat in Renfrewshire by a large majority but won't as it's in an area that returned a big Yes vote in the referendum. We did some canvassing then I gave a short speech to his team to try to gee them up. Good bunch of folk.

16 MARCH: To Rugby Park, home of Kilmarnock FC, for a Shadow Cabinet meeting. Jim insisted Ed Miliband will rule out a coalition with the SNP because they want to end the Barnett formula, and that we need constitutional stability.

Long discussion on election issues – people raised food banks, care tax, childcare, social care, NHS etc. Murphy said he had £100 million in his spending plans to allocate and was looking for ideas. He then said, 'This is the point that Ken (McIntosh) says spend it on ending the care tax, and Neil (Findlay) says spend it on social care. But we won't be spending it on either as it makes no impact on the focus groups, so we won't do it!' Well, if ever you wanted evidence of the complete lack of principle or conviction there it was. It's not about doing what is right by people. If I hear about focus groups one more time I will scream. There is no politics, just cynical misguided opportunism.

I raised a point about being asked to do election hustings, and asked why MSPs were expected to attend when it was a UK election. I said all hustings should be covered by MPs. I mentioned a request from the Lanarkshire *Morning Star* group to do one. Murphy said there was no point in doing such a meeting as there were no votes in it for us. If there are no votes for us at a *Morning Star* meeting then we are well and truly done for. When he said that, Cathy Jamieson and I looked at each other gobsmacked. There may not be many votes in it but there will be NONE if we leave an empty chair. I can't stand this much longer.

Murphy also said they were holding a low-pay summit that I have to chair – no discussion with me beforehand. Why do they do this? It is of course deliberate.

Miliband ruled out teaming up with the SNP, despite Sturgeon saying she wants an anti-Tory coalition, while urging a vote for the Greens in England. This is the woman who said she wants to end air passenger duty, has missed climate change targets and will build motorways between our cities!

Hilary Wainwright wanted to discuss the role of the left in a Labour-led Government. She believes Plaid Cymru, the SNP and Greens were all on the left and that Labour should work with them. She is typical of many on the English left who have bought this 'SNP are socialist' crap. I urged her to look beyond the rhetoric to the reality.

17 MARCH: Today, Rachel Reeves, the Shadow Work and Pensions Secretary said, 'Labour is not the party of welfare, we don't want to be the party of the unemployed, we want to be the party of working people.' Well of course we are the party of workers but we are also the party of people who can't work for whatever reason and we can't just abandon them. We should be the party that supports all people to live fulfilling lives; the party that helps people make a contribution to society. Is she saying we give up on people like my brother who, because he has MS, can't work? I hope not but that's how it came across. Who is advising these folk? How can we expect to win back people in our poorest communities? This will be thrown back at us during the election. I told Murphy of my displeasure, but he advised we say nothing as it will be seen as a split. Wait for it, but Rachel Reeves is coming to Scotland to campaign next week. Ah, the timing. She will go down like a bag of vomit if indeed anyone knows who she is. Highly likely Sean Clerkin and his militia will be there shouting 'witty banter' in her face.

18 MARCH: Morning spell campaigning in new housing scheme in Armadale. The place is really expanding with all the new builds. Met Archie Meikle from Ashwood Construction to discuss apprenticeships, the economic outlook and all things building trade. His company has a good employment ethos and have put some of their profits into a trust to disburse. He also sponsors kids affected by the Chernobyl disaster.

Visited the Sky academy at Livingston. Sky is a huge local employer and has set up an academy to give pupils experience of making a TV programme and working in the sector. Kay Burley showed us round the facility, which is an amazing asset. I dislike all Murdoch stands for, and don't have Sky TV in the house, but couldn't help be impressed by their set up.

To parliament to take part in Green debate calling for a £10 per hour minimum wage. Alison Johnston spoke for them – she is a decent, straight forward person but because there are only two of them, they get away with a lot. In the debate, Roseanna Cunningham came away with the usual guff 'we really want to increase wages and improve people's terms and conditions and if only we had the powers we would do so.' In debate, I pointed out Labour had cut in-work poverty by 10 per cent and absolute poverty by 40 per cent when we were in power in Scotland, whereas under the SNP it is increasing. The SNP have no redistributive policies, yet always blame others for poverty increasing. Patrick Harvie summed up for the Greens – he is a very able, prickly politician but often too sanctimonious and pious for his own good. He had a go at the failing of past Labour Governments through selective use of facts and figures and did not like it when I asked him to name anything the Greens have done in their history. The reality is they have achieved little or nothing. In Brighton, where they run the council, their great success is a long-running strike by binmen whose wages they slashed.

After the debate, there was members' business on the issue of racial discrimination, which gave everyone an opportunity to have a go at UKIP MEP David Coburg, who at the weekend referred to the SNPs Humza Yousaf as Abu Hamza, the convicted extremist preacher. Coburg is a dangerous fool who will say things like this to draw attention to himself. I despise UKIP and their false, man-down-the-pub act, which tries to disguise their far right, ultra-Thatcherite crap. They would privatise the NHS, end the welfare state, scrap the minimum wage, ban trade unions and send kids up chimneys in a heartbeat. I pray to God Farage doesn't get elected.

19 MARCH: To FMQs where Kez questioned Sturgeon on the GERS figures and the plummeting oil revenues. Finally Sturgeon admitted the SNPs oil forecasts were wrong – progress at last. But she also predictably flung back the Rachel Reeves and Ed Balls' quotes that there was nothing in Osborne's budget he would reverse. My Lord – nothing in a Tory budget to reverse. What the hell is going on? Ruth Davidson had a good line – calling out Sturgeon for demanding tax cuts for the oil industry in Scotland and a vote for the Greens in England!

20 MARCH: To the Govan Law Centre to meet Mike Dailly with my constituents Mr and Mrs Waddell. They have suffered 17 years of torture because their house was built on land the builder didn't own. There were conveyancing errors and a failure by lawyers to sort things out. The result is they have no effective title on their property (nor do many neighbours). They have been threatened with eviction, suffered years of legal wrangles and appear no further forward. As a couple, they have shown amazing tenacity and resilience. I'm determined to get a result for them.

Mike was very helpful – he is the chief solicitor at the law centre, which helps poor and vulnerable people with housing, consumer and other advice and representation. They do great work and Mike is one of those anti-establishment lawyers who likes to take on the big guys on behalf of ordinary people. We will write to the Minister and the Law Society seeking meetings and threatening to bring forward members' legislation to ensure this doesn't happen to anyone else. However, this won't help the Waddells. We need to meet the Law Society to try and pursue their case to conclusion.

21 MARCH: To Broxburn Chapel for my Uncle Pat's funeral. He was 91 and lived his last years as a blind double amputee due to diabetes. Right to the end he was cheerful, chatty and in great spirits. My cousin Pat, who is a mad, brilliant, eccentric priest, took care of the service. He does all our family services, my wedding, Chloe's christening and my da's funeral. He spoke about Pat's life in the army during the war, his work in the shale industry; at BP in Grangemouth and his love of dancing and family life. I did one of the readings and was very nervous. Had it been a speech I would have been fine, but it's amazing that something as simple as reading in strange surroundings has that impact.

22 MARCH: To Blackburn for leafleting. Afterwards, I watched *The Andrew Marr Show*, and Salmond said, 'he will write the first Labour budget!' I think he has completely lost the plot!

Today the *Sunday Mail* went big on zero hours contracts. When is Murphy going to launch the Charter of Workers' Rights I have been developing? It's a gift for us. Why the wait?

23 MARCH: James Kelly phoned to urge me to go to Clydebank Town Hall for the Miliband event. I would have preferred to stay and help in Armadale at the by-election with our candidate Andrew McGuire but agreed to go. Miliband dismissed Salmond's budget claim saying, 'I think he has a book to sell.' Not Miliband's biggest fan after the way he behaved with Johann etc. but he set out his case well – fairness, bankers' bonus tax, 50p rate, mansion tax, etc. He appeared with the local MP Jemma Doyle who is defending a 17,000 majority, but she won't win, of that I'm certain. I couldn't help notice Murphy's hair has changed colour – he must have binned the dye! Noticing this reminded me of something someone sent me just after the leadership election. It was an article from a newspaper in which the columnist said he wouldn't vote for any of the three candidates as 'they all died their hair, were all vegetarians and all teetotal!' Well I can't speak for Sarah but what I can say is he was way wide of the mark on all three counts when it comes to me – teetotal indeed!

24 MARCH: Disturbed to learn that a German plane crashed over the Alps killing all 150 on board. I'm always worried by air crashes given my sister's job as a stewardess. She loves her job and travels all over the world and hasn't had any major scares but after 30 years it still terrifies me.

Salmond says he is going to stop the Tories running a minority government. He was interviewed by the *New Statesman* and agreed to the interview only if they provided a bottle of pink champagne. His ego is running riot.

25 MARCH: Spoke to David Kelly about his review into social care. He is really frustrated at the lack of support from the Labour Party since I was moved from the health portfolio. I was speechless. Social care is the biggest issue in health care at the moment and David was at the forefront of developing West Lothian's ground-breaking approach to it and yet there is a reluctance to help him develop new policy in case it recommends tax rises!

26 MARCH: Into the chamber and asked Shona Robison a question about Dr Jane Hamilton, the sacked psychologist. Robison turned the question into a personnel issue rather than the whistleblowing and safety matter it is. The service she worked in has huge problems with poor training, management failure, several major incidents etc. We also need to look at how concerns in the NHS are dealt with. Too many who raise these concerns and go public are victimised, brow beaten and often hounded out of the job. I will need to put my thoughts into how we address this. Jane Hamilton has applied for several jobs in Scotland, many of which do not get filled because of a lack of psychologists, and each time she is refused or the job gets withdrawn – shocking stuff. Prior to recent events she had enjoyed an unblemished career spanning decades.

To Armadale St Anthony's Club to help with the by-election. A good turnout of party members to help out in the snow this morning, and while it cleared up later, it was sunny and freezing. We worked the doors all day. It is safe to say the flourishing of Scottish democracy after the referendum has not quite reached Armadale and Blackbridge as only 30 per cent turned out to vote. After the polls closed we went for a few beers to reflect on a campaign that had an excellent candidate, and a large number of people involved. We couldn't have done much more.

27 MARCH: To Howden Park Centre for the by-election count. On the first count, the SNP took 42 per cent and Labour 27 per cent. It was an STV count and took ages. Eventually the SNP got over the quota – 50 per cent to Labour's 42. I was gutted for Andrew, who should be proud of his efforts. His time will come.

28 MARCH: At the SNP conference, Sturgeon said the SNP will give Labour some spine, which is remarkable given not one of her MPs or MSPs has anything more than the backbone of a jellyfish. None of them stand up to

her, and not one has an independent voice or thought. None of them have broken the whip on any issue of substance in parliament since 2007.

29 MARCH: John Swinney says the SNP will agree to a 50p tax rate. Last week they said there would be no tax rises but this with full fiscal autonomy will impact on 16,000 Scottish taxpayers. Across the UK it will be 300,000 people and we will get a share of the money via Barnett if it were to remain.

31 MARCH: At last, the Charter of Worker's Rights is launched! It's a positive policy and set of proposals on issues such as zero hours' contracts, agency working, health and safety, blacklisting, apprenticeships, tribunal fees etc. – all very relevant to working people. It's something we can sell to trade unions and their members if we shout loud enough and sell it properly, but the reality is Murphy and McTernan don't believe in any of this stuff and will play much of it down.

2 APRIL: To parliament for the launch of Richard Simpson's alcohol bill. I like Richard, he's a sincere and consistent right-winger who was in the SDP, but he is a very straight person to deal with. He was a GP and psychiatrist working with people with drug and alcohol dependency and is a genuine caring person. He knows everything there is to know about the NHS and has brilliant connections throughout. He was really helpful and supportive when I did the Shadow Health job despite the reservations he would have had about my politics, which are different from his. He is just back after recovering from cancer of the oesophagus and is looking much better. His bill aims to introduce a wide range of measures to address alcohol-related issues.

At First Minister's Questions Kez led on full fiscal autonomy. Sturgeon is wriggling like a snake on this. It would mean a £7.6 billion black hole in Scotland's budget. All credible commentators see it is mad but as with everything else the SNP simply say black is white and white is black.

I asked Sturgeon to distance herself from the vile online abuse that is flying around but of course she just turned it on Labour and is completely unwilling to lead on this when she could have influence. Of course, after FMQs I was bombarded by yet more abuse from the cybernats. They demanded I condemn some idiot who tweeted about wanting Sturgeon hanged – of course I condemn such appalling behaviour, these folk are crazy. But what gets me is the belief that sending an email or tweeting abuse is somehow political activism. A lot of the new found army of keyboard warriors have never been involved in community activism, never volunteered for a local voluntary group, a community council, been on a picket line, supported people in struggle yet they now have the audacity to question the commitment and efforts of people who have been involved in their local communities for decades.

Leaders' election debate tonight. It wasn't as big a rabble as it could've been. Cameron was rubbish and posted missing; he said little of any substance and was pretty anonymous. Miliband did quite well. Sturgeon came across well because she was largely unchallenged on many of her sweeping assertions. The rest don't know what her government have and have not been up to; like the detail of the failing in our NHS, colleges etc. but she handles herself well in this format and is well briefed.

3 APRIL: Went out to Bathgate tonight with pals for a few drinks. It was great to get away from politics and have a laugh and a catch up – simple pleasures in life are the best. Both my pals' daughters have signed up for a school holiday to Peru. Peru? Whatever happened to school camp at Aberfoyle? How do kids whose parents can barely buy them a uniform and give them dinner money feel when some kids are going to Peru? Schools really have to think this through and be more sensitive to the plight of poorer pupils.

4 APRIL: *The Telegraph* has published a story quoting a leaked UK Government memo of a meeting between the French Ambassador and Nicola Sturgeon, in which it says 'Miliband is not Prime Ministerial material and she would prefer Cameron.' Labour now saying this is evidence of the SNP leader saying one thing in public and another in private, secretly wanting a Tory Government. Well of course they want a Tory Government as this would be the best way to push for another referendum! Social media has exploded with these claims. The cybernats and keyboard warriors are foaming at the mouth, indignant that anyone would say anything about the blessed Nicola. Both Sturgeon and the French Consul have denied it, but there is something strange about this story.

5 APRIL: Easter Sunday and it's a beautiful day. Mass at Stoneyburn with Father Haluka then home to make dinner. All the family and extended family came – Mum, Anna and Jim, John and Sharron, Martin (Lynne, Eilidh and Millie are in Tenerife). Wee Leo was there (a four-week-old miracle) and Eleana, Eva and Chloe appeared after their work. A lovely lunch then played some of my old albums from the loft on my new turntable; Goodbye Mr McKenzie, The Jam, Echo and the Bunnymen, the

Dubliners, Johnny Cash, Donovan and many more. Simple pleasures.

I had an interesting conversation with my niece Eleana about the election. She confirmed what I thought, that none of her peers (except Tommy's daughter Caitlin) are listening to Labour, they will all vote SNP. We need to offer young people hope and an alternative to austerity, job insecurity and living standards lower than their parents experienced. Apart from this depressing chat it was a lovely day.

6 APRIL: Another gorgeous day. Fiona in the garden so I left her pottering around and went to Murieston to canvass. It was okay but there are a lot of 'don't knows' who I suspect are closet Tories. The rumour is the SNP believe they are so far ahead in Livingston they are pulling resources out and moving them elsewhere. Probably true and frightening.

The polls suggest 43 seats for the SNP and 11 for Labour. If this is accurate then this will be a huge moment for the Scottish party, however I fear it could be worse because I have tried to name the 11 seats we will win and can't get past three. If it's as bad as I suspect, we need to face up to some very big issues. Do we accept independence; push the Red Paper line on federalism and a second question in a future referendum; should we fold up the tent and start again with a new or relaunched party and a new constitution, new branding and most importantly policy agenda? Do we become a stand-alone Scottish Party? In short, what the hell do we do?

7 APRIL: Tony Blair intervened in the election today opposing an in-out referendum on the EU. Sturgeon has said the same. So she wants a new referendum on an in-out of the UK but not in-out of the EU. No effort to answer why she wants to leave a small union, where our biggest market and closest neighbours are but remain part of a bigger union with all its well documented anti-democratic practices and a much smaller market.

8 APRIL: Got copy of the new Red Paper publication to be launched and distributed at the STUC conference. Later I took a call from a journalist who told me John McTernan is on £84,000 per year. I would rather put 84 grand on Labour to win every seat in Scotland with a 20,000 majority than pay him a penny.

9 APRIL: Visited Maple Villa dementia care unit in Livingston with a constituent whose dad is a resident. Was shown round by a nurse and spoke to a number of staff, residents and family members. It is a lovely place, and looks after some very ill men. The staff are run ragged because

there aren't enough of them, so the care they can provide is not of the quality it should be. Staff are angry and frustrated and families of these poor men are distraught. They can't even get bank staff to cover as the work is so hard. This is the reality of front line care in our health and social care system. It's heartbreaking and makes me angry as the government are in denial.

10 APRIL: Met William Lumsden and Scott Corrigan from Greenburn Golf Club. They have an idea for developing a golf education project based on the life story and history of Tom Morris, who has connections to West Lothian. An interesting project.

12TH APRIL: Sunday Politics leaders' debate had Sturgeon, Murphy, Rennie and Davidson all shouting at each other – terrible.

Got a call to tell me Salmond has met INEOS and their boss Jim Ratcliffe around 12 times – twice at his home in Switzerland. They are clearly cutting a deal on fracking. I have an FOI in on this but the government are blocking it so we have appealed. We are definitely onto something.

14 APRIL: Spoke to Libby Brookes at the *Guardian* who was wondering if I knew what the hell was going on as Murphy has said no cuts needed after 2015/16, whereas Chuka Umunna has said, 'The leader of the Scottish Labour Party won't set UK policy and doesn't hold the budget.' The SNP are in raptures with 'branch office' quotes flying out of their press office. What a fiasco! The SNP are on 54 per cent. It is clear we are stuffed and may need to take a hiding and start from scratch.

To Bents for canvassing – best night of the entire campaign to date. Really cheered me up. Met lots of folk I knew who were saying they would vote Labour.

17 APRIL: To Tollcross Leisure Centre to launch Scottish Labour's General Election manifesto – such a surreal event. Jim Murphy gave one of the most left-wing, anti-austerity, pro-public services speeches from a Scottish Labour politician in 25 years. He spoke of class politics, ending poverty, no tuition fees (he was the NUS leader who got them to abandon opposition to tuition fees), ending zero-hours' contracts – he even mentioned socialism! Things he has rarely mentioned in his political career yet here he was spouting lines he would previously have slated as impractical, utopian and unelectable. We then had former jailed miner David Hamilton give a

passionate speech about the miners' strike, his father's zero hours contract and socialism again. It was stirring stuff – all we needed at the end was 'three cheers for international socialism!'

Melanie Ward, a 'New Labour ultra', then introduced Ed Miliband, who took questions from the usual plants. They must have been pinching themselves and thinking 'what the hell is going on, I never signed up for this socialism malarkey!' I did find the whole thing pretty funny. The issues now being pushed, many of them through sheer desperation, are issues the left has pursued for years and been opposed or ignored by the likes of Murphy and McTernan, and now being claimed as their policies. I couldn't help but think back to a conversation with Anne McKechin and others during the leadership elections, telling me that I must 'talk about business and reach out to the business community', as if I was oblivious to that. I wonder what she thinks today – Murphy never mentioned business once.

Journalists asked if I had written Murphy's speech! Now, that was funny.

Ashcroft Poll suggests Douglas Alexander and Murphy will lose their seats. We could end up with Ian Murray and Willie Bain as our only MPs – the revolution is safe in their hands! If this happens all bets are off and we move into uncharted territory. New leader? No money? Goodbye McTernan and the rest of Murphy's recruits; Kez comes in – no one else likely to stand. What will the unions do? How will the party react? What will the public reaction be?

18 APRIL: To Loganlea Miners' Welfare to commemorate the 30th anniversary of the miners' strike. The club was packed with a broad mix of people. Locals who always support our events, ex-miners and their families, Labour Party members who were active during the strike, organising food collections, soup kitchens, women's support groups and much more. The council have passed a motion to commemorate the anniversary. It was proposed by Councillor Angela Moohan whose husband Brendan was a miner at Bilston Glen and who was sacked during the strike. NUM President, Nicky Wilson spoke of the strike, its struggles, the laughs, support from the community and the role of women. I called for an inquiry into the miscarriages of justice experienced by Scottish miners.

Emma Peattie, the council's libraries and museums officer, put an appeal out to all who attended to take part in a memorial book she is compiling. I hope she gets support for it as it would be a terrific way to mark such a huge event in our area's history.

19 APRIL: Speculation today that Murphy has taken legal advice on

whether he can remain leader if he loses his seat. He is obviously worried.

20 APRIL: At the STUC conference where I met Stephen Smillie of UNISON, and a group of Kurds who are lobbying about their plight in Turkey and surrounding areas. Stephen has done some excellent work raising the profile of their cause.

The new Red Paper publication got a good show in today's *Herald*. We must get the Labour Party onto the federalism agenda. Maybe someone might listen if we get an electoral hammering.

In the afternoon Ed Miliband spoke. The STUC is a tough audience but he spoke well, with real passion. This was the best I've heard him and he received a standing ovation.

Later, we went to the Unite reception and enjoyed great music and a right old trade union sing song. The type of event to cheer you up in the middle of an election!

22 APRIL: Canvassing today – very good response. There seems to be a bit of a fall out in the local election camp so David Cleghorn has taken over. Good move as he is experienced, committed and knows what he is doing.

23 APRIL: To Clydebank Trades Council for a debate on workers' rights with Martin Doherty of the SNP. During the referendum, Clydebank was a tough place and at public meetings and debates a lot of aggressive nationalists abused speakers who argued for a 'No' vote. Richard Leonard and Anas Sarwar were subjected to horrendous anti-English and borderline racist taunts and heckling.

Doherty was confident but with poor debating points. He used that typical SNP style of 'Scotch couthieness' to try and curry favour with the audience. He spoke of 'when he went to the shipyard gates with his mother, he passed by men shaped by misogyny, only 10 of whom would give their pay packet to their wives. The rest would be pissed up against the wall in Connolly's Bar!' I attacked this outrageous statement where he characterised the thousands of shipyard workers as drunken women haters. Perhaps some did as he described but to write off all men of this town was appalling.

24 APRIL: To Livingston for the opening of the new Carers of West Lothian Centre. They are a brilliant organisation who help so many people who care for family and friends.

Then to Glasgow to eventually launch the workplace manifesto with

Murphy. We should have been campaigning on this months ago as it is real policies that will affect working people in a very positive way. The event was nothing more than a press launch so I stayed for a short while and left Jim and his cheerleaders to it.

25 APRIL: To Livingston for canvassing but didn't get a good response. I fear we will lose Livingston heavily.

26 APRIL: I watched Miliband and Boris Johnston on the *Marr* show this morning. Miliband was quite good – he was confident, passionate and answered all questions well; announcing three year tenancies with controls on rent increases – all good stuff. The Tories are attacking the policy saying it would be similar to the bombing of our cities during the war.

Then we had Boris playing up to his loveable buffoon crap. He really is the world's worst actor, so why can't people see through the bullshit? Miliband has him on toast over the issues of non doms and their tax status.

To Bathgate Chapel for my niece Millie's confirmation. It was a really nice service with Archbishop Cushley, who spoke very well and came across as a decent and down to earth man.

An opinion poll out today has Labour on one seat. What on earth is going on? I am trying to give a realistic prediction and want to say we will win five seats but each time I try to name them I can't.

27 APRIL: Spent all day in bed with sickness and upset stomach – felt awful. I don't get ill very often and am very, very rarely off work but when I get ill I am not a good patient and am best left to feel sorry for myself alone until I get better.

28 APRIL: To Bathgate Balbardie Park for International Workers Memorial Day event. Robert Mooney from the community union spoke on behalf of the STUC general council. I spoke on the issue of blacklisting and health and safety. A lot of local trade union activists were present. Of course, since there is an election on, the two SNP candidates appeared, despite having never been there previously.

I really am having difficulty fathoming our election strategy. It appears they are trying to present the situation as a straight choice between Jim or Nicola and no one else is to get a look in. No shadow spokespeople leading on key issues. This is McTernan's master strategy. So we have Sturgeon being mobbed in Sauchiehall Street like Elvis, while Murphy can't go to his local petrol station at one in the morning for a pint of milk without being called a 'Red Tory'. Yes, that sounds like a real masterstroke.

29 APRIL: In Parliament and bumped into a senior Shadow Cabinet member, who told me one poll out today had us on zero seats and 20 per cent of the vote. She looked absolutely shattered. There are daily battles within the party, especially with McTernan. Internal polling is grim.

I attended a demonstration against TTIP; around 800 people there, and then spoke in a debate on MS. Given what is going on in the party, I better get thinking about what I do after the election on 7 May.

30 APRIL: To the last FMQs before the election. All party leaders asked about a second referendum and falling literacy rates in schools. I then hosted a members' business debate on the living wage, which was pretty uneventful to be honest.

1 MAY: I didn't attend the last Labour election rally in Glasgow tonight but it appears Clerkin and a band of his crazy followers were there jostling women with children and young people going in. Kids were crying and it all got ugly with shouts of scum, traitors etc.

2 MAY: To Broxburn for final street stall – both Labour and SNP out in numbers.

My brother John's stag do tonight so out for a curry with his pals and then back to the pub for drinks – really good to see lots of his mates together for the first time in years.

3 MAY: To the miners' welfare for the annual fundraiser for Survivors of Bereavement and Suicide. Brilliant event with around 300 there to hear the cream of local talent. Raised around £5,000.

4 MAY: I didn't see the leaders' debate tonight but apparently Sturgeon said if a Labour budget didn't suit her she would vote it down. There you have it loud and clear. The SNP would vote with the Tories against a Labour budget!

Got a text from Alex Rowley asking me to meet Gordon Brown tomorrow when I am over in Fife campaigning for my mate Kenny Selbie, who is standing to succeed Gordon in Kirkcaldy. I wonder what it's all about.

Leafleting in Stoneyburn with Kevin Lindsay, who had just come from a canvass session in Livingston which was awful. I feel sorry for our candidate, Graeme Morrice, as he has been a diligent MP and was a good councillor for decades before that.

I see the 'Scottish Resistance' were out today in Glasgow giving Murphy and Eddie Izzard a hard time. Apparently they were tipped off by Sturgeon's press officer Campbell Gunn. I also hear the 'Resistance' leader is called Piers Doughty-Brown. Always thought revolutionaries and resistance leaders had names like Che, Fidel or Hugo. Piers Doughty-Brown disnae quite cut it I'm afraid!

5 MAY: To Kirkcaldy in the pouring rain to campaign for our candidate Kenny Selbie. Every time I go up to help I feel worse. Kenny is a top bloke and great candidate but you can sense the tide is rapidly going out and there is nothing we can do to prevent it but put on a brave face.

After canvassing Alex, Gordon and I went to the Parkland Hotel for a curry lunch and a very interesting and wide-ranging chat. I have only briefly spoken to Brown before and it was small talk but this was serious political discussion. He is worried about the election and the fall-out from it for Scotland and the UK. He wants to develop thinking on the future of the UK and the intellectual case for the UK remaining together and Labour to lead in Scotland. He wants us to attack poverty and inequality and argue for full employment and quite remarkably wants us to expose the failings of neo-liberalism. I just wish he had done that more when he and Blair were in power. He said he had to support Murphy for leader as he had previously been in his Shadow Cabinet (poor argument) but that he was all over the place on policy and couldn't carry a consistent message. He said he agreed with much (not all) of what I put forward in the leadership election but he now wanted me to work with people I might not usually work with. I gave as good as I got in the discussion and challenged him on a number of things, and urged him to use his contacts to help us rebuild the party. Reading between the lines, I think there was some coded language in there, but I might just need an enigma machine to crack what was being said.

6 MAY: At FMQS I asked Sturgeon about her relationship with INEOS, the company that wants to frack gas across the central belt. Sturgeon was uncomfortable with this and there is no doubt we have much more to come.

7 MAY: It's General Election day so I'm out leafleting very early in Broxburn, Seafield, Blackburn, Stoneyburn and Fauldhouse. Huge effort put in all day and there is a high turnout in good weather.

Afterwards we went for our traditional 'close of poll' pint in Bathgate before heading to Balbardie Sports Centre for the count. As the boxes were opened the scale of our defeat was immediately apparent. We won the East Calder box, drew in Fauldhouse, and lost every other box in the Livingston constituency. Seat after seat fell across Scotland. Kenny lost Kirkcaldy by 10 per cent on a 35 per cent swing against us. The dominoes started to topple. Danny Alexander, Ian Davidson, Jim Sheridan, Katy Clark and Douglas Alexander all lost. Michael Connarty lost (and gave a very dignified speech) and of course Murphy lost. In the end the SNP won every seat except three: Murray for Labour, Mundell for the Tories and Carmichael for the Liberals. Across the UK, Cameron is back in with a majority.

I said to Graham Hope, chief executive of the council, that now that the Tories had won, and the SNP will dominate Scotland, he would now be implementing turbo-charged austerity and cuts to services – and his face said it all.

I could weep today, although not for my party or my friends and colleagues who have lost seats (which is bad enough), but for the poor, the disabled, the elderly and those who rely on public services. More jobs will go, education standards will fall, food bank queues will grow, social care will deteriorate and our communities will splinter. The post-rational politics in the aftermath of the referendum will see divisions grow as people maintain allegiance to one side or the other, dismissing fact as propaganda and for that we will all lose out. Miliband will resign and be replaced by another bland middle-of-the-road New Labourish type; Cameron will be put under huge pressure from UKIP and his right wing, and Sturgeon will push for another referendum. I, of course, dodged the biggest bullet ever by losing the leadership election.

8 MAY: Awoke to see Miliband has resigned. Clegg has gone too, as Lib Dems almost wiped out.

Listened in to a conference call by Murphy at 9.30am, where he insisted he would be staying on. He said at the election he would retain 41 seats and win East Dunbartonshire, but he retained one, lost his own and every other, and now wants to stay on – it's nonsense. I was so stunned I said nothing. Afterwards I sat gathering my thoughts. I cannot be part of this anymore. I have to be free to express my views on how we rebuild and can't do this from within the Shadow Cabinet. I spoke to Fiona, Tommy and my brother-in-law, Jim about it: I will resign tomorrow. I don't have any other choice.

9 MAY: Up early and drafted a resignation statement, which I shared with Tommy. Called Jim Murphy but there was no reply so I left a message. Took lots of calls, texts, Facebook messages all urging Jim to go. I spoke to a few close colleagues and told them I was going to resign, and all were supportive. At 3pm I got a call from Jim. I told him I was going to resign and talked him through why – poor strategy, McTernan, the campaign's failings, political issues, lack of authenticity and leadership style. I said I could only play my part in rebuilding the party from out-with the Shadow Cabinet. He responded by saying I was doing this at 3pm on a Saturday to get maximum publicity and that it was a pincer movement between me and Unite – complete bollocks on both counts!

I put out the statement and later that day ASLEF and Unite called on Murphy to go.

Went out with Tommy and Diane and Norrie and Phyllis for a few drinks – feeling quite liberated.

10 MAY: Up early for the papers. Cameron busy filling his cabinet with right wingers. Awful.

Took lots of phone calls from people who reckon Jim has to resign.

15

General Election Fall Out: May–June 2015

AS FAR AS the Labour Party in Scotland is concerned, the General Election of 2015 was a disaster. In the 117-year history of the party, it's difficult to think of a more depressing moment.

The result of the election in Scotland was as follows:

Scottish National Party 56 seats, 1,454,436 votes
Labour one seat, 707,147 votes
Conservative one seat, 434,097 votes
Lib Dems one seat, 219,675 votes.

We lost a staggering 40 seats and took a 24.3 share of the vote, but after the election, Jim Murphy said he would continue as Scottish Labour leader!

11 MAY: To Glasgow for a Labour group meeting. TV cameras outside, but it's 'no comment' from me. Spoke with some trade union people and Alex Rowley. They think Murphy has to go. Some colleagues were warm and friendly; others, as expected, were sub-zero.

There was a wide ranging debate and discussion about why we lost and what happened during the campaign. The leadership team said that staff, candidates and activists had given their all – people are grieving. The defeat reflected the referendum result with the worst coming in Yes-voting areas. We knocked on 2.5 million doors and contacted 650,000 voters, delivered 20 million leaflets, two million direct mails and employed 35 organisers. Resources went to areas based on seat winability and when polls failed to close, money was directed to so-called 'safer seats' – no doubt Murphy and Margaret Curran's.

People believed or wanted to believe the polls in England but not in Scotland. The view is 'that we will get English votes for English Laws'

(Cameron had already raised this, boundary changes, no Lords' reform and an EU referendum). All of this makes future Labour wins even more problematic. While the election was supposed to be about Cameron, it became about the SNP. 1.6 million Yes voters became 1.4 million SNP voters. Labour was crushed by competing nationalisms. Union Jack British Nationalism versus Saltire Scottish Nationalism. Cameron tried to delegitimise the SNP but drove many towards them. Should we have ruled out a Labour/SNP deal earlier? Voters in Scotland didn't like it so the timing may have been irrelevant.

The extent of the problem is this: pre-referendum, in 2010, the Labour Party had been in power for 13 years; involved in four wars, and in the middle of a global economic crisis. We won 42 Scottish seats. Post-referendum and out of power for five years, during years of austerity, we lost all but one!

Massive challenges lie ahead. How do we learn and act upon it? What can we learn from other parties and organisations? How will we deal with the financial hit from the loss of short money that comes with a higher number of MPs? How do we raise funds, employ staff and develop better policies? How do we deal with the post-referendum landscape? How do we support and develop our frontline councillors? What do we offer in our 2016 manifesto? We need to stop being angry and shrill and be more principled, complemented by better tactics and strategy. We didn't lose because of our values and we shouldn't abandon or lose confidence in them. I didn't speak because I thought it would just provoke attacks on me and anyway I have had enough. Many did speak and quite a few weren't there. Jackie Baillie left and told the press, 'the vast majority of MSPs support Jim', which did not at all reflect the position of the majority at the meeting.

12 MAY: To parliament, but a bad day lay in wait. Alex Rowley resigned his shadow post and called on Murphy to go. He released a robustly worded letter about leadership, McTernan etc. This will be explosive. I think the best option is for Murphy to go, Kez to step up and we have an election for deputy. This would prevent a leadership contest and get things moving forward quickly. The news is carrying the story of Alex's letter: there is now real pressure on Murphy to go.

I was in the debating chamber and was approached by a close ally of Jim's, who asked what I think he should do. She also asked if I would stand in a contest. I said I would give anyone my commitment in blood, but would never, ever stand again.

One MSP said Jim wants to go but doesn't want to be seen to be forced out by the trade unions! He really does hate them, largely because he doesn't understand them and has never made any effort to work with them. If Kez comes forward I will give her my full support. We have many political differences, but there is mutual respect, and at this stage there is no one from the left in a position to challenge.

The Scotsman carried a piece from me on the debate around an independent or federal Labour Party and country. I went on *Scotland 2015* with David Henderson and repeated again that Better Together was a disaster and that we needed a federal UK.

Apparently a spontaneously called meeting of over 100 members in Glasgow unanimously called for Murphy to go. McTernan, who dislikes Kez, is trying to bind her to Murphy saying they were elected together and should resign together. No one I know is calling for that.

13 MAY: People in and out my office all day wanting to discuss the situation. Went into the chamber for Sturgeon's statement on the election result. Kezia did well in appallingly difficult circumstances. Sturgeon tried to sound like a stateswoman but I'm sure she was bursting to shout 'get it up ye – we hammered yeez'!

14 MAY: I was approached by Rhoda Grant, one of the most straightforward, decent and honest people I know. She couldn't make Monday's meeting and asked for another group meeting to discuss the leadership issue, but it was refused. Murphy, James Kelly and Neil Bibby are said to be touring the corridors turning the thumbscrews, 'urging' people to back Jim. Rhoda called an informal meeting and invited all group members. Margaret McCulloch, Margaret McDougall, Cara Hilton, Jayne Baxter, Claudia Beamish, Elaine Smith and amazingly Duncan McNeil all signed a letter asking Murphy to go. Johann Lamont, Paul Martin and Jenny Marra are in agreement.

Earlier in the day McTernan held a meeting with researchers, saying we ran a good campaign, full of ideas, energetic, with excellent media and social media but we just got caught up in a perfect storm. He said there was no issue with Jim and Kez's leadership and that we were in a good place for the 2016 campaign! Astonishing. What world does this guy live in? Tommy Kane and David Leitch, from Alex Rowley's office, challenged this crap and apparently a verbal battle erupted. McTernan was furious. This delighted me as he thinks people are complete fools and he would do all in his power to intimidate these young researchers. Apparently Rhoda's letter has been leaked to the *Herald*.

To Livingston to meet with the West Lothian Prostate Cancer Support Group. An excellent group helping men with the condition. I met my Uncle Leonard, my da's twin. He is recovering from treatment and was looking well.

15 MAY: Len McCluskey has called for Murphy and his team to clear off in a newspaper interview. While I agree with this sentiment, it may make him dig in more.

Spoke to Tom Watson. He is going for the national Labour deputy leadership. Ian Lavery MP, who is a friend and a decent man, has been approached to stand from the left but has decided to opt out. I had a long chat with him and understand his personal reasons. So far the declared candidates for UK leader are Andy Burnham, Chuka Umunna, Yvette Cooper, Liz Kendall and Mary Creagh. God, it's going to be dull. Umunna released an amateurish video announcing his candidacy and then almost immediately withdrew. The tabloids apparently have something on him and are camped outside his parents and grandparents houses. I don't blame him.

16 MAY: My CLP met last night and after a long and very intelligent, good-natured debate, decided by 18–10 in a vote of no confidence in Murphy. The motion was sent to General Secretary Brian Roy for debate at the weekend Scottish Executive Committee meeting. However, Roy has said it's not competent as the meeting should have had 25 per cent of members present (i.e. 60 members). This is a perfect example of how the right wing of the party operates when desperate. They don't defeat opposition with political argument but by organisational gerrymandering. It's the worst type of political fixing. If this principle was applied to the last 10 years across Scotland then we could write off the entire decade of history of the Labour Party, as 25 per cent of members in attendance at meetings is rare.

Now that we are down to one MP, there is a vacancy for one of the Parliamentary Labour Party rep positions on the party's Scottish Executive. I was told something quite amazing today by a friend who sits on the executive. The right wing have recruited and parachuted in (given her background, possibly quite literally parachuted in) Baroness Meta Ramsay of Cartvale, former spook and MI6 officer and member of the House of Lords, as the new rep from the PLP on the Scottish Executive. You couldn't make it up. Today's SEC meeting should be quite something.

The news came through that Murphy survived a no-confidence vote by three votes. He voted for himself and was supported by Agent Ramsay and the chair, Jamie Glackin. If Murphy goes on from this, he will take revenge and there will be a concerted purge against those who went against him. I will be near the top of his list. After the meeting Murphy came out and spoke to the media. He blamed Unite and Len McCluskey for bringing him down, called for one member one vote, and said Unite were full of grudge and grievance. He said he would stay on for a month to write a report on the way forward for Labour and then resign. It is clear he wants to implement a Blairite suite of changes before he goes. He came across as bitter, resentful, deluded and sanctimonious.

17 MAY: Media full of Murphy's absurd and bitter attack on Len. A lot of folk calling and texting urging me to stand but I want to nip this in the bud, so I put out a statement making it clear I would not be standing. It's very kind of people to ask but it's a job which demands your whole life and I have too much else going on with family and friends and too many interests as well as politics. I love the Labour Party, and put my heart and soul into my work, but I've had my go and never, ever again.

18 MAY: On the way into Edinburgh I heard on the radio that the SNP are trying to steal Dennis Skinner's seat in the House of Commons. Dennis, an 83-year-old ex-miner, is as tough as old boots and knows the Commons inside out having been there for 46 years. No matter how much the SNP try they won't succeed, he is far too wily for that to happen. I tweeted a message of support saying 'In solidarity with Comrade Skinner. I think I will sit in Nicola Sturgeon's seat at FMQs today!' Well, the cybernats went apeshit. I received torrents of abuse and tweets telling me how stupid and infantile I am. In post-rational Scotland there is no room for humour when it comes to Saint Nicola!

Astonishingly, Ken McIntosh is going to stand for leader again. He stood against Johann before and was beaten. If he goes for it again he will lose badly. I like Ken, he is a decent and good natured man. If he comes to see me, I will as a friend urge him not to stand.

Kezia Dugdale called and I told her I would be supporting her. The bookies have her at 6/5 and me at 9/4 even though I'm not standing. I might pay Ladbrokes a wee visit. I'm not sure who will go for deputy, although rumour has it Jackie Baillie will, but I couldn't support her. I hope Drew Smith throws his hat in the ring.

19 MAY: I phoned Dennis Skinner to fill him in on some of the people who are trying to oust him from his seat. He now has much more information to take them on politically. They are playing tig with a fox and there will only be one winner.

To the group meeting. Murphy once again said he would resign after writing a report on the way forward. Duncan McNeil, an old right-winger, is very good on these matters and said it wasn't for Murphy to do this. It would be for the new leader. Apparently at the Shadow Cabinet, Murphy attacked Sarah Boyack for speaking out in a private meeting. He then said he had chosen to attack Len McCluskey, but that there were many others he could have attacked instead! No doubt he had me and a few more in his sights.

20 MAY: Marion, my parliamentary case worker, called in very upset. Her husband George has fallen in the back of a lorry and broken his arm just under the shoulder. He works for the blood transfusion service and fell in one of their vehicles. He is to have major surgery on it but may not be able to get a plate fitted because of where the break is. It may have to be left to heal itself. She will be off for a while to look after him. Frank and Tommy will cover for now.

A head of steam is building behind Kez in the leadership race. I hope Ken is listening and withdraws. If he does he will save the party thousands of pounds (elections are costly affairs) and the contest could be over with quickly. Apparently Kez has 30 MSPs committed to date. Ken will struggle.

Today, the *Daily Record* ran a full report of yesterday's group meeting; no doubt briefed by Murphy's press people. The article raised the issue of selections for Scottish Parliament elections and getting rid of third-rate MSPs, naming Anne McTaggart and Hanzala Malik as examples. It's typical Murphy. Anne put her name to articles supporting him, and was generally helpful in the vain hope he would save her, but when it came to the crunch, McTernan and the press team hung her out to dry. All so predictable – she has been used by them. Group members are rightly unhappy at the leak.

I spoke in the education debate. Colleges have lost 130,000 places, teacher numbers are falling, classroom assistants losing their jobs in huge numbers and the attainment gap growing and the 'steady hand' of Angela Constance on the tiller. Sturgeon knows Constance is poor but won't sack her. Apparently she has strips torn off her regularly at the Cabinet. Some SNP backbenchers must wonder what they have to do to gain promotion!

After the debate I met with Kez and advised her to be the unity candidate who will work across the party respecting all members and affiliates. That she should build relationships with people who are not natural allies and get a big list of supporters to launch the campaign, which would pull the rug from Ken at the outset. I said I don't want anything from her, only a fair crack at the whip for left candidates when selections come round.

21 MAY: To parliament and the group seem more positive following last night's meeting. I think it allowed people to get things off their chest. Murphy is being seen as taking a wrecking ball to the party in the time he has left as leader. His list deselection story was classic McTernan. It backfired spectacularly and got plenty of backs up.

22 MAY: Today, Ken McIntosh was complaining in the media that his supporters are being 'bullied' by the party machine not to support him. The word bullying must be one of the most abused and misused words in the dictionary. Anyone who disagrees with someone, robustly criticises or takes issues with what they have said or done now claim they are being bullied. These folk must have gone to a pretty tame school if this is what they class as bullying.

That night, Fiona and I went with pals to see a David Bowie tribute band, who were excellent.

24 MAY: To Fauldhouse Cricket Club for their 160th anniversary match against a President's XI. The club is the second oldest in Scotland and was established by a Church of Scotland minister to give young boys something to do. It thrived when Yorkshire and Lancashire miners came to work in the local pits. Now a lot of young guys from nearby schemes play and are pretty good. It is definitely a working class sport here. We had a great day watching them and I hope they go on for decades to come.

25 MAY: Fiona and I went for a walk around Lanark Loch before having a fish tea. Lovely day out.

26 MAY: At the group meeting, Paul Martin challenged Ken McIntosh's claim that people were being bullied out of supporting him and asked him to name who he was talking about. Ken failed to do so and got people's backs up with his unsubstantiated claim.

27 MAY: Today is the debate on assisted suicide. We have received

thousands of emails from each side but the clear majority are calling for it to be introduced. The bill was originally promoted by Margo McDonald, but after her death Patrick Harvie has pursued it. I have tortured myself with this issue. I'm very sympathetic and moved by the personal stories of people seeing their loved ones fade away in pain from cancer, dementia, MND etc and wishing they could have helped their relative fulfil a wish by dying with dignity, but I cannot get my experience with my da out of my head. When he was dying he was in a hospice in Edinburgh and a few of us had gone to see him. He had gone from a big bear of a man to skin and bone and was unconscious. He didn't respond when we spoke. We stayed half-an-hour and left. No one said anything but we all believed he might not last the night. The family wanted him home but it was taking a few days to sort out. Overnight there was no change so I went to work. After lunchtime I received a phone call which went like this: 'Hello, how are you daeing?'

'I'm fine... who is this?'

'Who the hell dae ye think it is, it's yer faither. I'm back fae the deid. I'm sitting here with a glass of Laphroaig!'

I nearly collapsed. I could NOT believe it. I was stunned, gobsmacked, astonished; words failed me. He really was 'back fae the deid', and was coming home that night.

Later that evening he came home in the hospice ambulance and went to sleep in his own bed. Two nights later Fiona and I dozed in the room next door and listened to his breathing get shallower and shallower before he died with the family around him. This very personal episode had a big influence on my vote, as had assisted suicide been legal we may have missed those last few days together. It may be totally selfish; it may be that those few days were good for the family but only prolonged my da's decline, but it was a profound moment for my family I would not like denied to others.

Patrick Harvie gave a very good speech and then I spoke about how tortured I was with the decision and how I had wrestled with it for a long time and that I would vote against, but with a heavy heart. I took a long time to write my speech and thought long and hard about it. The debate was a good one, very passionate with lots of good speeches. In the end the bill was defeated 82 to 36.

I was congratulated on my speech by Patrick, Siobhan McMahon, Fiona Hyslop and Clare Adamson, which was greatly appreciated as I wanted to do a serious issue justice. The debate showed the parliament at its very best; good, thoughtful, informed speeches with a great deal of compassion shown. Many people will have had Margo in their thoughts today – I know I did.

28 MAY: Met with the striking Dundee hospital porters over the pay grading that will hammer their wages. A good turnout from Labour MSPs – but not a single SNP MSP in sight.

30 MAY: Brilliant night at John and Sharron's wedding reception in the golf club. They were married earlier in the month in a small private service at Loch Lomond with just their best friends in attendance. Great to see them happy and with lots of friends and family enjoying themselves. Back to our house for the after party.

1 JUNE: Scotland play Qatar in a football match on Friday. The World Cup will be hosted there in 2022. It's a farcical situation and lots of questions have been asked about corruption, FIFA and the decision to give it to Qatar. Trade unions have been campaigning over the slaughter of migrant workers building stadia there. Thousands have died in accidents and many workers are terribly treated in conditions akin to slavery. Apparently 62 workers will die for every game of the cup, and all the while the Scottish Government courts the Qatari regime. I put down a motion calling for the game to be cancelled on the basis of the workers' deaths. Immediately the media picked up on this with STV, *The Sun*, the *Daily Mail* and BBC all covering the story. I went on *Scotland 2015* for a discussion with representatives from Supporters Direct.

2 JUNE: To my mate Scotty's mum's funeral. Lots of locals there, lovely service, hymns and eulogy – all round good funeral, as it should be.

To STUC General Council to discuss the General Election. I opened by asking members their views on why we lost so badly. Replies ranged from a lack of hope and vision, failure to offer a second question in the referendum, Better Together, the Stevie Deans/Unite issue, failure to listen and learn from past mistakes and the lack of appeal of Miliband and Murphy. It was challenging and depressing but also interesting. I asked them to campaign with us and challenge the SNP on council budgets, the social care crisis, failures in education and the NHS and lack of delivery on the fair work agenda.

I spoke with one of the members of the General Council about Qatar, and they said the game against Scotland was to be an 'inaugural' match and part of a business deal involving the Scottish Government and the Qataris. Apparently Humza Yousaf is heavily involved. They have developed an air route from Edinburgh to Doha. I think there is much more to this than meets the eye and that it's all a bit murky. I will need to get Tommy to do some FOI's on this.

3 JUNE: 38 degrees running a petition calling on the Qatar match to be cancelled. It is all over social media and newspapers are running with it. The SFA are keeping their heads down and not one SNP MSP will sign my motion. It's obvious they have all been told not to go near it and of course they like to do what they're told.

4 JUNE: To the House of Commons for a series of meetings. Had coffee with Ian Lavery, an ex-miner who increased his majority by 10 per cent at the election. We spoke about a range of policies, the direction of the party, Labour in Scotland and the leadership election. Ian had been asked by many on the left to stand for leader but refused for personal reasons. There is huge pressure on people who put their head above the parapet.

5 JUNE: To the Saltire pub in Livingston for a night out to recognise Michael Connarty and Graeme Morrice's combined 66 years of elected office. Michael was first elected in 1977 and Graeme in 1987. Both were council leaders and then MP's, and are good friends of mine. It's a sad loss to public service. I was a councillor alongside Graeme when West Lothian Council was named UK Council of the Year – a significant achievement.

Tonight was the Scotland v Qatar match, and there was a poor crowd. The STUC held a demo at the match. Yesterday, Malcolm Chisholm asked Sturgeon at FMQs about this and now Tommy has found that both Humza Yousaf and Salmond's ministerial diaries have not been filled in for the time they were in Qatar – this is getting interesting!

7 JUNE: A home win as the SFA announce they are dumping their links with Qatar. In the same paper, Marion Scott reports on the research Tommy has unearthed that the Scottish NHS has been using the same surgical mesh as has been found defective in the US, where women have been paid up to £100 million in compensation for their horrendous injuries. This could have huge implications for the Scottish NHS.

I travelled into the office by bus today – an eight-mile journey which cost an astonishing £3.20! Public transport really is a scandal. The privatisation of bus and rail services has been an expensive disaster.

Nice afternoon in the garden with Fiona putting in plants. The simple things…

8 JUNE: Fourth year pupil from one of the local schools in at the Scottish Parliament today for a week's work experience. I've had some really clever and impressive pupils in over the last few years and Steph is no different; exceptionally bright and picks things up quickly.

9 JUNE: To parliament and I'm really concerned about the Labour position on the EU referendum. Our people are all gushingly positive about the EU with no mention of issues like TTIP, the role of the European Central Bank, austerity or the exploitation of workers, mass youth unemployment, low pay etc. Incredibly, the SNP are arguing that they want to remain in the EU – a large distant, undemocratic body, but want out of the UK because it is distant and undemocratic? They have completely forgotten the arguments of last year and are now arguing for unity, solidarity and working with neighbours, although just not our nearest neighbours and biggest market. Completely inconsistent and I believe many of their supporters do not support their position.

I met a group of Norwegian students who are over in Scotland with a friend of mine, who is their lecturer. We had a great discussion about politics, parliament, socialism, democracy, religion, assisted suicide and much more – it was great fun and very interesting.

11 JUNE: At the House of Commons, the SNP have moved an amendment demanding full fiscal autonomy – unbelievable. Last week Tommy Shepherd MP called it 'nonsense' and George Kerevan MP said it was 'suicide', but I guarantee this week both of them, and every one of their compliant, sheep-like MPs will vote for it. I fear the Tories might actually give them it which would be a disaster for Scotland.

12 JUNE: After two-and-a-half years and evidence of perjury, wrong doing, violence, lies and cover up on behalf of South Yorkshire Police, the IPCC have said there will be no inquiry into Orgreave. 95 people were arrested on 18 June 1984; 71 with rioting, and all were acquitted, but senior police officers have never been held to account for their actions. The Ogreave Truth and Justice Campaign will now redouble their efforts. A lot hinges on the outcome of the Hillsborough inquiry, which will expose their wrongdoing. The pressure for an Orgreave inquiry will be stepped up if there is a damning report from Hillsborough.

Heard today that Jackie Baillie will stand for deputy leader – I really hope this isn't true. She is a very capable and committed MSP but not what we need if we are to try and win back Yes supporters.

13 JUNE: Today, there are gala days in both Fauldhouse and Blackburn. The weather was a bit overcast but there were lots of families and children out dressed up and enjoying the fun. A fantastic atmosphere at both and afterwards Fiona and I went down to Jimmy and Kate's with a group of pals and sat around a blazing fire outside chatting for hours – lovely relaxing evening.

14 JUNE: Alex Rowley is thinking of standing for deputy leader, which would be a good move. Alex is an ex-gardener who retrained at Newbattle College, then Edinburgh University. He is a close friend of Gordon Brown but has moved to the left during his time in parliament. I get on well with him. We have had our differences but always maintained a good friendship. Richard Baker is also to stand. I like Richard on a personal level but will support Alex.

Murphy resigned today at the Scottish Executive and presented his proposals for change. These were:

- Leader and Deputy should top the list in their region
- One member one vote for leadership election
- Scottish Parliament List process to be opened up to attract new candidates (the inference being the current MSPs are crap)
- Councillors to go before a national selection panel
- The current qualifying criteria of having to be a member for six months before putting their name forward as a candidate to be waived

In standing down he had a swipe at Johann Lamont, saying she left behind chaos without doing the hard work to sort out the party, and 'the boss politics of Unite'. My reflections on Jim Murphy: He was a capable communicator; a fixer who saw himself as a big beast. From being a student activist he set out to be an MP and believed his own PR. Every move was about his power and bolstering his control. He saw everything as the next tactic; little was about principle. Politics was an exercise in PR. He was insincere and indulged in every trick and manoeuvre he learned from the Blairite recipe book. He would brief and undermine colleagues if it suited him. At the election he thought he had only to bring in the manual from the 1990s, complete with McTernan and a new Clause IV, and things would turn around. He was the NUS leader who supported tuition fees only to now claim he supported their scrapping. He supported the Iraq war only to say that had he known then what he knew now he would never have voted for it. He supported tax cuts then said he would increase taxes. No one was fooled. I'm pleased he has gone.

15 JUNE: Took phone calls from five MSP colleagues, Vince Mills and other friends on the left asking me to stand. I'm getting a bit frustrated. I WON'T BE STANDING! But of course it's good of them to call. I told Alex Rowley I will support him especially as we now know Gordon Mathieson, leader of Glasgow Council, is putting his name forward. He is the Murphy candidate for deputy.

16 JUNE: So, Alex Rowley, Richard Baker and Gordon Mathieson are the candidates for deputy with Kez and Ken McIntosh up for leader. Mathieson says he wants it because a councillor should be deputy, but he wants to be an MSP so that contradicts that argument.

17 JUNE: Spoke to Alex Rowley who now has enough nominations and has started to get a backroom team in place. Not getting too involved but will offer advice based on my experience of a year ago.

18 JUNE: After FMQs I went to a group meeting to hear Liz Kendall's campaign pitch. Against all my better judgement, I couldn't help but be impressed by her, not any of her policies, I hasten to add, but by the fact she at least has a political philosophy, and is prepared to articulate it and back it up. She was asked about issues like welfare, Trident and immigration and she took them on, fell back on her philosophy and answered them articulately. Her answers were almost all very different from my views: she said she wasn't right wing and that it wasn't right wing to want to balance the books, control immigration and want strong defences, especially against ISIS. As if you can take on ISIS with a nuclear bomb! She will get support from the uber-new Labour outriders but won't win. I don't think the Labour Party is quite ready to morph into the Democratic Party just yet!

20 JUNE: To George Square, Glasgow for the anti-austerity rally. 250,000 at the rally in London and 4,000 in Glasgow. SNP flag wavers tried to shout down Denise Christie of the FBU, the Labour Campaign for Socialism speaker. She was excellent. I really like Denise and hope she puts her name forward for parliament. The rally was okay but a poor turnout. Heard later it had coincided with the annual Bannockburn rally and that, wait for

it, Tommy Sheridan was speaking there. Even more astonishingly, so was Brian Quail of Scottish CND, a representative from a peace organisation commemorating a battle where thousands of people died. You couldn't make it up.

22 JUNE: To the RMT Conference in Newcastle. As a member of the RMT Parliamentary Group, I was invited to give the group's annual report. The meeting started with tributes to Bob Crow and moving music from the RMT brass band. The event was fascinating and impressive. The RMT are a strong, coherent and no-nonsense union. They are robust in standing up for their members and win far more battles than they lose.

At lunchtime I did a fringe meeting on the trade union bill with John McDonnell and Mick Cash before heading to Durham for the ASLEF Scottish and Northern Region meeting at the fantastic Redhills, the Durham Miners headquarters. We were met by Davey Hopper, Durham Miners leader – a brilliant guy who I have met on a number of occasions and who is someone I love talking to and learning from. A meal, a few beers and some great crack ended the perfect evening.

23 JUNE: Met this morning at Redhills and spoke to ASLEF members after Davey. Redhills is a beautiful and amazing place, dripping in history. The main chamber was effectively the Parliament of the Durham NUM with a numbered seat for every union delegate from each pit in the region – 290 seats. It was a huge honour to speak in such a place. I raised issues around the General Election and Labour's failures, the manifesto, Ed Miliband, Jim Murphy, the challenge of the Tories and SNP in Scotland. I urged ASLEF members to come forward as candidates. Afterwards I met Dave Douglas, a former miner who showed me around Redhills. The photographs, murals, miners' banners, statues, plaque to the volunteers of the International Brigades etc. were fantastic to see. There was even a telegram from Stalin thanking the Durham Miners for the donation of an X-ray machine! This is a real hidden gem of a place that anyone interested in the history of the Labour movement should visit.

News today is that a mother who had been in the perinatal ward at St John's killed her baby after being unable to access services. Tragic. This was the very service Dr Jane Hamilton blew the whistle on. I am convinced there is much more to come on this story.

24 JUNE: Last day of parliament before the recess. We had a group meeting to hear the deputy leadership candidates speak. Stella Creasy, who put

forward a Progress/Movement for Change line; Ben Bradshaw, who spoke about the way to victory being knocking more doors (Yip, we have been doing nothing else for the last three years). Angela Eagle, who said very little that was memorable; Caroline Flint, who has an interesting back story as a young parent and the daughter of an alcoholic mum; and Tom Watson, who understood the need for us to listen to what the electorate are saying and who came across as decent and human.

16

Enter Stage Left: May 2015–September 2016

WHEN THE YOUNG people of today look back at the British political landscape of 2015, they will identify a group of politicians who changed our country, our mindset and our attitudes towards current affairs. They might debate the merits or otherwise of Cameron, Osborne, Sturgeon, Miliband, Clegg and Farage, but they were merely bit-part players, because the biggest impact of post-election 2015 came in the shape of a 66-year-old bearded vegan who had spent the previous 30 years in relative obscurity on the backbenches at Westminster.

Enter stage left: firmly left, Mr Jeremy Corbyn.

When this keen cyclist, allotment enthusiast and jam maker declared he would stand for the Labour leadership, his team's ambition extended to getting him on the ballot paper. Accomplishing that would provoke a genuine debate within the Labour Party. The first goal was achieved due to the heroic efforts of his team, as well as a clever social media campaign designed to put pressure on MPs to nominate him. Ironically he wouldn't have succeeded without the help of right wingers like Frank Field and 'Blue Labour' advocate Jon Cruddas. Mind you, their 'crime' would make them the target of abuse from New Labour 'Ultras'.

Objective number two for Corbyn and his Scottish team was to avoid finishing last when votes were cast north of the border. Given the politics of the Scottish Labour Party – not traditionally the most radical or left wing of groups – dodging the 'wooden spoon' would be an achievement. In the end, Corbyn's camp miscalculated the outcome on a grand scale, although not as grand as the Labour right.

I'd met Jeremy just a couple of times prior to the leadership election. He had been around left politics for many years and was active in the peace movement, where he played a leading role in opposing the Iraq war. Those meetings had left a favourable impression on me. He was someone completely without ego (a rare commodity in a politician); he was friendly to everyone he met, and came across as calm, authentic and gentle. He conducted himself well and always took time to chat to people, but more importantly to listen to their stories, their views and life experiences. He was very much like his great friend and mentor Tony Benn. I took to his style and manner immediately. He also clearly held an ideological position, which he has stuck to all his political life. Tony Benn described people like Jeremy as a signpost – someone with a clear direction, standing firm and showing others the way. The alternative, the weathervane, blows around in the wind, heading one way one minute, then the other the next. Jeremy was no weathervane, but his rise to prominence put the wind up a few on the Labour right.

8 MAY 2015: Ed Miliband's election defeat has prompted his resignation and is the catalyst for a summer leadership battle. This will involve a number of candidates who will, in policy terms, be pretty much indistinguishable from one another. I expect Chuka Umunna, Yvette Cooper, Andy Burnham and Hilary Benn to come forward. There will be the usual attempt by my comrades on the left to try and get on the ballot but this won't happen as there is almost no chance of any candidate such as John McDonnell securing the votes necessary to challenge. All very depressing.

10 MAY – 2 JUNE: Candidates start coming forward to declare themselves as potential leaders. First out the traps is Blairite-Ultra Liz Kendall, then Chuka Umunna (who withdraws a few days later) Andy Burnham, Yvette Cooper and Mary Creagh. Others like Tristram Hunt flirt with the idea.

3 JUNE: Out of the blue, Jeremy Corbyn, the most unlikely candidate from the Labour left, announces he will run for leader. I expected McDonnell or Lavery, but Corbyn? Anyway, it's game on so let's do all we can to try and get him on the ballot. A day or so after the announcement I agreed to be his Scottish campaign manager.

3 JUNE – 15 JUNE: A clever – and massive – social media operation designed to lobby and put pressure on undeclared MPs sweeps into operation. This clever strategy starts to bear fruit. Corbyn receives nominations from the left – Skinner, Meacher, Abbot; from the centre – David Lammy, Sadiq Khan, Gordon Marsden, and from the right – Frank Field and Neil Coyle, but by decision day he is still one or two short. As the 12 o'clock deadline approaches, John McDonnell, his campaign manager, gets down on his knees and begs the last few undecided MPs to swing towards Jeremy. To everyone's astonishment, they oblige. Jeremy is on the ballot. When news

filtered through to my office, we all punched the air with delight. We could now have a full and proper debate on the future of the Labour Party.

25 JUNE: In agreeing to take on the role of Scottish campaign chair, I was keen and upbeat but realistic about our chances. They're not high. We appointed Martyn Cook as Scottish organiser, and the team included Vince Mills, Pauline Bryan, Denise Christie, Jackson Cullinane, Stephen Low, Lesley Brennan, Elaine Smith MSP and Tommy Kane. We were up and running pretty quickly with the contribution of the Scottish Labour Young Socialists outstanding. This group had come together two years previously to help in my campaign for leader, and it didn't take much for them to self-organise for this campaign.

Jeremy's first leadership visit to Scotland coincided with the last day of our parliamentary term. He met the MSP group in the Serenity Café and then the Edinburgh Council Labour group. Walking from Holyrood to the council chambers normally takes around 15–20 minutes but in the height of the tourist season the route was packed with people. During the walk only one person recognised Jeremy and stopped him for a chat.

15 JULY: Acting Labour leader Harriet Harman insists Labour won't fight plans to cut child tax credits. All leadership candidates follow the party line, except Jeremy, who loudly resists and says he will vote against the Tory plans. Good on him.

21 JULY: Jeremy's series of rallies around the UK are commanding huge crowds: news channels, papers and pundits sit up and take notice. A YouGov poll rocks the party establishment by putting him 17 points ahead: something big is happening. His odds have fallen from 100/1 to 4/1.

22 JULY: Commentators initially treat Jeremy as a joke figure but every time another Labour grandee or media outlet warns against a Corbyn victory, his popularity rises. Today, Anthony Charles Lynton Blair warned he could not support a Corbyn-led Labour Government and said people who 'vote Corbyn with their hearts should get a transplant'. How stupid can intelligent people be? As a result, Jeremy's popularity rises – again. I'm reminded of Dennis Skinner's great line about Boris Johnson having been 'educated beyond his intelligence'.

1 AUGUST: One of the most significant events of the campaign is a rally in Liverpool where 5,000 folk turn up, many of them young people. Hundreds are turned away as the venue is packed to capacity.

Neither Burnham, Cooper nor Kendall are capable of drumming up anywhere near that kind of support, news coverage or interest. People are joining Labour in droves or taking up registered supporter status for £3 to ensure their vote. As Corbyn tours the country, his mantra of 'straight talking, honest politics' and a 'gentler, kinder politics', is gaining huge traction. On issues such as nationalisation of the railways, ending tax avoidance, housing for all, no privatisation etc, he is talking real Labour language that many in the party have been waiting decades to hear. His agenda sounds new and fresh and he is appealing to young and old alike. The other candidates don't have a clue what to do to stop it. It is invigorating and inspirational.

2 AUGUST: 2,500 pack out Camden Town Hall and Jeremy is forced to go out and speak to 500 more who are locked out from the roof of an old fire engine provided by the local Fire Brigade Union.

5 AUGUST: Andy Burnham – who I like a lot (he passes the 'pint test' with ease) and had worked with during my time as Shadow Health spokesman – started his campaign by trying to appeal to the New Labour right with tough talk about financial responsibility and tighter immigration controls. Today, though, he has swung to the left and is talking renationalisation of the railways. A clear indication that Jeremy is in a strong position and is picking up votes.

9 AUGUST: The Scottish Labour leadership battle is also underway following Jim Murphy's demise. Ken McIntosh secures the nominations needed, but is way behind Kez. Neither candidate is on the left, and I am close to neither personally nor politically, but have no hesitation in backing Kez. I had previously arranged for her to meet key people on the left to discuss how she could take the party forward respecting all views. It is clear she is going to win and win handsomely, so you can imagine my frustration when I read comments attributed to her in the papers two days before Jeremy arrives in Scotland, saying a Corbyn victory would leave Labour 'carping from the sidelines'. I told her it wasn't the cleverest of moves since it looked like they would both win and have to work together! Within 12 hours of our exchange she had registered for the Corbyn event in Edinburgh.

13 AUGUST: Jeremy is in Scotland and more than 300 people turn up at Aberdeen Arts Centre for a Friday lunchtime event on the warmest day of the year (not a spectacular claim as anything over 12 degrees qualifies

for the warmest day of the year in the Granite City!). Dexter Govan of the University Labour Club, Tommy Campbell and Katy Clark spoke while I chaired the event. The reception was as warm as the weather and encouraging. Many people remained behind afterwards for a chat and photos.

That night, we are at Dundee University for a rally, and I'm anxious about this more than any other. Dundee was a big 'Yes' voting city with activists reporting a lot of anti-Labour hostility from hard-line nationalists. If any event was going to kick off, this was the most likely. The place is rammed to the door with 400 people and another 200 in an overspill room watching on a live feed. Jeremy speaks for half an hour covering a wide range of issues from austerity to public services, war and peace and how to create a fairer, more equal society. The crowd lap it up. Jeremy is not a natural orator; his style is not structured or heavy on flowing rhetoric or imagery. As someone who has spoken at thousands of public meetings over the years, he hasn't been used to doing set piece crafted speeches. His style is more 'write a few words on a scrap of paper as prompts' and then off he goes. But the audience loved it. As with all public meetings it's the Q&A session which flashes up warning signs and none more so than in post-referendum Scotland. But Jeremy handles each question well and respectfully and gives serious answers.

Only one moment gives cause for concern. A particularly aggressive nationalist, who is well known to Labour activists in Dundee, shouts and jabs his finger wanting to know if Jeremy supports a second independence referendum. As Corbyn says no and explains why, the guy starts shouting and heckling at which point I think, 'Here we go!' But he only manages a few words before the crowd turn on him and he's told to shut up. Because of that, the incident was over in a flash. The rest of the evening went fantastically well and again ended with photos and friendly chat. We enjoyed a few drinks afterwards to celebrate. Just one red wine for Jeremy, though.

14 AUGUST: Edinburgh is busy with people visiting the world famous International Arts Festival, but the weather was awful, with rain bouncing off the cobbled High Street. The original plan was to walk through the town to the Conference Centre, as we had time to spare, but just as we set off, Jeremy remembered he had to write his *Morning Star* column. I was flabbergasted. 'Can't someone else do it?' We are in the middle of a leadership election, traipsing round the country on public transport, and he announces he has a weekly column to write! We settled on a quick visit

to the Arts Café, behind Waverley Station and he huddled in a corner and began typing. He didn't get very far. Soon, there was a steady trail of folk keen to chat, get a selfie, or simply wanting to say hello and wish him good luck. Fair play to Jeremy as he stopped typing whenever someone approached, and picked it up again straight away. One hour later, we were on route to the centre, where 600 folk were waiting patiently. It was a fantastic attendance, considering we were competing with thousands of festival shows. TV footage showed a guy in the audience moved to tears as he said he had waited 30 years to see the Labour Party return to its socialist roots.

Before the event, Kez texted to ask if she could meet Jeremy, so when we finished I asked everyone to vacate the backstage room and left her and Jeremy alone to chat. Both agreed it had been an excellent meeting and regardless of what is written in the media, they maintain good personal relations to this day. I would like to think that initial meeting helped a lot. Apparently Liz Kendall was also in Scotland today, although no one really noticed!

Later that night, we travelled through to Glasgow for an event at the Old Fruitmarket – and this was on a different level from the rest. Around 1,200 people were there and the atmosphere was electric. Speeches from Owen Jones, Sam Ritchie, Denise Christie, Katy Clark and I preceded Jeremy, and he rose to the occasion. Socialist songs from the great Arthur Johnstone, Stephen Wright and the greatest 'moothy' player I have ever heard, Fraser Spiers, brought a fantastic event to a close. The place was bouncing. One of the best Labour events in decades.

Observing Jeremy at such close quarters for a couple of days, I was amazed at how anyone can put up with such constant pressure but he carries it off without an apparent care in the world. It was my responsibility to make sure the tour went well, while working with the rest of the team to manage the campaign. Martyn Cook did a tremendous amount of work in the day-to-day running of the campaign, while I was more involved in the political side, but it was a great team effort.

15 AUGUST: Today is deadline day to register to vote, and the other candidates have issued a warning for people to vote anyone but Corbyn! They are clearly panicking.

With the Scottish tour behind him, work continued apace in the leadership battle and returns from phone banks in Scotland are encouraging. Constituency parties are starting to nominate for leader, and we are picking up nominations we couldn't have dreamed of, particularly in Edinburgh, Glasgow and Dundee. Our hope and optimism is growing.

18 AUGUST: During the leadership election it was my job to secure positive media opportunities in Scotland. I had discussions with several newspapers and had hoped get at least a fair hearing from them. The ground work paid off as the *Daily Record*, one of Scotland's biggest papers, endorsed Jeremy for leader – a major coup. Apparently 'Team Corbyn HQ' went into a frenzy when the front page appeared on their social media feed!

9 SEPTEMBER: Ballot closes amid all sorts of claims of infiltration of the membership by candidates who know there are losing. It all looks a bit desperate as they seem afraid of a party that now has over 600,000 people contributing to its leadership election. The fact we are now the biggest political party in Western Europe should in itself be cause for celebration.

10 SEPTEMBER: After First Minster's Questions at Holyrood, I rushed to Edinburgh Airport and flew to London to attend Jeremy's final campaign rally in the Grand Rock Tower Gospel Church in Islington. It was packed to the rafters, and outside it seemed as though every window in the borough was displaying a poster saying 'Vote Corbyn'. Jeremy's local branch now has a staggering 3,000 members! The speakers resembled a Who's Who of left-wing politics: Len McCluskey, Owen Jones, Rebecca Long Bailey MP, Clive Lewis MP, Richard Burgon MP etc. It was inspirational stuff and the atmosphere was electric. I was proud to contribute my two minutes' worth on behalf of the Scottish team but the moment the meeting finished, I had to dive along to the station to get the sleeper train up the road.

11 SEPTEMBER: I did my Friday constituency work before attending a charity event in the Fauldhouse Miners Welfare, and later that night I was back on the sleeper to London for the result the following day.

12 SEPTEMBER: I felt no tiredness as I rolled up at the Queen Elizabeth Conference Centre, near Westminster. The crowds outside were remarkable and the reception for Jeremy was like a football crowd. In the main hall I stood at the side near the media prior to the big announcement, close to a large group of MPs, and their faces spoke a thousand words. They looked so crestfallen I knew we had won. When the announcement came, Jeremy secured a remarkable 59 per cent of the vote with the closest challenger Andy Burnham on 19. It was a landslide. Tom Watson, who I had voted for, won the deputy leadership pretty comfortably.

And then it began. Jamie Reid, a Blairite-ultra MP, announced his resignation from the front bench. This was, of course, all pre-planned: designed to undermine Corbyn, just 10 minutes after the result had been declared.

The moment the announcement was made, I grabbed Kezia Dugdale and hauled her through a frenzied media scrum to a back room where Corbyn had just come off stage, and we got a photograph taken of the pair for the Scottish media the following day. Team Corbyn then celebrated all afternoon and evening in a pub near the conference centre and when Jeremy appeared, after his media duties, the place erupted. He gave a speech and announced that his first act as leader would be to go up to Parliament Square to a rally in support of Syrian refugees. Typical of the man, thinking of others during *his* big moment.

2 DECEMBER: Jeremy has always tried to work towards peace, and doesn't believe that raining more bombs on top of people achieves that aim. When Miliband was leader, the Commons had voted to oppose military action in Syria, which was seen as a great coup for Labour. Today, there was a second call for military action and some elements of the Parliamentary Labour Party were all for it, saying the time was now right, but when they couldn't get everyone to agree they decided to have a free vote on the subject culminating in Jeremy speaking against military action, while Hilary Benn, his Shadow Foreign Secretary, made a theatrical speech in Parliament calling for the immediate bombing of Syria by UK forces. The speech was aimed at undermining Jeremy and creating division. At the end of his speech we had the sickening sight of Tory MPs giving Benn a standing ovation – enough to make a pig vomit.

3 DECEMBER: Oldham and West Royton by-election caused by the death of Corbyn ally Michael Meacher. Despite warnings from Corbyn critics that we were facing defeat, Labour held the seat and secured a 10,000 majority.

5 MAY 2016: I didn't keep a detailed diary of the 2016 Scottish Election – I was far too immersed in it as a constituency candidate to have time – but this is my entry from the day after:

> After months of campaigning, door knocking, 100,000 leaflets delivered – and a dog bite when delivering the *very last* leaflet of the campaign to my neighbour's house – the Scottish Parliament election was held today against a backdrop of increasing turmoil within the Labour Party, and the polarisation of Scottish politics between two forms of flag-waving nationalisms. Despite its most

radical Scottish manifesto in decades, Labour was badly squeezed at the polls. A resurgent Scottish Tory party led by Ruth Davidson pushed Labour into third place. The SNP failed to secure a majority and was forced to govern as a minority Government albeit bailed out by their unofficial backbenchers in the Scottish Green Party.

On a personal level we put in a huge effort to try and win the Almond Valley seat from the SNP's Angela Constance. We worked extensively on local health issues and policy areas relevant to constituents and enjoyed a lot of help and support from members on the left as well as the trade unions. Without doubt people were prepared to give us a fairer hearing than in 2015 but the legacy of the independence referendum still hangs heavy in the air. In the end we lost 13 seats and our constituency share of the vote was down over nine per cent. This was a historic low for the party. Locally, I lost by over 8000 votes but retained my seat via the regional list. As parliament reconvened with a smaller group of Labour MSPs, there was much head scratching, tough talking and analysis required.

I declined the opportunity to serve on our front bench, preferring instead to focus on my campaigning work and chairing the Parliament's health committee, whilst simultaneously working across the broad left of the Labour movement to support and promote the Corbyn agenda.

As I have always been convinced that Labour's fortunes in Scotland hang on two things – a radical and coherent, socialist programme and a constitutional settlement that people can enthusiastically buy into – I knew the Corbyn team was in for a rough ride, but things were to come to a head sooner than I expected.

24 JUNE, 2016: Those scheming against Jeremy got up to some awful things, but one of the worst has to be the leaking of regular reports to the press on the weekly Parliamentary Labour Party meetings. These are private meetings to discuss the parliamentary agenda, tactics and developments; an opportunity for people to speak freely and frankly in private. However, almost every word and criticism was being relayed to journalists outside or tweeted on social media. It was a disgrace and a betrayal of hard-working party members. Many on Corbyn's side would be first to admit they have made mistakes, so if the criticism coming from those orchestrating the coup had been legitimate then fine, but it was poisonous. And it would go on for the best part of a year until the schemers saw the European referendum as an opportunity to go in for the kill. The referendum itself was awful. That ham actor Boris Johnson, along with the little squirt Michael Gove, teamed up with Nigel Farage and his bunch of UKIP loonies to push a racist

campaign full of lies and deception. The biggest lie of all being that with a leave vote £350 million extra would go into the NHS every week. My limited vocabulary can only describe this claim as utter bollocks! As a long time sceptic of the EU, Corbyn is in a difficult position. His critique of the EU is similar to mine – it is a remote, undemocratic institution that pursues neo-liberal economic policies that have caused havoc in countries like Greece, Spain and Italy. It has been a major contributory factor in the crisis of capitalism following the financial crash and promoted competition and privatisation. But despite this the Parliamentary Labour Party, and party in general, are pro-EU, so Corbyn took a pro-EU position and spoke at meetings and events arguing for Remain. But none of this was enough for his critics. The UK voted Leave by 51 per cent to 48 per cent, and PM David Cameron resigned.

26 JUNE: Hilary Benn is outed by a newspaper as one of the chief plotters against Corbyn and was rightly sacked late last night. MPs Margaret Hodge and Anne Coffey have laid a motion of no confidence in Jeremy, which will be voted upon if enough MPs support it. Then, out of the traps springs none other than Scotland's only Labour MP, Ian Murray, resigning live on television. How gracious of him! How to inflict maximum damage. Here we had David Cameron resigning after being defeated in the referendum, the Tory party are on the ropes and we should be kicking them up and down the corridors of Westminster, but those behind the coup decide it is far more important to seize the moment to get rid of a decent and honourable man. It is like being on the verge of winning the Champions League and turning round and blootering the ball into your own net. Complete lunacy, and party members were wondering what the hell was going on!

27 JUNE: The coup is in full swing and all day Shadow Cabinet members have been resigning at half hourly intervals in an attempt to create maximum damage. All carefully coordinated and TV stations lap it up. Now, a lesser person might have said, 'bollocks to this, I'm off', but not Jeremy, and you have to admire the courage of the man in saying: 'I was elected on a massive mandate. Members are behind me so I'm not going anywhere.' A new Shadow team was appointed and he dug in.

10 JULY: Angela Eagle announces she will be the latest from the Labour right to stand against Jeremy. The coup has been a mess from start to finish. I mean, when the Tories do coups, they do them right. They don't knife you in the back. They go straight in through the heart. Look what

they did to Gove and Johnson. They absolutely annihilated them and had their election over in a week with a new Prime Minister in place before you can even blink. The new Labourites are bungling amateurs by comparison.

12 JULY: Angela Eagle claims her office windows have been smashed by Corbyn supporters. It later transpires her office was in a communal building and it was the window in the stairwell of the building that was smashed, and not her office window. Far from it being a politically motivated act, it looked more like the work of vandals. She then delivered the campaign launch from hell, with folk comparing it to the unveiling of a new perfume!

13 JULY: Next! Owen Smith declares he is to stand for Labour leadership saying 'he believes in Corbyn's policies but doesn't believe Jeremy can win an election.'

20 JULY: Angela Eagle withdraws from the contest. I actually feel sorry for her because she probably didn't want to stand in the first place. She comes across as a decent human being and I believe she was put up to it by people who would never normally have supported her.

29 JULY: As the plotters realise Corbyn is going nowhere, they do what they do when they lose a political argument – try to manipulate the rules to get their way, but today the courts rule Corbyn was entitled to a place on the ballot. Great news!

25 AUGUST: While all this was going on I was astonished at how Corbyn was able to continue. It showed his genuine qualities; his calm self-belief, a clear set of principles and impressive steely resilience. God knows how I would have coped with such a situation. I wouldn't have slept a wink. In hindsight, if anyone was going to handle that type of pressure, it was going to be him.

At one point, I sent a text to him and John McDonnell saying 'whatever happens in all of this, look after your health and your family – everything else is secondary.' People tend to overlook the fact that these prominent politicians are human like the rest of us and have lives and families. Okay, they are in the public eye, but they still have feelings and human frailties like everyone else. They need to have time for themselves and their loved ones.

The Labour Party need a second leadership election like a hole in the head. Mind you, what tends to be overlooked is the massive increase in membership just after Corbyn took charge. When Tony Blair was in charge, party membership had dipped below 200,000. Just after the second leadership battle, we were hovering around the 600,000 mark. Corbyn has helped make Labour the biggest political party in Western Europe. For many, the party has become something worthwhile, something to believe in again. We have regained some of the credibility lost over Iraq. Corbyn was consistent in his views throughout the Iraq crisis and in his claims that it would be a disaster, and one of the best things he did as leader was to apologise to the families of the soldiers who died during the war. The day after the Chilcott Inquiry had reported, he went into a room full of families and said, 'On behalf of the Labour Party, I want to apologise to you all,' and he left to a standing ovation. It was very moving and typically humble. The families responded to his message: but he only did what Tony Blair should've done.

But we are now in the grip of a second leadership battle. To be honest, it isn't long after the previous one so we know exactly what needs to be done in Scotland. We get the organisation back up and running and bring in Joe Cullinane as chief organiser. Again we have a great social media campaign, phone banks, donations, etc.

Prior to Jeremy's return to Scotland a few of us went to London to brief his team on the impending trip, and the main issues. One of the issues we wanted to nail was the talk of a 'progressive alliance' between Labour and the SNP. Some on the English left believe we should be teaming up in an anti-Tory alliance with the Nationalists and Green Party, but we were dead against it. If people believed they could get a Labour Government by voting SNP then why vote Labour in Scotland? And you can only be in a 'progressive' alliance with parties that are progressive. The SNP have cut 70,000 council jobs, are slashing local government budgets more than Osborne, have cut 130,000 college places and do nothing on the redistribution of wealth or power. How can we have a progressive alliance with such a party? Nationalism and socialism are two completely different ideologies: we can have no truck with free market conservatism nor divisive nationalism. We want to ensure this is dead in the water before it has a chance to grow arms and legs, and to that end we have put out a series of articles to rule it out before Corbyn even sets foot across the border.

26 AUGUST: As we leave Euston Station for Glasgow, the furore over a video showing Corbyn sitting on the floor of a Virgin train after failing to get a seat is in full flow. I knew that when we arrived at Euston there would be media watching our every move. They would know we were heading to Scotland, and that Jeremy didn't like flying, so they would be hanging around the station – and we weren't disappointed. But we managed to get

on the train without too much hassle, just a few folk wanting photographs, which was fine. Oh, and it was a Virgin train!

There were six or seven of us and I was keeping a wee eye out for the hacks. Around 90 minutes into the journey, Jeremy was writing the obituary of one of his constituents for the local paper when the guard told us about a reporter and photographer at the end of the carriage 'asking questions'. I kept an eye on them for a while, but a further half hour into the journey the photographer walked straight up and started clicking away. I got up and told him to move, but the reporter started shouting, 'I want to ask Mr Corbyn why he wants to steal Richard Branson's railway from him,' and on and on he went. I asked them again to move, and the reporter was insistent he wanted to ask questions. I said to him, 'there are families and children in this carriage and you're disturbing them, so would you please sit down and we will speak to you in an hour. Jeremy is writing an obituary at the moment.' I then reported the pair of them to the guard for hassling us and the other passengers. A few minutes later, the guard warned the newspaper folk that any more nonsense and they would be off the train. It transpired they were from the *Daily Mail*. They were fuming, but had just gone about it the wrong way. They didn't come near us again, but when we arrived in Glasgow I knew 'all bets were off'. It would be rammed with journos and snappers but we decided to throw a ring of steel around Jeremy to protect him from the *Daily Mail* hack as he was a right obnoxious git. We got off the train and sure enough, he was straight up screaming and shouting. We kept him at bay, but when we got up to the gate there was an absolute sea of media. TV cameras, radio, snappers, reporters. It was unbelievable, and easily the worst I have ever experienced. It was like a rugby scrum. I don't know who it was, perhaps Virgin, but someone had called the police and three officers showed up to help, and we were very grateful. Thankfully, Ian Davidson was waiting nearby with his car and we bundled Jeremy in and they got away okay, but it was just awful.

Jeremy was in Glasgow for a rally at the Crown Plaza Hotel with trade union speakers and activists, and he was on good form. We then headed to the SECC for a hustings with Owen Smith. It was dreadful, because while Jeremy stuck to policy, hope and vision, Smith sadly focused on more personal attacks.

27 AUGUST: We were in Edinburgh for an event hosted by comedian Susan Morrison. Jeremy launched his new arts policy amongst a group of musicians, producers, comedians and directors, all in town for the Festival. Many said it was the first time they'd heard any political leader speak so

positively about the arts, and arts funding, music and literature.

It was then over to Lochgelly, in Fife, to meet Alex Rowley and Mary Lockhart, who had won a council seat for Labour the night before. Mary is a big Corbyn supporter so we had some nice photographs taken. Afterwards, we travelled to Dundee for the final rally in the Caird Hall, which completed a tough couple of days, although everything had gone well.

24 SEPTEMBER: We were at the Liverpool Conference Centre for the result of the second leadership contest, where Jeremy secured a huge mandate to again lead the Labour Party. The coup had failed miserably and Corbyn had both strengthened his position and humiliated his detractors. Make no mistake, this was a huge moment in the history of the Labour Party and I was proud to play my part.

17

As One Parliamentary Legend Leaves Us, Another Emerges

ON THE EVENING of 26 January 2017 I was speaking at a miners' justice event at the Jewel Miners Welfare on the outskirts of Edinburgh when news broke that my greatest political friend and mentor Tam Dalyell had died. When someone reaches their 80s you realise bad news isn't far off, but the passing of such a great man had a profound effect on me.

From my first tentative steps in the Labour Party we struck up a great friendship. He was always supportive and listened carefully to my arguments and views. He would call the house for a chat about the latest issues and ask my opinions. A great role model, he showed me how to be a dogged campaigner and was everything a parliamentarian should be.

I was privileged to write an obituary for Holyrood magazine and some local media, but while in conversation with Tam's wife Kathleen and their son, Gordon, I was humbled to be asked to speak at his memorial service in Linlithgow, his body having been donated to scientific research. I was determined to do Tam's career justice and myself proud.

As the service drew closer, I learned that the other speakers were Oxford professor Lord Peter Hennessy, the Right Honourable Brian Wilson, a former Government Minister, and Tim O'Shea, Principal of Edinburgh University. No pressure then.

The church was full of politicians from across the political spectrum, including Sir Menzies Campbell, Sir Patrick Cormack and Alistair Darling. The service was a fitting tribute to Tam's career. Tim O'Shea spoke of his contribution to education as a teacher and university rector. Peter Hennessy focused on Tam's brilliance as a parliamentarian, while Brian Wilson covered his role in the anti-devolution campaign of the 1970s, where he became famous for the so called 'West Lothian Question'.

The following is my contribution, which I hope captures the man and his relationship with local people over many decades as their constituency MP.

Good afternoon ladies and gentlemen, brothers and sisters, comrades and friends; it is a great honour and privilege to have been invited by Tam's family to speak at this service about his immense contribution to West Lothian life in over half a century of public service in education and politics.

I was speaking at a miners' justice event near Edinburgh when news of Tam's passing came through. I couldn't help but reflect on how fitting it was, given Tam's lifelong relationship with the miners of West Lothian and across the country, and his unwavering commitment to shale and coal industry workers throughout his life.

Tam became our MP with the endorsement of many miners and was not only loyal to them throughout but became a great personal friend to many. During the seismic events of 1984/85, Tam was a regular on the Polkemmet picket line, supporting local workers in that titanic struggle for jobs and communities, and in doing so exposed the role of the Thatcher Government and how forces of the state, including the security services and police, were directed by Thatcher to defeat the strike at all costs. Famously, he exposed the future head of MI5, Dame Stella Rimington, as a regular security services agent on the picket line at the Whitburn Pit.

As news of Tam's passing filtered into the mainstream, glowing tributes poured in. Labour Leader Jeremy Corbyn said, 'Tam was a titan of parliamentary scrutiny, fearless in pursuit of the truth.'

Shadow Chancellor John McDonnell added, 'He was a fine socialist and a parliamentarian of the first order.' Dr Jim Swire, on behalf of the Lockerbie families, called him, 'A righteous and fearless soldier in the cause of what is right.' And his old sparring partner and friend Jim Sillars said, 'Tam was a man of rock-hard integrity and a wonderful parliamentarian.'

These few examples highlight his legendary campaigning, dogged determination and political and parliamentary skills – all appropriate and absolutely right, but to us, the people of West Lothian, yes, he was our representative, our MP, our voice in parliament, but more important than all that, he was our trusted, reliable, honest, supportive and consistent pal. Loyal, but not uncritical friendship is one of the greatest gifts one human being can give to another, and Tam gave it to many.

I first met him when I was in my late teens, having just joined the Labour Party, and no matter my youthful rantings, naivety or idealism, Tam never once looked down on me, never dismissed my views or the views of anyone else. He treated everyone the same – with total respect, listening carefully to them and taking on board their comments.

He was no fan of New Labour and once said to me, 'Neil, you and I aren't Old Labour, we're not New Labour either, we are Jurassic Labour!' I liked that.

He spoke of his first brush with local politics. Having taken up an issue that was clearly the remit of the council, he received a note from Jimmy Boyle, leader of West Lothian County Council, saying, 'Foreign affairs yours, dog shit mine.' The demarcation lines of responsibility established very early on in his tenure. He did of course go on to be a great champion of local government, and build good relationships with regional and district councillors across the county.

During his time as MP he dealt with literally thousands of local cases. These were not the days of email, texting and Twitter – no sir, for Tam it was a brief scrawled letter in fountain pen sent to the relevant government minister, public agency or company. And very effective it was too.

He took great pride in his constituency work, and surgeries, very rarely missing a constituency party meeting, as hearing directly from constituents was invaluable to Tam and one of his top priorities. On one occasion, my brother visited his surgery for help. However, the stench in the small community centre office was horrendous. Tam, clearly oblivious to the pungent odour, took details of the case and had a chat – my brother all the time trying not to heave – and only on leaving did he notice that Tam had a large peacock shite on the front of his shoe. He kept a number of peacocks in the grounds of The Binns, and while he can claim many firsts in his career, he is surely the only MP to have conducted his surgery with a peacock's doings on his shoe!

Tam was a great politician, but couldn't have managed such a huge caseload without the help of his beloved wife and soulmate, Kathleen. They were very much a double act and a hugely effective one at that. There is not a chance that Tam could have made the impact he did in his life were it not for Kathleen's massive intellectual, as well as practical, contribution to her husband's work, and for that we thank her.

There are so many positives to pick out from Tam's life, but for a moment I would like to focus on one area where Tam was absolutely dreadful – amongst the worst you are ever likely to come across – and that was his driving skills. He had none. He would often ask some unsuspecting conference delegate or party member if they wanted a lift to the conference or home from a meeting. And before that unsuspecting comrade had time to think, they had accepted a lift. Big mistake. The journey in the wee blue Mini Metro was something to behold. Tam had a car with a manual gearbox but would drive permanently in third gear, either from a standing start or along the motorway. Like his politics he remained doggedly in the same gear until the journey's end, but he must have gone through more gearboxes than petrol!

Constituency party meetings with Tam were an education. We held them in Glen's Bar on a Sunday afternoon, around the same time as the Karaoke phenomenon was hitting Scotland. Downstairs in Glen's, the afternoon singers would be warming up as we were having our monthly party meeting. By the time we got to Tam's parliamentary report, the drink had kicked in downstairs and the sing-song was at fever pitch. At this point, Tam was heavily involved in trying to prevent what would become the disastrous Iraq war and was pursuing issues around the Lockerbie bomb. So he would begin his report by saying to Alistair Mackie or Ian Grant, 'Mr Chairman, my constituency report may take a bit longer than usual this month,' at which point we knew we were in for at least an hour of global politics, espionage and intrigue that would take us across many continents. There was something magical and apt about Tam's oratory taking us from Iraq to Kuwait and Malta to Libya and Latin America, set against the backdrop of someone downstairs murdering Gloria Gaynor's 'I Will Survive' or Abba's 'Dancing Queen'. It often resembled an episode of Peter Kay's *Phoenix Nights*.

At election time, I recall Brian Fairley's vain attempts to bring some razzmatazz to Tam's election campaign by hiring an open-top double decker bus to tour the constituency. Brian's plan hit the buffers immediately, as Tam refused to go upstairs, instead spending his time hiding on the lower deck. If there had been a toilet on the bus, I think he would have locked himself inside. The words razzmatazz and Tam Dalyell did not belong in the same sentence.

He did his electioneering differently but with great skill, building relationships and friendships across the constituency. We were campaigning in Blackridge one afternoon where we came across an old guy leaning on a gate having a fag. Tam walked up and said, 'Hi, you must be Mr Collins, brother of Willie Collins, former NUM delegate at Woodend pit'.

Completely taken aback, the man replied, 'How the hell dae ye ken that?'

'You look like him. I would recognise that face any day.'

'Well, there ye go,' said the man, amazed, and on we walked, Mr Collins' vote secured and no doubt that of his family and half the street too.

Tam's kindness, generosity and courtesy saw him build lifelong friendships with Liberals, Communists, Tories, Nationalists and Unionists, and across the broadest spectrum of the Labour movement at home and internationally. Although a staunch opponent of devolution, he was one of the first to congratulate and encourage me when I was elected to the Scottish Parliament.

I have no doubt that, when selected as the Labour candidate in 1962, people questioned how an ex-Tory, old Etonian who lived in a grand family home and who spoke with an accent that wasn't exactly 'Stoneyburn or Armadale' could represent the industrial working class of West Lothian. Well, he did, and with some aplomb. He gained their trust, showed them loyalty and commitment and he did it through hard work. Whether it was the women at Plessey, the car workers at Leyland or the miners at Polkemmet, Tam took up their cause and put heart and soul into it; and they repaid his loyalty election after election.

So many people across West Lothian will miss Tam and we of course mourn his passing, but we must genuinely celebrate a life packed with experiences, a life totally committed to public service, a life dedicated to advancing the cause of the working people of West Lothian and seeking truth and justice in all he did.

In 2004, Tam's great friend Tony Benn wrote a book called *Dare to be Daniel*, challenging us to be like Daniel in the bible and stand up against big, powerful forces. I believe a fitting tribute to Tam is this: no matter what you do in life, no matter where you live or how rich or poor you are, seek truth and justice, speak up when you believe in a cause and 'Dare to be Tam'.

A couple of months after Tam's death, I was in the middle of chairing a session of the Scottish Parliament's Health and Sport committee when SNP MSP Tom Arthur slipped me a piece of paper to say that Theresa May had called a General Election for 8 June. My first reaction was unparliamentarily. I mumbled, 'F**king hell!' to myself. This was incredible news and took everyone by surprise, including May's own cabinet. Clearly the tactic was to take advantage of a Labour Party that appeared hopelessly divided, with opinion polls consistently showing the Tories leading by more than 20 per cent.

Immediately, we had the usual suspects like Tom Blenkinsop and a few of his New Labour Ultras standing down and describing Corbyn as an 'unelectable disaster', and John Woodcock saying he would stand as a Labour candidate, but never support Corbyn as PM. It was a disgrace. The Lib Dems saw this as an opportunity for a comeback and played the pro-Europe, anti-Brexit card, while Sturgeon and the SNP claimed it was all about independence. Bloody hell, this was going to be a tough one. Given that we were right in the middle of a council campaign, MSPs from all parties looked a bit deflated but put on a brave face, despite seeming to have been in one continual campaign for the previous seven years.

As the news of the election sank in, Labour candidates were hurriedly put in place via emergency measures, with surprisingly little fuss. Given where we were in the polls in Scotland (around 16 per cent), those who came forward were the real heroes of the movement, because a great many more took one step back when the call came.

Across Scotland we saw the advantage of having people from the left on the party's Scottish Executive Committee. For the first time in decades, we had a properly balanced slate of candidates with members from both wings of the party. In the broad church that is the Labour Party, this is exactly how it should be.

Having witnessed Jeremy at close quarters throughout two leadership elections, I was convinced what he had to do was recreate the vibe and buzz of those heady days of 2015. He is by nature a calm person who doesn't get rattled or nervous, even in the face of extreme provocation. He is humble, decent and compassionate, but he has to get his personality across. If we could do this, then we might just begin to get a fair hearing and build some momentum. The campaign needed to look young, exciting, dramatic and vibrant. Tommy Kane described the atmosphere down south as 'completely mad'. Whatever was to happen it would be one helluva ride.

At First Minister's Questions following the election announcement, Ruth Davidson was cocky, Sturgeon was showboating and our team put a brave face on it.

As the election campaign got under way, Jeremy spoke at the annual STUC congress in Aviemore, where despite plummeting temperatures and heavy snow, he was warmly received by delegates. He set out a progressive agenda on workers' rights, including a £10 per hour real living wage, an end to zero hours contracts and the repeal of the Trades Union Bill. The contrast with the cool response later that day to Nicola Sturgeon was very noticeable. The only problem with the visit was that his people wanted to keep him away from the Scottish media and he left without speaking to them – which frustrated me, as he is excellent with the media. They have to let him build a relationship with the media and be himself. The more people see and hear him the better.

Labour's performance at the council election was much better than many expected. In West Lothian we were only one seat behind the SNP, but the story of the night was the Scottish Tories making a breakthrough across Scotland. In West Lothian they rocketed from one seat to seven – nauseating and astonishing. We lost Glasgow and North Lanarkshire, but not by much. Despite the losses there were definitely signs of green shoots of recovery.

A few days before the national Labour campaign launch, the party manifesto was leaked to the media. Was it sabotage, incompetence or a stroke of genius? Whatever, it proved to be brilliant as the manifesto was fantastic. It was a document written in Corbyn's image reflecting the politics he has believed in all his life – fair taxes, Keynesian economics, an end to student fees, free school meals, a pensions triple lock, ending the public sector pay cap, mass council house building, public ownership of rail, water and energy, investment in health and social care, workers' rights and a whole range of policies that put clear and deep red water between not just Labour and the Tories but Labour and the rest, including the SNP. I have never been more proud to campaign on any manifesto in almost 30 years of party membership.

The official manifesto launch a few days later looked and sounded superb, with a positive image being portrayed on TV and in the media. The slogan 'for the many, not the few' reflected perfectly the values of the manifesto and the politics of Jeremy and his Shadow Cabinet. The lack of kickback or criticism from the Blairites and the media was noticeable. Jeremy came across as confident and spoke with real clarity. He had a manifesto he could proudly promote and did so relentlessly with huge energy. Opinion polls on some of the main policy areas showed it was very popular – things were getting interesting.

In contrast, the Tory manifesto launch was awful. More austerity, cuts to public services, a grim Brexit, ending the pensions triple lock, cutting winter fuel allowance for older people, cutting foreign aid and a social care policy dubbed the 'Dementia Tax'. It was dire, austere and utterly miserable. The launch was low key and extremely dull. It looked like it took place in an abandoned bus depot. The contrast with Labour was there for all to see.

Labour activists fed up with years of bland third-way politics – where voters found it difficult to see any major differences between the parties – went out campaigning with a spring in their step. They were enthused and motivated.

As the ideas in the manifesto were already out there following the leak, they started to penetrate the voters' psyche, which was noticeable from the response on doorsteps. The voters wanted to talk to us again. Yes, some did bring up Jeremy Corbyn as a barrier to voting Labour, just as they did Kezia Dugdale, but every leader has their followers and detractors. What was crystal clear, though, was that the SNP vote was softening up. The antagonism of 2014/15 had gone, the 'Red Tory' jibe was redundant, and we had the SNP on the defensive over economic policy (they won't introduce a 50p higher tax rate in Scotland but wanted it introduced at UK level), over their record on public services and their focus on the constitution. The Labour manifesto opposed another independence referendum – that should have put it to bed and got us onto public services and the economy but it didn't. The Scottish Labour strategists instead continued to fixate on the independence referendum issue with almost every press release, speech and party election broadcast banging on about it relentlessly. This was all part of a strategy set out over a year prior to target No voters – a strategy which I had opposed. We had to win back voters from across the spectrum and not give up on working class Yes voters in particular as they are the people who have most to gain from a Labour Government, especially a Corbyn-led one.

Of course, during the campaign there were some stressful moments. The right-wing media continually brought up Jeremy's role in working with Sinn Fein, the Middle East and the Stop the War Coalition. They failed to mention that he also worked with Unionists in Northern Ireland to try and bring about peace, was repeatedly proven to be right on Iraq and Afghanistan and throughout his life has been at the centre of the peace movement. Their squalid attempts to portray him as a terrorist sympathiser and lentil-munching pacifist continued right up to polling day.

In the middle of the election campaign the sickening suicide bombing of a Manchester pop concert full of teenage girls brought the election to a shuddering halt and put things into perspective. What kind of crazed person would do such a thing? The country was left speechless and stunned and many tears were shed. What a depressing world we live in when such things happen.

As the election resumed, Team Corbyn took a major strategic gamble by correctly addressing the issue of terrorism, foreign policy and cuts to police and public services. The speech was brave, measured and very credible, addressing both the horror of what happened but also the future and how to prevent further atrocities. The Tories were forced into trying to defend their record on police cuts, most of which were implemented by one Theresa May. If the Tories could not reassure people on law and order, traditionally their strongest card, they were in deep trouble.

And it was clear that Tory smears were not working: people saw right through the Tory strategy that tried to present Theresa May as 'Strong and Stable' and Corbyn as weak, chaotic and soft on terror. After four days of appalling headlines on the 'Dementia Tax', the Tories performed a major U-turn by setting a £100,000 cap on charges, but it made them look shambolic. The press had a field day: the mantra of 'Strong and Stable' blurted out by May and every one of her candidates was wholly discredited. 'Weak and Wobbly' became the new catchphrase on everyone's lips.

Problems for Labour arose with Diane Abbot's poor performances on radio and TV, where she didn't know her budget numbers, with a similar failure by Jeremy on *Woman's Hour*. But compared to the Tory campaign, all was going well. May was having a real stinker and the polls were closing.

One of the key contrasts in the campaign was how the two party leaders engaged voters. Corbyn is a people person. He likes to listen to people, discuss ideas and hear their experiences. He is at his best amongst people. I was always of the belief that the more people got to know him the more they would like him. So when he embarked on a series of rallies and meetings around the country he was able to meet thousands of voters. At West Kirby on the Wirral, thousands stood on the local beach to listen. At Tranmere football stadium he spoke to thousands of young people at a music concert, receiving a rapturous reception. At Hebdon Bridge, almost the entire town came out to see him, and at Gateshead 10,000 people were locked out of a full meeting. In Glasgow, we filled the Old Fruitmarket again. Jeremy was clearly enjoying himself. I asked him this question in the green room at the Old Fruitmarket and he said he was 'bloody loving it'. We were on a roll.

Meanwhile the Tory campaign was going from bad to worse. Theresa May looked as though she would rather be anywhere else than meeting the voters. She repeatedly attended small meetings with hand-picked Tory activists acting as sycophantic cheerleaders. It didn't make for good press or TV. Journalists were only allowed to ask presubmitted questions and access to the Prime Minister was limited. They were however still well ahead in the polls but they were closing to within 10 percentage points. When May refused to turn up for the leader's debate and Corbyn performed pretty well in front of a very receptive BBC audience, her stock fell further.

Positive UK Labour election broadcasts, a vibrant and lively social media campaign and articles on alternative news sites created a really positive buzz. Rap artists, comedians, artists and actors came out in their droves for Labour. Full credit to the much criticised and maligned Momentum organisation, which supported Jeremy's leadership and who were behind much of this new campaigning. In Bristol, where one my relatives was involved, 150 people turned up for a Momentum day of action in support of candidate Kerry McCarthy, one of the MPs who had tried to get rid of Corbyn, which shows how committed and unified people were around the manifesto. The rivalries and bitterness of two years of division were set aside for the greater good: a Labour victory.

In Scotland the campaign continued with leaders' debates dominated by independence and the questions of another referendum. On the doorsteps, the worm had turned and people were warming to the radical manifesto; and concerns about Jeremy, while still a theme, was much reduced.

I visited campaigns in Fife and the Lothians and in each constituency the atmosphere was positive. This was in such contrast to 2015, where hostility to Labour hung heavy in the air. In Kirkcaldy, Dunfermline, Edinburgh, Linlithgow and Livingston our stock was clearly on the rise and reports back from Glasgow, Lanarkshire and Ayrshire were good. Lots of people, especially the young, were reacting to a manifesto of hope, while older voters were prepared to vote tactically to keep the SNP out.

In the run-up to polling day the last Scottish Labour election broadcast was screened – and it was dreadful. Once again it focused completely on Sturgeon and another referendum, depicting a broken record and Sturgeon obsessively repeating lines about another referendum. Now there is little doubt Sturgeon's star has seriously fallen, and that there are groups of people who genuinely and vocally don't like her, but at this stage the Scottish Labour team must have had the data to tell them that the Corbyn campaign was cutting through on policy and vision and optimism. We should have at that point, or even earlier, changed tack and promoted the positive agenda of 'for the many not the few'. We should have promoted real and genuine progressive change, a vision of hope and a vision that no one would be left behind. If we believe, as I do, that the needs and ambitions of our class are the same in London, Lisburn and Llanelli as they are in Livingston and Lanarkshire, then people would react in the same way. We needed to embrace that and drive home that message. Instead, the Scottish strategists fought the election like a by-election in Edinburgh South, trying to defend Ian Murray's position as our sole MP rather than seizing the opportunity to capitalise in other areas. The evening before the poll I compered an election event at Òran Mór, which linked up to six other towns and cities across the UK, for a live speech from Jeremy. The reaction was brilliant. Our Glasgow candidates Paul Sweeney and Pam Duncan reported that they were in with a real chance as people were coming over to us from the SNP.

The following day epitomised how far we had come in just a few years. In 2015 had we advertised an 8am election event in the centre of Glasgow, we would have met with a gang of nationalists screaming abuse about 'Red Tories' and trying to run us off the streets. This time 600 people turned up to cheer and support Jeremy as he embarked on a six-stop UK tour, ending his day in the church in his Islington constituency where I spoke with him on the platform on the eve of his election as Labour leader. What a fabulous contrast.

On election day, the UK polls showed Labour with anything from a +3 per cent lead to a 10 per cent deficit. The polls opened amidst some of the worst polling day weather in my political lifetime. It poured all day, until a brief respite in the evening brought out the infamous Scottish midges – and we prayed for more rain! Despite this, voters were out and the feeling was good, and we had a number of new helpers on polling day – a very healthy and promising sign.

In keeping with tradition, we went for a pint after the polls closed and waited nervously on the exit poll. When it came, Tommy and I nearly fell off our chairs. It showed the Tories down 12 seats; the SNP down 22 and Labour up to 266. We were in hung parliament territory. Gulping down our pints we ran across to West Lothian College to begin our local count.

It soon became clear that the SNP's big majorities in Livingston and Linlithgow were no more. We were taking them close in areas of Livingston where we had previously lost by huge margins, and winning boxes in places we were nowhere near last time. As the first results came in, the exit poll was proving to be accurate. Predicted pre-election losses in north of England 'Leave' voting areas failed to materialise. The first Scottish deceleration saw Ged Killen take Rutherglen for Labour – totally against expectations. Further results showed huge Labour majorities stacking up in seats in London, Merseyside and Greater Manchester and some Midland marginals going our way. Corbyn was having a fantastic night. Then a series of shocks hit Scotland: Angus Robertson, the SNP Westminster leader, lost in Moray; Eilidh Whiteford lost Banff and Buchan, but the big one was Alex Salmond's loss in Gordon. A huge political figure had watched his career ended by the Tory party he loved to lambast. For Scottish Labour it proved a good night, with Paul Sweeney winning in Glasgow North East, Marin Whitefield in East Lothian, Lesley Laird in Kirkcaldy, Ian Murray in Edinburgh South (with a 15,000 majority), Danielle Rowley in Midlothian; for me, the best of them all was seeing postman, and CWU rep, Hughie Gaffney winning in Coatbridge.

As Theresa May's result was declared, she looked physically broken. We were heading for a hung parliament with the Tories the biggest party but having to rely on support from some of the smaller parties. Her cynical attempt to secure a bigger majority by cashing in on Labour division had proved disastrous. On an election panel, her sacked former Chancellor, George Osborne, now editor of the *Evening Standard*, declared her a 'dead woman walking'.

Just as in the aftermath of the Scottish referendum, politics was turned on its head when the winners, the Tories, became the losers and the losers, Labour, became the winners. All night I took quiet pleasure in hearing Corbyn's greatest critics, and those who plotted and backed the coup, gagging on gargantuan portions of humble pie. John McTernan, Alistair Campbell, John Woodcock, Peter Mandelson, Chuka Umunna, Neil and Stephen Kinnock, Hilary Benn, Yvette Cooper and many, many more were paraded on TV and invited to apologise for getting it spectacularly wrong.

In the immediate aftermath, Theresa May was forced to court the reactionaries of the DUP from Northern Ireland in what looks to everyone like a squalid and unstable deal that will not last. In the meantime, Corbyn has galvanised the Labour Party with post-election parliamentary meetings now resembling fan club rallies rather than the weekly brawls they previously were.

What a difference, what a turnaround. As I've always said, 'You can't be a pessimist *and* a socialist!' The last few years certainly confirm that.

APPENDIX

My World

MY FATHER-IN-LAW LIVES in the French city of Aix-en-Provence and Fiona and I had gone out there to visit him for a few days in October, 2015, during a parliamentary recess. We were getting ready to head out for a spot of sightseeing one morning when I spotted what looked like an abnormality on one of Fiona's breasts. When she was 17, she'd had an operation to remove what they call a 'breast mouse', which is like a wee lump or a bit of gristle, and naturally she thought it was that again. She promised she would get it checked out when we got back to Scotland.

We enjoyed the rest of the break and when we got home, Fiona was as good as her word and went to see our doctor, who referred her to hospital. She was working that day and popped along to the appropriate department after a break in her shift. She was very relaxed but the surgeon took one look and issued her with a follow-up appointment for the following week, saying, 'I don't like the look of that at all.' Fiona hadn't been prepared for that response, especially as she was there herself, but didn't call me because she knew I would be in at First Minister's Questions. If I'm completely honest, before she left that morning I had a feeling all wasn't well, although there's no way I could have convinced her to allow me to come to the hospital. Anyway, as soon as I got out of FMQs, I saw the missed call and phoned her straight away. She was in a right state but mentioned the hastily-arranged follow-up appointment. I told her I would be right home but she wanted me to stay at work, as she was doing the same. I wasn't having any of that and headed straight home. When I got there, Fiona was already in, and as soon as I walked into the living room, we looked at one another and burst into tears. We had a long chat but decided not to tell anyone, because nothing had been confirmed at that point. It was a long seven days until the follow-up, but they more or less confirmed what we already knew: Fiona had breast cancer. To be honest, I felt nothing at that point. I was completely ready for it. If the doctor had told me it wasn't what we thought it was I would've fallen straight off the chair. We asked a few questions and came out of the meeting feeling a bit strange. I was neither up nor down, which I think was because we'd already had such an outpouring of emotion the week before. So we had to then tell loads of folk and that was the difficult part. There was a lot of crying and talking to family and friends, but we were ready to get on with it and beat it. We were relatively confident we would do so, as the consultant had told us the size of it, how they planned to deal with it and that they expected Fiona to live for another 40 years, so it certainly wasn't a case of 'the end is nigh'. It was a hammer blow, no doubt about that, but there was a lot of hope. Almost immediately, we had a procession of people at the door offering help and support. Our house was full of flowers and cards. People genuinely cared and were 100 per cent behind us. Yet we thought of those who receive similar news but who leave the surgery and return to no one; to a cold, empty flat. No support, no cuddles, no cards, no flowers. How do they cope? I can't even begin to imagine.

Once we got past telling everyone the bad news, Fiona sat Chloe and I down, and said, 'Right, here's the deal. We are going to carry on as normal. You're going to work, and you're going to uni, and we are going to do everything just as before, and I don't want to see anyone moping around the house.' She then looked at me and said, 'And I don't want to see you going about ironing and dusting, and loitering about the house looking after me. You've never done it before, so don't start now!' A harsh judgement on my domestic efforts, but the message was clear, 'we continue as normal.' In hindsight, that was the best call she made. She isn't the type who sits there saying 'look how terrible this is for me', that isn't her. Chloe agreed 100 per cent. She is probably the most practical and straight talking of us all, and would regularly remind me of the need to act 'normal'.

But even though we were all getting on with it, I won't pretend we didn't have our moments, because we did. I think if you asked any of us now, we would say it was bad, it was certainly tough, but probably nowhere near as bad as we thought it was going to be.

Fiona has naturally thick hair and when she started chemotherapy her hair was coming out in big clumps. I feared the worst, because as a former hairdresser she has always taken great pride in her locks. After a few weeks of treatment, the inevitable started to happen and she immediately called the girl who did her hair and asked her to come over and take the lot off. I had been at work and when I got home, I realised Susan the hairdresser was in, so I braced myself, walked in and they were just about to start. Susan said, 'Will I just take it down and keep it quite short?' I thought, 'here we go, this will be awful,' but Fiona was great, and afterwards admitted it was actually better getting the lot off than having to look at handfuls of hair in the shower each morning. She said it was more traumatic losing her eyebrows than her hair!

From diagnosis to the end of her treatment was probably about seven months. She still has tablets to take for the next 10 years, but apart from that she is great. We went to a follow-up meeting at the end of the treatment and they said it had gone as well as expected. They told us about the next stages and of all the classes she could attend to help regain her fitness.

At the end of September, 2016, an organiser from Breast Cancer UK's Race for Life called to ask if Fiona would act as starter for their Edinburgh race. She also agreed to make a speech and did very well. She had decided to embrace it and I was very proud of her.

One thing Fiona did say right from the start was that she would shout it from the rooftops, to ensure that the message to 'check yourself' got out. Chloe would come in with her pals and Fiona would be harassing them all, saying, 'Check your tits, always, because it really can happen to girls as young as you.' And they would all just stand there looking at her, or more than likely staring down at their shoes!

One of her colleagues at the hospital, who also lives in Fauldhouse, was diagnosed the week after Fiona, so the two of them helped each other a lot, and a guy we know across the road was also dealing with stomach cancer, so there was a wee group of them who kept each other going throughout.

When you're living through something as serious as that, you tend to have a cry at times and then get on with it. It's only really afterwards that you look back and say 'wow, we went through quite a bit there', but we are constructed to deal with situations at the time and worry about them later.

Cancer rates in our country are high and will get higher. It is likely that one in three of us will experience cancer over our lifetime. The message from my family is to take all the help you are offered, support each other best you can and provide support to others in the same boat. Stand up to it with all the physical and emotional strength you have and you have a real chance.

#FuckCancer

Some other books published by **LUATH PRESS**

What Would Keir Hardie Say? Exploring his vision and relevance to 21st Century politics.
Edited by Pauline Bryan
ISBN: 978-1-910745-15-1 PBK £9.99

The Wey Forrit: A Polemic in Scots
Stuart McHardy
ISBN 978-1912147-01-4 PBK £8.99

My work has consisted of trying to stir up a divine discontent with wrong.–KEIR HARDIE

Has the Labour Party stayed true to Hardie's socialist ideals and vision?

What would Hardie make of the recent developments in Scottish politics?

If he were active today, what would Keir Hardie say about attacks on welfare • trade union rights • immigration • privatisation • European Union • the economy?

A passionate leader who fought for justice, Keir Hardie, founder and first leader of the Labour Party, was a stringent critic of the world he saw around him. A socialist, a trade unionist and above all an agitator, he gave unstinting support to the women's suffrage movement and risked all in his commitment to anti-imperialism and international peace.

Now, 100 years after Hardie's death, editor Pauline Bryan gathers together essays from writers, trade unionists, academics and politicians to reflect on Hardie's contribution and what it means today.

The Wey Forrit is a political work written in Scots which examines the current British political climate, with a particular focus on how the inner workings of Westminster affect Scotland and her people. Arguing from a communitarian perspective, Stuart McHardy meticulously pulls apart the long-standing political ideas and traditions which many citizens of the United Kingdom have automatically accepted as correct or justified. He challenges his readers to re-think the consensus.

Focusing on some of today's most highly discussed and potentially divisive topics – such as Brexit and Scottish Independence – McHardy lambasts the 'peelie-wallie politicians and lickspittle journalists' who protect the needs of the rich and sneer at those outside the realms of money and power. His views on the sovereignty of the Scottish Nation are also put forward, considering both the past and future implications of the way in which Britain came into being and the way in which it has been run for the three centuries since the Act of Union.

Citizens United
Henry McLeish
ISBN 978-1910021781 PBK £8.99

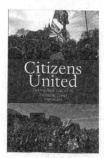

Poverty Safari
Darren McGarvey
ISBN 978-1912147-03-8 PBK £7.99

The early years of the 21st century have erupted into a spectacular period of seismic political unrest which challenges our sense of purpose, shreds our certainties, and questions our path to progress. Volatile and angry citizens are contesting social democracy and progressive politics. It is a wake-up call to those who believe that humans are capable of achieving much higher levels of social, economic, political and cultural wellbeing.

The future of Scotland is at a crossroads as Brexit creates more complexity and confusion. The SNP has lost momentum and a window of opportunity has emerged for a wider and deeper debate about the current political situation both in Scotland and the UK.

This book examines the most pressing issues facing us today in the context of the political and constitutional upheaval that is coursing throughout Western democracies. The shock politics of Trump and Brexit demonstrate that the political landscape has changed and we face an uncertain future. Henry McLeish offers a new approach to get us out of the mess we're in.

People from deprived communities all around Britain feel misunderstood and unheard. Darren McGarvey AKA Loki gives voice to their feelings and concerns, and the anger that is spilling over. Anger he says we will have to get used to, unless things change.

He invites you to come on a safari of sorts. A Poverty Safari. But not the sort where the indigenous population is surveyed from a safe distance for a time, before the window on the community closes and everyone gradually forgets about it.

I know the hustle and bustle of high-rise life, the dark and dirty stairwells, the temperamental elevators that smell like urine and wet dog fur, the grumpy concierge, the apprehension you feel as you enter or leave the building, especially at night. I know that sense of being cut off from the world, despite having such a wonderful view of it through a window in the sky; that feeling of isolation, despite being surrounded by hundreds of other people above, below and either side of you. But most of all, I understand the sense that you are invisible, despite the fact that your community can be seen for miles around and is one of the most prominent features of the city skyline.

Details of these and other books published by Luath Press can be found at:
www.luath.co.uk

Luath Press Limited

committed to publishing well written books worth reading

LUATH PRESS takes its name from Robert Burns, whose little collie Luath (*Gael.*, swift or nimble) tripped up Jean Armour at a wedding and gave him the chance to speak to the woman who was to be his wife and the abiding love of his life. Burns called one of the 'Twa Dogs' Luath after Cuchullin's hunting dog in Ossian's *Fingal*. Luath Press was established in 1981 in the heart of Burns country, and is now based a few steps up the road from Burns' first lodgings on Edinburgh's Royal Mile. Luath offers you distinctive writing with a hint of unexpected pleasures.

Most bookshops in the UK, the US, Canada, Australia, New Zealand and parts of Europe, either carry our books in stock or can order them for you. To order direct from us, please send a £sterling cheque, postal order, international money order or your credit card details (number, address of cardholder and expiry date) to us at the address below. Please add post and packing as follows: UK – £1.00 per delivery address; overseas surface mail – £2.50 per delivery address; overseas airmail – £3.50 for the first book to each delivery address, plus £1.00 for each additional book by airmail to the same address. If your order is a gift, we will happily enclose your card or message at no extra charge.

Luath Press Limited
543/2 Castlehill
The Royal Mile
Edinburgh EH1 2ND
Scotland
Telephone: +44 (0)131 225 4326 (24 hours)
email: sales@luath. co.uk
Website: www. luath.co.uk